ESSENTIALS
OF
MANAGEMENT

£17.95,

ESSENTIALS
OF
MANAGEMENT

fourth edition

Joseph L. Massie
University of Kentucky

PHI Prentice-Hall International, Inc.

This edition may be sold only in those countries to which
it is consigned by Prentice-Hall International. It is not to
be re-exported and it is not for sale in the U.S.A., Mexico,
or Canada.

© 1987, 1979, 1971, 1964 by Prentice-Hall, Inc.
A Division of Simon & Schuster
Englewood Cliffs, NJ 07632

Printed in the United States of America

10 9 8 7 6 5 4

ISBN 0-13-286691-9

Prentice-Hall International (UK) Limited, *London*
Prentice-Hall of Australia Pty. Limited, *Sydney*
Prentice-Hall Canada Inc., *Toronto*
Prentice-Hall Hispanoamericana, S.A., *Mexico*
Prentice-Hall of India Private Limited, *New Delhi*
Prentice-Hall of Japan, Inc., *Tokyo*
Prentice-Hall of Southeast Asia Pte. Ltd., *Singapore*
Editora Prentice-Hall do Brasil, Ltda., *Rio de Janeiro*
Prentice-Hall, *Englewood Cliffs, New Jersey*

FOREWORD

With the rapid growth in recent years of courses in such areas as personnel, organizational behavior, production, decision science, labor relations, and small business management, there has developed an increased need for a viable alternative to the standard 500- or 600-page, casebound textbook. The Essentials of Management Series has been designed to fill that need. The Series consists of brief, survey books covering major content areas within the management discipline.

Each book in the Series provides a concise treatment of the key concepts and issues within a major content area, written in a highly readable style, balancing theory with practical applications, and offering a clarity of presentation that is often missing in standard, full-length textbooks. I have selected authors both for their academic expertise and their ability to identify, organize, and articulate the essential elements of their subject. So, for example, you will find that the books in this Series avoid unnecessary jargon, use a conversational writing style, include extensive examples and interesting illustrations of concepts, and have the focus of a rifle rather than that of an encyclopedic shotgun.

The books in this Series will prove useful to a wide variety of readers. Since each covers the essential body of knowledge in a major area of management, they can be used alone for introductory survey courses in colleges and universities or for management development and in-house educational programs. Additionally, their short format makes them an ideal vehicle to be combined with cases, readings, and/or experiential materials by instructors who desire to mold a course to meet unique objectives. The books in this Series offer the flexibility that is either not feasible or too costly to achieve with a standard textbook.

Stephen P. Robbins
Series Editor

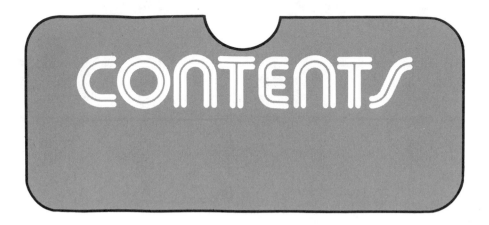

CONTENTS

PART

BACKGROUND OF MODERN MANAGEMENT   1

1

NATURE AND IMPORTANCE OF MANAGEMENT   1

2

DEVELOPMENT OF MANAGEMENT THOUGHT   11

3
ETHICAL AND ENVIRONMENTAL FOUNDATIONS

PART
& 23
FUNCTIONS IN THE MANAGEMENT PROCESS

4
DECISION MAKING

5
ORGANIZING AND STAFFING

11
MARKETING MANAGEMENT 168

12
FINANCIAL MANAGEMENT 187

13
MULTINATIONAL MANAGEMENT 201

17

MANAGEMENT
INTO THE SECOND CENTURY

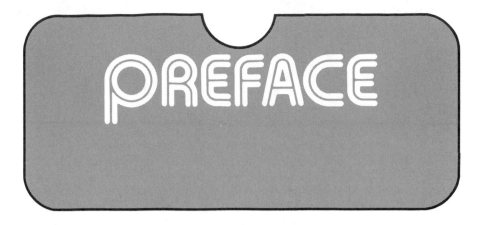

PREFACE

This book summarizes the essential elements of management. Its primary aim is to provide the reader with a synthesis of the traditional and quantitative and behavioral approaches to the subject of management by focusing attention on basic concepts and techniques of analysis. It proposes a framework for integrating the contributions of the various disciplines interested in the study of management; yet, it encourages a critical attitude toward all administrative thought, with the hope that the reader will reach a synthesis of his own.

The author adopts the view that management must be based on interdisciplinary study. Important advances have been made in economics, accounting, sociology, social psychology, statistics, and mathematics in areas directly related to management. These areas have been integrated within the traditional, functional framework.

This fourth edition has retained the basic material from the first three editions; the disciplinary foundations and behavioral and quantitative elements, however, have been integrated into the discussion of the various functions of management. The fact that most chapters needed only minor changes supports the proposition held by many users of the previous editions that the original text included essentials of lasting importance.

Two groups of major changes in this edition include (1) expanded coverage of the international dimension and complete reorientation in managing information with computers, and (2) a greatly enlarged part on applications of managerial functions. This last change has been made desirable because management has branched out into many applications, each with its own concepts and terminology. Thus, we have included from the first edition separate chapters on operations (production) management, marketing management, and financial management. In addition, we have completely new chapters on entrepreneurship and small business, health services administration, and multinational management.

The reader will find that several techniques have been used to present as much useful information as possible in this volume. The index, for example, includes many of the terms one must know in order to understand the meaning of management. These terms appear in **boldface type** in the text where they are first used. Tables and charts are frequently used to summarize important information that would otherwise require many pages to present.

The author hopes that this volume will be a stimulating and

provocative experience for the reader and will prompt further study in order to secure a more comprehensive knowledge of the field of management.

With this end in view, references have been updated at the end of each chapter. The reader will find in these books a more elaborate treatment of the subjects and more extensive bibliographies for further study.

As a summary of the essentials of management, this book will prove useful to a wide variety of readers. It will be understandable to the lay person who has had no formal education in management. It will be helpful to students in various management courses who feel the need for a concise integration of subjects covered in other books. It will be of particular help to students in "case" courses who need some references to concepts and techniques of analysis to apply in specific situations. In addition, it will provide a useful summary of ideas for the person who is in, or hopes to be in, a managerial position.

The author gratefully acknowledges contributions to past editions by Dr. James L. Gibson and Dr. Marc Wallace, Jr., of the University of Kentucky; Dr. John Douglas of Miami University, (Ohio); and Dr. Martin Solomon of Ohio State University. Although the reorganizaiton of the fourth edition required the omission of their direct contributions, the author has received a lasting impact from their ideas. Special appreciation is extended to contributors of new chapters in the fourth edition: Dr. Marc Dollinger for the chapter on entrepreneurship and small business; Dr. Lawrence X. Tarpey, Sr., for the revised chapter on marketing management; and Ms. Rachael Massie of Duke University Hospital for the chapter on administering health services. Finally, the support and feedback from the users of the first three editions were essential to the improvements in this fourth edition.

J.L.M.

ESSENTIALS
OF
MANAGEMENT

1

NATURE AND IMPORTANCE OF MANAGEMENT

Management is universal in the modern industrial world. Every organization requires the making of decisions, the coordinating of activities, the handling of people, and the evaluation of performance directed toward group objectives. Numerous managerial activities have their own particular approach to specific types of problems and are discussed under such headings as farm management, management of health delivery systems, college management, government management, marketing management, production or operations management, and others. All have elements in common. This book summarizes some of the essential concepts and techniques of management that are fundamental to various applications.

Management has become more important as labor has become more specialized and as the scale of operations has increased. Technological developments have continually created new challenges. The complexities of human relationships constantly challenge those who perform managerial functions. The dynamics of management, therefore, should be characteristic of any study of its theory and practice.

Because of the increasing importance of management, and because of the new challenges it faces, many researchers in various disciplines have concentrated their attention on parts of the subject. The result is that managerial approaches to such subjects as psychology, economics, and accounting have helped to improve the thinking in relation to the overall field of management. Research on subjects important to management since World War II offer renewed hope to those who must face the complexities that confront the operating manager. On the other hand, managers face new challenges to established doctrines and dogmas as the result of research which requires them to adapt their approaches.

Certain fundamental changes in society have altered the relative opportunities in management. In the past, management developed in the industrial and business sector. In the 1980s opportunities are developing more rapidly in the following ways:

1. *Post-industrial society*—Service-oriented organizations now are the dominant and most dynamic parts of the economy.
2. *Growth in the public sector*—Although the profit-oriented firms remain important in the U.S., public agencies, Health Maintenance Organizations (HMO's), and non-profit associations are increasing at a more rapid pace.
3. *Women in management*—The role of women as managers has increased in the 1980s and this new factor has made a significant impact on management thinking.
4. *Emergence of the information society*—New technology is revolutionizing the flow of information and organizational structure.
5. *Entrepreneurship*—Small new businesses provide the leading edge for the American economy.

MEANING OF MANAGEMENT

The chief characteristic of management is the integration and application of the knowledge and analytical approaches developed by numerous disciplines. The manager's problem is to seek a balance among these special approaches and to apply the pertinent concepts in specific situations which require action. The manager must be oriented to solving problems with techniques tailored to the situations; yet he must develop a unified framework of thought that encompasses the total and integrated aspects of the entire organization.

What, then, is management, and what does it do? In general usage, the word "management" identifies a special group of people whose job it is to direct the effort and activities of other people toward

2

common objectives. Simply stated, management "gets things done through other people." For the purpose of this book, **management** is defined as the *process* by which a cooperative group directs actions toward common goals. This process involves techniques by which a distinguishable group of people (managers) coordinates activities of other people; managers seldom actually perform the activities themselves. This process consists of certain basic functions which provide an analytical approach for studying management and is the subject of Part 2 of this book.

The concept of management has broadened in scope with the introduction of new perspectives by different fields of study. The study of management has evolved into more than the use of *means* to accomplish given *ends*; today it includes moral and ethical questions concerning the selection of the right *ends* toward which managers should strive.

Harbison and Myers[1] offered a classic threefold concept for emphasizing a broader scope for the viewpoint of management. They observe management as (1) an economic resource, (2) a system of authority, and (3) a class or elite.

1. As viewed by the economist, management is one of the *factors of production* together with land, labor and capital. As the industrialization of a nation increases, the need for management becomes greater as it is substituted for capital and labor. The managerial resources of a firm determine, in large measure, its productivity and profitability. In those industries experiencing innovations, management must be used more intensively. Executive development, therefore, is more important for those firms in a dynamic industry in which progress is rapid.

2. As viewed by a specialist in administration and organization, management is *a system of authority*. Historically, management first developed an authoritarian philosophy with a small number of top individuals determining all actions of the rank and file. Later, humanitarian concepts causes some managements to develop paternalistic approaches. Still later, constitutional management emerged, characterized by a concern for definite and consistent policies and procedures for dealing with the working group. As more employees received higher education, the trend of management was toward a democratic and participative approach. Modern management can be viewed as a synthesis of these four approaches to authority.

3. As viewed by a sociologist, management is *a class and status system*. The increase in the complexity of relationships in modern

---

[1] Frederick Harbison and Charles A. Myers, *Management in the Industrial World* (New York: McGraw-Hill Book Company, Inc., 1959), pp. 21–86.

society demands that managers become an elite of brains and education. Entrance into this class is based more and more on education and knowledge instead of on family or political connections. Some students view this development as a "managerial revolution" in which the career managerial class obtains increasing amounts of power and threatens to become an autonomous class. Some observers view this development with alarm. Others point out that as the power of managers increases, their numbers expand, so that there is little need to worry about this tendency toward a managerial autocracy. A broad view of management requires that the student consider this larger perspective of the place of management in society.

These three perspectives are not the only important ones for the manager to recognize. An industrial manager would argue that the technological viewpoint is of prime importance. A psychologist would emphasize the needs of the human being and adjustment to organizational pressures. The theologian would concentrate on the spiritual implications of managerial actions. A politician would look to what is feasible and acceptable.

Many chief executives and educators contend that the most important perspective of top executives should be based on a "liberally educated outlook on life." The total concept of management requires an understanding of the meaning of liberal education and its relationship to management functions. A **liberal point of view** is not merely the sum of a finite number of narrow approaches. Its emphasis is on freedom to choose from the widest range of possibilities by discovering new possibilities, and by recalling possibilities previously developed but forgotten. The liberally oriented executive continues to expand his horizons with utmost freedom in an effort to strive toward an ultimate in life. Because management must be concerned with ends as well as means, it is clear that it must maintain a broad perspective, unfettered by specialized restrictions. The paradox of management is that it is based on identifiable and rigorous frameworks of concepts, but at the same time it continues to strive toward breaking out of any set discipline. This paradox makes management an extremely interesting subject.

FUNCTIONS OF MANAGEMENT

One way to view the process of management is to identify the basic functions which together make up the process. These functions will be discussed in greater detail in Part 2 and will serve as elements for all applications of management concepts in Part 3. These functions

4

are basic to managerial activities at all levels from the immediate supervisor to the chief executive. They are fundamental in all types of cooperative endeavor, including business firms, government agencies, and benevolent institutions. They form the core of activities in various applications such as marketing, manufacturing, financing, and public agencies.

Different authorities offer different names for the key functions of management; however, there is general agreement on most of the actual duties of a manager. In this book, the following seven functions will be used to describe the job of management:

1. *Decision making*—the process by which a course of action is consciously chosen from available alternatives for the purpose of achieving a desired result.
2. *Organizing*—the process by which the structure and allocation of jobs are determined.
3. *Staffing*—the process by which managers select, train, promote, and retire subordinates.
4. *Planning*—the process by which a manager anticipates the future and discovers alternative courses of action open to him.
5. *Controlling*—the process that measures current performance and guides it toward some predetermined goal.
6. *Communicating*—the process by which ideas are transmitted to others for the purpose of effecting a desired result.
7. *Directing (leadership)*—the process by which actual performance of subordinates is guided toward common goals. Supervising is one aspect of this function at lower levels where physical overseeing of work is possible.

All these functions are closely interrelated; however, it is useful to treat each as a separate process for the purpose of spelling out the detailed concepts important to the whole job of the manager. At times it may be desirable to consider several functions jointly in order to show their close interrelationships. For example, communicating and controlling must be considered together in systems planning; organizing, communicating, and staffing may be viewed together in studying organization behavior.

A list of management functions is merely a useful analytical device for stressing the basic elements inherent in the job of management. At times it might be desirable to identify subfunctions for purpose of emphasis. For example, each of the above seven functions assumes that management has a certain set of objectives. In this book, objectives are considered in Chapter 3 as the foundation for the performance of the seven functions. Motivation of human beings is considered a subfunction of staffing and directing.

It should be obvious that the seven functions stated above do relate to what might be called "leadership"; however, for our purposes, it is important to distinguish between leadership and management.

Leadership involves personal qualities which enable one person to induce others to follow. These qualities are particularly important to the directing function of management. Styles of leadership are important to the study of management, but management is a more comprehensive concept than leadership. Development of a manager can be achieved through academic study. The essence of leadership is interpersonal and action-oriented, and therefore can best be developed in practice.

ROLES OF MANAGERS

In 1973, Henry Mintzberg provided one of the first comprehensive studies of the nature of managerial work.[2] A summary of Mintzberg's findings gives us a more complete picture of what a manager actually does. Based on his study of the activities of five practicing chief executives, Mintzberg generalized his description of the nature of managerial work in current practice.

Mintzberg found that about one-third of a manager's time is spent in dealing with subordinates, about one-third in dealing with external (outside the organization) matters, and the other third in a variety of activities, including contacts with superiors, tours of the workplace, and thinking.

Mintzberg grouped ten basic roles performed by managers as interpersonal, informational, and decisional. These roles—organized sets of behaviors belonging to a position—describe what managers *actually do*, whereas functions of managers had historically described what managers *should do*.

The **interpersonal roles** were these: (1) A manager is a symbol, or a *figurehead*. This role is necessary because of the position occupied and consists of such duties as signing certain documents required by law and officially receiving visitors. (2) A manager serves as a *leader*—that is, hires, trains, encourages, fires, remunerates, judges. (3) A third interpersonal role is that of serving as *liaison* between outside contacts—such as the community, suppliers, and others—and the organization.

The **informational roles** found by Mintzberg were these: (1) As *monitors*, managers gather information in order to be well informed.

---

[2] Henry Mintzberg, *The Nature of Managerial Work* (New York: Harper & Row, 1973); *The Nature of Managerial Work* (Englewood Cliffs, N.J.: Prentice-Hall, 1980).

(2) Managers are *disseminators* of information flowing from both external and internal sources. (3) Managers are *spokespersons* or *representatives* of the organization. They speak for subordinates to superiors and represent upper management to subordinates. All three of these informational roles provide a communications network for the organization.

Mintzberg's **decisional roles** were these: (1) Managers as *entrepreneurs* are initiators, innovators, problem discoverers, and designers of improvement projects that direct and control change in the organization. (2) As *disturbance handlers*, managers react to situations that are unexpected, such as resignations of subordinates, firings, or losses of customers. (3) A third decisional role is that of *resource allocator*. (4) Finally, managers are *negotiators*. At times, this role can be partially delegated; however, managers assume it when conflicts arise.

Probably one of the most dramatic changes in the performance of managerial functions in the last few decades has been the technology with which information is managed. In earlier editions, this technology was included in the discussion of computers and management information systems. In the 1980s the view is increasingly one of managing information, not merely processing data or computerizing systems. Often the layman has worried about the computer's becoming his or her manager. The view of this book is that both the rapid developments in computer hardware and software and the speed of data transmission via satellites and lasers provide managers with powerful tools for performing their functions. Therefore, the final chapter in the discussion of managerial functions is devoted to a conceptual view of managing information which necessarily covers computers as a major means of handling information.

DEVELOPING FUTURE MANAGERS

The need for managers will increase with the development of more complex enterprises. Rapid growth of knowledge useful to management will demand a higher quality of managers. Greater effort is being given to the development of persons who can better perform managerial functions. This book directs attention to the essentials of developing future managers. It provides some of the available knowledge useful to future managers and indicates the attitude and point of view of good managers.

Executive development programs have long been a useful means for supplying the needed manager personnel. More recently, attention has been given to **Organizational Development** (OD), which includes the process of reeducation and training to increase the adaptability of the organization to environmental requirements. Organizational development thus is a broad subject area of management, since its focus is on group adaptations rather than personal leadership qualities.

The characteristics of a good manager may be described in broad terms of initiative, dependability, intelligence, judgment, good health, integrity, perseverance, and so on. The trouble with this broad approach is that it is not very useful in describing how a given individual can develop into a better manager. Two more useful approaches provide conceptual help to those aspiring to managerial positions.

One approach, suggested by Robert Katz,[3] is to explain the *skills* which can be developed. In this approach three skills are fundamental: (1) technical, (2) human, and (3) conceptual. **Technical skills** relate to the proficiency of performing an activity in the correct manner and with the right techniques. This skill is the easiest to describe, because it is the most concrete and familiar. The musician and the athlete must learn how to play properly and must practice their skills. The executive, likewise, develops skills in such areas as mechanics, accounting, selling and production that are especially important at lower levels of an organization. As the executive rises to more responsibility, other skills become relatively more important. A second required skill involves **human relationships**. The executive deals with people and must be able to "get along" with them. Human relations concentrates on developing this skill of cooperating with others. However, if colleagues notice that the executive has read a book on "how to win friends" and is consciously attempting to manipulate them, trouble develops. A third skill involves **conceptual ability**: to see individual matters as they relate to the total picture. This skill is the most difficult to describe, yet is the most important, especially at higher levels of an organization. Much of this skill can be learned, and is not "just born into a person." Conceptual skill depends on developing a creative sense of discovering new and unique ideas. It enables the executive to perceive the pertinent factors, to visualize the key problems, and to discard the irrelevant facts.

A second approach to analyzing factors important in developing managers is suggested in an early work by Charles E. Summer.[4] He emphasizes knowledge factors, attitude factors, and ability factors. *Knowledge factors* refer to ideas, concepts, or principles that are

[3] Robert L. Katz, "Skills of an Effective Administrator," *Harvard Business Review* (January-February 1955), pp. 33–42.

[4] Charles E. Summer, *Factors in Effective Administration* (New York: Graduate School of Business, Columbia University, 1956).

conscious, able to be expressed, and accepted because they are subject to logical proof. *Attitude factors* relate to those beliefs, feelings, desires, and values that may be based on emotions and that may not be subject to conscious verbalization. Interest in one's work, confidence in one's mental competence, desire to accept responsibility, respect for the dignity of one's associates, and desire for creative contribution are some of the attitudes that can be acquired by proper education. *Ability factors* are too often treated as being unaffected by environment. Executive development depends upon attention to four major ability factors: skill, art, judgment, and wisdom. These ability factors are abstract, but they direct one's thinking to factors that can be developed by the individual who takes the trouble to consider them.

The basic proposition of this book is that the development of managers can best be achieved through a directed effort in the study of the subject of management. True, some people may be born leaders; others may be able to learn as apprentices while working with a mature manager; others may become successful managers with education in the law, engineering, medicine, and so on. Yet, these leaders with innate abilities, varied practices, or education could more rapidly become superior managers if they acquired the necessary knowledge and attitudes in the most efficient manner—some formal recognition of the complex role of managers. Furthermore, in modern complex organizations the demand for managers is so great that reliance on elite leaders results in a deficiency in the supply of managers.

THE STRUCTURE OF THIS BOOK

Part 1 of this book consists of three chapters that provide the historical background of management thought and the philosophical and social setting in which management activities take place. Part 2, consisting of six chapters, offers the essentials of the seven managerial functions, which form the central theme of managerial activities. In these chapters, the reader will find some of the basic concepts that are useful in all management applications. These concepts should be considered as first approximations. The modern manager will do well to recognize that the subject of management is developing rapidly and that new ideas are being formed. This fact should be exciting and promising; it surely should not be discouraging or frustrating.

Part 3 consists of chapters that concentrate on important operational activities. These chapters include concepts and analytical devices of special importance to particular areas of operations. Each of the sub-areas of management has developed unique methods of applying the general concepts of management. Marketing managers use key terms of special significance to them; financial managers apply economic and accounting concepts in handling money and other resources; operations managers focus on the production and manufacturing aspects of operations; public administrators develop unique approaches to fit organizations in the public sector with a non-profit orientation; multinational managers need understanding of cultural differences and knowledge of international monetary and economic mechanisms; entrepreneurs and small business managers must adapt quickly to changes, searching for niches in which they can maintain advantages; and administrators of health delivery services serve as the managerial interface for patients, the medical staff, and the community.

REFERENCES

LEAVITT, H. J., W. R. DILL, and H. B. EYRING, *The Organizational World.* New York: Harcourt Brace Jovanovich, 1973.

MAGAZINER, IRA C. and ROBERT B. REICH, *Minding America's Business— The Decline and Rise of the American Economy.* New York: Harcourt Brace Jovanovich, 1982.

MASSIE, JOSEPH L. and JOHN DOUGLAS, *Managing: A Contemporary Introduction,* 4th ed. Englewood Cliffs, N.J.: Prentice-Hall, Inc., 1985.

MINTZBERG, HENRY, *The Nature of Managerial Work.* New York: Harper and Row, Publishers, Inc., 1973; *The Nature of Managerial Work.* Englewood Cliffs, N.J.: Prentice-Hall, Inc., 1980.

NAISBITT, JOHN, *Megatrends—Ten New Directions Transforming our Lives.* New York: Warner Books, 1984.

PETERS, THOMAS J. and ROBERT H. WATERMAN, JR., *In Search of Excellence.* New York: Harper and Row, Publishers, Inc., 1982.

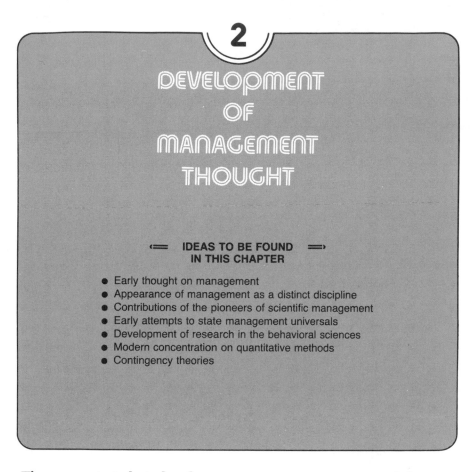

2

DEVELOPMENT OF MANAGEMENT THOUGHT

<== **IDEAS TO BE FOUND** ==>
IN THIS CHAPTER

- Early thought on management
- Appearance of management as a distinct discipline
- Contributions of the pioneers of scientific management
- Early attempts to state management universals
- Development of research in the behavioral sciences
- Modern concentration on quantitative methods
- Contingency theories

The concentrated study of management, as a separate and distinct field of endeavor, is a product of the last century. Most writers agree that the origin of this young discipline was the work performed by Frederick W. Taylor and his associates during the scientific management movement that developed around 1900. In this chapter, the review of the development of the thinking about management will provide historical perspective for an understanding of the concepts discussed in later chapters.

PRESCIENTIFIC MANAGEMENT ERA Problems of administration were of interest to students of government even in ancient Greek and Biblical times. The Bible, for example, explains organizational problems faced by Moses in leading his people. Histories of the Roman Empire contain information on how administrative problems were handled. Table 2–1 summarizes the basic managerial ideas as they responded to situational demands from early times to the twentieth century.

Table 2-1
Early Streams of Managerial Ideas Responding to Situational Demands

Dates	Sources	Ideas	Situational Demands	Relevance to Today's Management
5000 B.C.	Sumerian civilization	Written records	Formation of governments and commerce.	Recorded data are essential to life of organizations.
4000–2000 B.C.	Egyptian	Planning, organizing, controlling	Organized efforts of up to 100,000 people for constructing pyramids.	Plans and authority structure are needed to achieve goals.
2000–1700 B.C.	Babylonians	Standards and responsibility	Code of Hammurabi set standards for wages, obligations of parties, and penalties.	Targets of expected behavior are necessary for control.
600 B.C.	Hebrews	Organization	Leaders organized groups to meet threats from outside.	Hierarchy of authority is a basic idea.
500 B.C.	Chinese	Systems, models	Commerce and military demand fixed procedures and systems.	Patterns and procedures are desirable in group effort.
500–350 B.C.	Greeks	Specialization, scientific method	Specialization laid foundation for scientific method.	Organizations need specialization; scientific attitude promotes progress.
300 B.C.–300 A.D.	Romans	Centralized organization	Far-flung empire required communication and control by Rome.	Effective communication and centralized control are necessary.
1300 A.D.	Venetians	Legal forms of organization	Venetian commerce required legal innovations.	Legal framework for commerce serves as foundation for ventures.

Date	Individual or group	Major contribution		
1400	Pacioli	Double-entry bookkeeping	Effective classification of cost and revenue demanded by increased trade.	Accounting systematizes record keeping.
1500	Machiavelli	Pragmatic use of power	Governments rely on support of masses. Expectations of leader and people must be clear. Opportunistic use of personal power makes leaders effective.	Realistic guidelines for use of power are a key.
1776	Adam Smith	Division of labor	The competitive system resulted from specialization.	Specialization and profits are key to private enterprise.
1800	Eli Whitney	Interchangeability of parts	Mass production is made possible by availability of standard parts.	Modules, segments, and parts are building blocks for organizations.
19th Century	Western nations	Corporation	Large amounts of capital required by entity with long life and limited liability.	Separation of owners from managers increases demand for professional managers.

Source: Based on Claude S. George. *The History of Management Thought*, 2nd ed. (Englewood Cliffs, N.J.: Prentice-Hall, Inc., 1972).

In spite of the fact that administrative problems received attention in ancient times, no important managerial tools of analysis developed until the end of the Dark Ages, when commerce began to grow in the Mediterranean. In the thirteenth and fourteenth centuries, the large trading houses of Italy needed a means of keeping records of business transactions. To satisfy this need, the technique of **double entry bookkeeping** was first described by Pacioli in 1494. The roots of modern accounting, therefore, were planted four centuries before they were to form an important field of knowledge for the modern manager.

Not until after the rise of the capitalistic system did students rigorously give attention to the field of economics. In 1776, Adam Smith wrote *The Wealth of Nations*, in which he developed important economic concepts. He emphasized the importance of **division of labor**, with its three chief advantages: (1) an increase in the dexterity of every workman; (2) the saving of time lost in passing from one type of work to the next; and (3) the better use of new machines. The development of the factory system resulted in an increased interest in the economics of production and the entrepreneur.

In the Middle Ages (and even until recently in many countries) the family unit was the basic production organization. A skilled craftsman taught his sons a trade, and the family was known by its particular trade and skill. Modern surnames such as Carpenter, Goldsmith, Butcher, Farmer, and Taylor are evidence of this development. Production functions were not distinguished from social functions; there was still no need for separate attention to managerial activities. The inventions of the eighteenth century initiated a change which Toynbee later called the Industrial Revolution. Production moved from the home to a separate installation—the factory—where machinery was concentrated and labor employed. In the early stages of the Industrial Revolution, owners of factories directed production but generally did not distinguish between their ownership functions and their management duties.

Some of the first factory owners concentrated on improving methods of production and introduced concepts that proved fundamental to modern manufacturing methods. Before 1800, Eli Whitney and Simeon North developed the concept of **interchangeability of parts** in the manufacture of pistols and muskets. This concept led to the producing of parts to close tolerances, thus making possible the exchange of one part for another without fitting or further machining. In 1796, Matthew R. Boulton and James Watt, Jr., organized the Soho Foundry, in which product components were standardized, cost records kept, and management of the factory improved.

In the early nineteenth century, the need for larger aggregations of capital to support factory operations resulted in increased applications of a special legal form of organizing a business. The **corporation**, as a separate legal entity, could sell shares of stock to many individuals and thus raise large sums of capital. Stockholders then became so numerous that all could not actively manage a business. By the middle of the nineteenth century, general incorporation acts made it possible for many businesses to use this legal form of organization at a time in which technological developments were forcing an increase in the size of the manufacturing unit. If the family fortune was insufficient for the family owners to expand, the corporation provided a means by which capital could be secured from owners who were not managers. The distinction between the function of owners and the function of managers became clear. This distinction set the stage for students to concentrate on the management process as a separate field of study.

The social evils of the Industrial Revolution received wide attention in the early nineteenth century. In England, social reformers sought legal regulation of employment practices in the Factory Acts of 1802, 1819, and 1831. One reformer also became a pioneer in management. Robert Owen, as manager of a large textile firm in New Lanark, Scotland, concentrated on the improvement of working conditions and on the development of a model community. The social impact of modern productive methods became an important interest of such men in operating management.

By 1832, scientists and other persons not directly related to ownership of manufacturing firms began to consider improvements in management. In that year Charles Babbage, a mathematician and a teacher, wrote *On the Economy of Machinery and Manufactures*, in which he applied his principles to the workshop. This early work introduced the idea of using scientific techniques to improve the managing process. Such developments before the twentieth century were, however, exceptional and did not include any integrated effort to study management. The social, legal, technical, and economic environment had not provided the necessary conditions for concentrating on management improvements. By the end of the nineteenth century, the stage was set for a group of people to tackle management problems in a systematic manner.

CLASSICAL MANAGEMENT

By 1886 the American Society of Mechanical Engineers was an established professional society, holding meetings at which leaders presented technical papers. In that year Henry R. Towne, President of Yale & Towne Manufacturing Company, presented a paper, "The Engineer as an Economist," and made a plea to the society to recognize management as a separate field of study.

At the time that Towne's paper was presented to the ASME, Frederick W. Taylor was an operating manager at the Midvale Steel Works. He had progressed from the level of worker in the plant—where he had been able to observe the accepted practices of the time—and had obtained an engineering degree in 1883 by studying evenings at Stevens Institute of Technology. With his strong will and keen powers of observation, he rebelled against the restriction of production that he called "soldiering." Taylor noticed that managers were supposed to "pick up" their management skill through trial and error. "Rules of thumb" were their only guides. Above all, he argued that too much of management's job was being left to the worker. He felt that it was management's job to set up methods and standards of work and to provide an incentive for the worker to increase production. Two of Taylor's specific contributions resulted from this thinking: (1) experiments with Maunsel White led to the development of high-speed cutting steel that trebled production; (2) interest in motivating the worker to greater effort led to a piece-rate system of wage payment based upon a definite time standard.

Taylor would have been remembered for his early work in providing specific techniques for managers; yet his contributions leading to his recognition as the "father of scientific management" were two books written after he had resigned as a practicing manager: *Shop Management* (1906) and *The Principles of Scientific Management* (1911).

Until his death in 1915, Taylor expounded his new philosophy, stressing that the core of scientific management was not in individual techniques but in the new attitude toward managing a business enterprise. The essence of **scientific management** was in four general areas:

1. The discovery, through use of the scientific method, of basic elements of man's work to replace rules of thumb.
2. The identification of management's function of planning work, instead of allowing workmen to choose their own methods.
3. The selection and training of workers and the development of cooperation, instead of encouraging individualistic efforts by employees.
4. The division of work between management and the workers so that each would perform those duties for which he was best fitted, with the resultant increase in efficiency.

Scientific management was an innovation and, as such, generated tremendous opposition. During Taylor's lifetime and in spite of the support of such other leaders as Louis Brandeis, James Dodge, and Henry Towne, opposition to change retarded the spread of its basic ideas. Public opposition was demonstrated before special Congressional committee hearings in 1912. At these hearings, Taylor's testimony in defense of his ideas contained some of the most lucid explanations of the central ideas to this first stage of management as a separate and identifiable discipline.

Taylor was a major contributor to scientific management, but by no means was he alone. Henry L. Gantt, a contemporary and associate of Taylor, joined in the attack on existing management practices and emphasized the psychology of the worker and the importance of morale in production. Gantt devised a wage payment system, which stimulated foremen and workers to strive for improvement in work practices. He developed a charting system for scheduling production that remains the basis for modern scheduling techniques.

Other leaders in the scientific management movement had independently developed improved techniques of management before being influenced by Taylor. Frank Gilbreth made studies in applying principles of motion economy and is considered to be the originator of motion study. Starting in the construction industry, he revolutionized the techniques of bricklaying and later applied his new approach in a variety of industries. His wife, Lillian Gilbreth, not only helped her husband develop his ideas but also contributed to a new dimension in her writings on the psychology of management. Both Gilbreths took an analytical approach and stressed the importance of giving attention to minute details of work. This approach was to become an important characteristic of all scientific management.

Morris L. Cooke and Harrington Emerson were among the founders of scientific management and are important for their applications of the philosophy to a wider group of activities. Cooke demonstrated the applicability of scientific management in nonindustrial fields, especially in university operations and city management. Emerson concentrated on introducing new ideas to the Santa Fe Railroad and later developed what he termed twelve principles of efficiency.

Scientific management's effect on unemployment rapidly became a national and social issue. Dedicated disciples of the movement took an aggressive mechanical view of production and immediately created opposition by organized labor. The result was that the spread of scientific management was not as great as it could have been.

By 1924, when the first International Management Congress was held in Prague, scientific management had become international in scope. Henri Fayol had previously led a French movement in the improvement of work at the administrative level of organization. Lenin had seen the advantages of the techniques of scientific management and introduced the ideas in Russia.

During the 1920s and 1930s, scientific management fell into the hands of "efficiency experts," who concentrated on the mechanical aspects of production. Critics of the movement pointed out that this approach neglected the elements of the psychological needs of workers and the sociological aspects of cooperation. They also observed that scientific management, by concentrating on the details of the shop, had neglected improvements at higher levels of the organization. During these decades, some management thinkers and practitioners attempted to remedy this defect by formulating generalizations deduced from their understanding of what management should be. A number of books attempted to collect these universals and state them as tight and complete prescriptions.

Lyndall Urwick, a British consultant, Ralph C. Davis, a college professor, James D. Mooney and Allan C. Reiley, industrial executives, and many others expounded their views concerning the principles of organization and management. These views were considered authoritative and were widely quoted as basic readings for the education of managers. Later, they served as points of departure for students who were intellectually skeptical of the universality of the observations when applied to actual business cases. Thus the groundwork was laid for a multiple attack on the study of essentials of management.

BEHAVIORAL AND QUANTITATIVE APPROACHES TO MANAGEMENT

In the last 50 years, many disciplines have been active in making contributions to the development of management thought. The fields of public administration and business education have felt, more than any others, the impact of the diversified attack on current practices and past thought by disciplines that previously had little to offer the practicing manager. Barriers to communication among these disciplines were pierced by joint research and the publication of findings in both academic journals and popular periodicals. The streams of thought, together with their principal exponents, that have contributed to this development appear in Figure 2–1. A partial integration of these streams has been attempted by some of their exponents as they developed interests in fields outside their major discipline (indicated by arrows and repetition of their names in the fields in which they have made important contributions).

One of the earliest and clearly most important events in this trend of interdisciplinary activity in the study of management was the Hawthorne Experiment, conducted between 1927 and 1932 at a plant of the Western Electric Company. Elton Mayo, a Harvard sociologist, and a team of social scientists conducted a series of experiments and worked with management in an attempt to explain variations of productivity in the plant. Physical factors, such as lighting and working conditions, were the first aspects to receive attention, but psychological factors emerged as the more important.

An early contributor to the psychology and sociology of management, Mary Parker Follett, attempted to interpret classical management principles in terms of the human factors. She proposed four principles as guides to management thinking.

1. Coordination by direct contact of the responsible people concerned.
2. Coordination in the early stages.
3. Coordination as the reciprocal relating to all the factors in the situation.
4. Coordination as a continuing process.

Central to the thinking behind these principles was the idea that management must continually adjust to the total situation. Follett observed that conflict is usually present in management situations and offered a process for resolving it. The manager must handle conflict by (1) domination, (2) compromise, or (3) integration. The first two never satisfy everyone, but integration can achieve a new approach to the problem that will satisfy all parties. In order to achieve integration (1) the differences must be brought into the open; (2) a "re-evaluation" must be made by all parties; (3) all parties must anticipate the responses of the others and seek a new position that suits not only the parties but the relationship among the parties. In other words, each party should avoid the limitations of his own position and seek a new, integrated position acceptable to all.

Later, behavioral scientists developed new approaches to the study of management. Kurt Lewin developed theory and research under the heading of "group dynamics." His study with small groups led him and his followers to concentrate on the advantages of group participation and increased interaction among members of a group.

More recently, psychologists have improved the validity and reliability of tests used for the selection and placement of individuals in industrial and government organizations. Other recent developments in the behavioral sciences will be summarized in a later chapter. It is clear that the modern manager has access to new

MANAGERIAL ACCOUNTING	MANAGERIAL ECONOMICS	ORGANIZATION STRUCTURE AND SYSTEMS	ORGANIZATION BEHAVIOR	MANAGEMENT SCIENCE (MATH. & STAT.)	TECHNOLOGICALLY ORIENTED DISCIPLINES
Pacioli (1494)	A. Smith (1776) A. Marshall (1890)			C. Babbage (1932) (1886)	C. Babbage → H.R. Towne F. Taylor
		Taylor →		Taylor →	F. Gilbreth L. Gilbreth H. Emerson
		Weber →	M. Weber L. Gilbreth		
			H.L. Gantt →	K. Pearson	H.L. Gantt
		H. Favol O. Sheldon J. McKinsey		W. Shewhart L. Tippet	
J. McKinsey J.M. Clark →	J.M. Clark	M.P. Follett →	M.P. Follett		
1930					
J. Canning → E. Cammon	J. Canning →	Mooney and Reiley L. Gulick	E. Mayo J. Moreno T. Parsons K. Lewin		
		L. Urwick C. Barnard R. Davis	C. Barnard F. Roethlisberger L. Warner R. Merton		L. Urwick
A. Littleton W. Paton					
1940	G. Terborgh		A. Bavelas W.F. Whyte H.A. Simon P. Selznick	A. Wald H.A. Simon N. Wiener C. Shannon G. Dantzig E. Deming W. Feller	R. Barnes E. Grant H.A. Simon Holt Modigliani Muth H. Maynard
H.A. Simon → C. Devine W. Vatter	H.A. Simon →	H.A. Simon			
	G. Shackle W. Leontief T. Koopman				

20

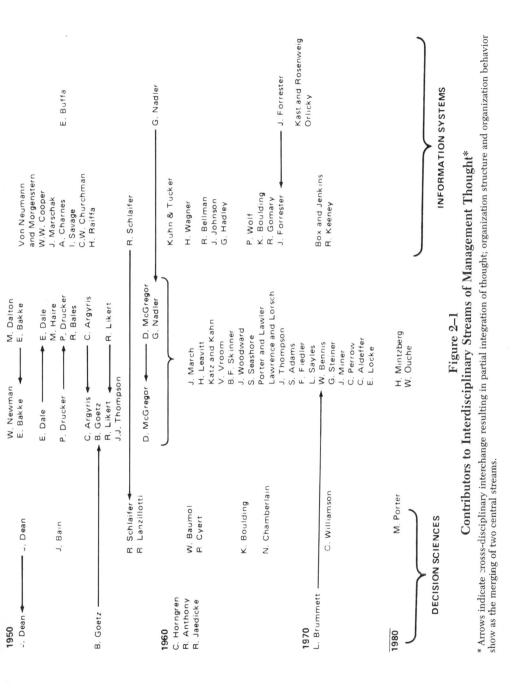

Figure 2–1

Contributors to Interdisciplinary Streams of Management Thought*

* Arrows indicate cross-disciplinary interchange resulting in partial integration of thought; organization structure and organization behavior show as the merging of two central streams.

21

techniques that have scientific basis, thus eliminating the need to depend solely on intuition and guesses.

Much of the modern development in management can be traced to the theoretical work of a practicing executive, Chester I. Barnard, who in 1938 published a classic in management literature, *The Functions of the Executive*. In this work he introduced the concepts of informal organization, decision making, status, and communications that became important topics for management consideration. His influence on the thinking of other leaders with regard to new developments cannot be overemphasized.

Concurrent with the developments in the behavioral sciences were other developments, quite separate and independent, that affected management. Economics, the basic discipline of business for a century, began to direct its attention to business decisions. New meanings of old economic principles began to have practical implications for the manager. Accounting, too, took on a new outlook. It no longer looked only to past transactions but began to offer answers to problems dealing with the future. In the early 1920s J. O. McKinsey developed budgeting as a basic tool for management's use. Although McKinsey died at an early age, he was able to develop budgetary theory as a college professor, expand its use through a consulting firm that he founded, and apply it in practice as Chairman of the Board of Marshall Field & Company. In a short period of time, both economics and accounting became basic fields of study for the manager.

Modern developments in management have promised help to the manager in still another area that has long caused management worry, that is, how to handle uncertainty. Here, the maturing of the field of statistics proved to be of great help. After W. A. Shewart had applied statistical theory to the area of quality control during the early thirties, the use of statistical samples expanded and enabled the manager to estimate probabilities with mathematical accuracy in other types of problems. Recently the manager has been offered a way of using this same approach in handling problems about which his information is very uncertain.

With the availability of electronic computers, the manager now can deal with theoretical questions in a more definite and rigorous manner. This new hardware permits him to state his theory in terms of a clearly definable model and to handle the constants and variables of his problem with more precision. New mathematical tools of analysis, such as linear programming, which G. B. Dantzig developed in the late 1940s, enable the manager to find the best answers to problems of resource allocation, which he previously had to approximate through application of judgment and experience.

Other developments in quantitative analysis are being brought forth by researchers and are rapidly being adopted by practicing managers. In fact, the approach of a team of specialists, working together to frame quantitative techniques for making decisions on companywide issues, has led to the creation of a new analytical profession called **operations research (OR)**. The limits of operations research are ill-defined, because its applications are continually breaking out of previously conceived frameworks and deal with a wide range of problems including defense systems, outer space, and management. **Management science** is a term of more recent origin and refers more specifically to application of quantitative techniques to management problems. The terms tend to be used interchangeably yet OR is more general and theoretical in its orientation while management science is more application- and problem-oriented to management.

This short survey of management should make it clear that the subject is faced with growing pains. These pains result from the continuous process of having to accommodate new ideas that spring from many new sources. Management thought, therefore, continually requires restatement and consolidation. One of the leaders in this modern development of progressing from one fruitful stream of thought to another is Herbert A. Simon. Trained as a political scientist, he was faced first with problems of public administration. These problems led to questions of organization, and his publication in 1947 of *Administrative Behavior*—a book that proceeded to challenge the existing thought on the subject and became a classic in the field. Concurrently, economic questions were central to topics of his interest, and thus he presented research in that discipline. However, psychological aspects of organization and economics became so important that he intensively began to handle specific issues in that discipline. Throughout his research, he felt the need for the rigorous tools of mathematics and statistics. His techniques, therefore, employed these basic tools together with experimentation on the applications of computers in management research. His approach, thus, has been interdisciplinary and can be categorized primarily as involved with "decision making," a term that he has been influential in establishing as a major subject for management attention. Others in management thinking are finding it necessary to take a similar interest in many disciplines.

The development of management thought has accelerated and diversified to an extent that defies comprehensive treatment in a single volume. Table 2–2, however, summarizes the pioneers in disciplines closely related to management and identifies their contributions.

Table 2–2
Pioneers in Management and Their Contributions
(chronological by birth date)

Name	Chief Publications	Major Contributions
Henri Fayol (1841–1925)	*Administration Industrielle et Generale* (1916).	Stressed that the theory of administration was equally applicable to all forms of organized human cooperation.
Harrington Emerson (1853–1931)	*Efficiency as Basis for Operation and Wages* (1900). *The Twelve Principles of Efficiency* (1912). *The Scientific Selection of Employees* (1913).	Studied the Sante Fe Railroad and promoted "scientific management" in general usage.
Frederick W. Taylor (1856–1915)	*A Piece-Rate System* (1895). *Shop Management* (1903). *On the Art of Cutting Metals* (1906). *The Principles of Scientific Management* (1911).	Father of Scientific Management. Developed high-speed cutting tools. Introduced time study to industry.
Karl Pearson (1857–1936)	*On the Correlation of Fertility with Social Value* (1913). *Tables for Statisticians* (1933).	Developed basic statistical tables and early statistical techniques, including the chi-square test and the standard deviation concept.
Henry L. Gantt (1861–1919)	*Work, Wages, and Profits* (1910). *Industrial Leadership* (1916). *Organizing for Work* (1919).	Emphasized relation of management and labor. Stressed conditions that have favorable psychological effects on the worker. Developed charting techniques for scheduling.
Max Weber (1864–1920)	*The Theory of Social and Economic Organization* (translated by Henderson & Parsons in 1947). From Max Weber: *Essays in Sociology* (translated by Gerth and Mills in 1946).	The foremost pioneer in the development of a theory of bureaucracy.
Frank Gilbreth (1868–1924)	*Concrete System* (1908). *Motion Study* (1911).	Searched for "the one best way." Introduced motion study to industry.
Mary Parker Follett (1868–1933)	*Dynamic Administration* (edited by Metcalf and Urwich) (1941).	Led in practical observations about the value of human relations to the basic principles of organization.

Table 2–2—(continued)

Name	Chief Publications	Major Contributions
G. Elton Mayo (1880–1949)	*The Human Problems of an Industrial Civilization* (1933). *The Social Problems of an Industrial Civilization* (1933).	Stressed the importance of human and social factors in industrial relationships. Questioned the overemphasis on technical skills at the expense of adaptive social skills. Led a team of researchers in extensive studies at the Hawthorne plant of Western Electric Company.
Chester I. Barnard (1886–1961)	*The Functions of the Executive* (1938). *Organization and Management* (1948).	Leader in stressing sociological aspects of management. Concentrated on the concept of authority, the importance of communication, and informal organizations in management.
Kurt Lewin (1890–1947)	*Resolving Social Conflicts* (1948). *Field Theory in Social Science* (1951).	Developed research and theory of group dynamics.
Ronald A. Fischer (1890–1962)	*Statistical Methods for Research Workers* (1925). *The Design of Experiments* (1935).	Pioneer in the use of statistical methods in research. Made valuable contributions to the design of experiments.
Walter A. Shewart (1891–1972)	*The Economic Quality Control of Manufactured Products* (1930).	Applied theory of probability and statistical inference to economic problems at Bell Laboratories. Developed statistical control charts.
F. J. Roethlisberger (1898–1974)	*Management and the Worker* (with W. J Dickson) (1939). *Management and Morale* (1941) *A New Look for Management* (1948).	Made a comprehensive report on the Hawthorne experiment. Led in experimental research on human factors in management.
Peter Drucker (1909–)	*The Practice of Management* (1954). *Innovation and Entrepreneurship* (1985).	Developed concept of management by objectives. As a consultant and writer, popularized new developments in management.
G. B. Dantzig (1914–)	*Maximization of a Linear Function of Variables Subject to Linear Inequalities* (1947).	Developed the basis for practical applications of linear programming.

Table 2–2—(continued)

Name	Chief Publications	Major Contributions
Claude Shannon (1916)	*The Mathematical Theory of Communication* (1948).	Laid the theoretical foundation for information theory.
Herbert A. Simon (1916–)	*Administrative Behavior* (1947). *Models of Man* (1957). *Organization* (with J. March) (1958).	Winner of Nobel Prize in Economics. Developed theory building from behavioral and quantitative bases for modern management.

OVERVIEW OF SHIFTS IN FOCUS IN MANAGEMENT THOUGHT   The development of management thought over the last hundred years has not been a single continuous stream from one source but has been a process of integrating ideas from a number of streams, as indicated in Figure 2–1. Furthermore, during this development the focus of attention has shifted from one stream to another. (1) From 1900 to 1930, the major focus was on the physical factors as viewed from industrial engineering and economics. (2) Between 1930 and 1960, the focus shifted to the human factors affecting productivity, with supporting efforts from managerial accounting and classical concepts of personnel and finance. (3) During the 1960s, as a result of reports prepared for the Ford and Carnegie Foundations, emphasis was placed on achieving precision through the use of quantitative methods (mathematics and statistics) and the behavioral sciences (psychology, sociology, anthropology). Computers and systems thinking developed rapidly during this decade as techniques for management. (4) The trend in the 1970s focused on organizational behavior (built on the behavioral approach) as almost synonymous with management. In the last decade **contingency** theories, that is, theories of management which are dependent upon the environmental situations in which they are applied, received major attention. The classical approach of a single universal theory of management has given way to a number of contingency theories. Legal aspects, cultural considerations, and the emerging field of public administration have received new emphasis. (Table 2–3 outlines some of the many bases for managerial thought).

This overview of the historical development of management indicates two concurrent, opposing trends over time: first, periodically, specialists in one or two streams of thought have attempted to narrow management topics to their particular stream of research, e.g.,

Table 2–3
Disciplinary Bases for Management

Discipline	Special Emphasis
Industrial Engineering	Measurement and analysis of physical factors in achieving efficiency.
Economics	Allocation of scarce resources with orientation to future.
Financial Accounting	Recording, reporting, analyzing, and auditing of past transactions.
Public Administration	Formation of a rational hierarchy for the accomplishment of activities.
Legal Profession	Development of a consistent course of action based on precedents to achieve stability, order, and justice.
Statistical Methods	Employment of probability theory to infer facts from samples and to handle uncertainty.
Mathematics	Construction of models which state explicitly one's assumptions, objectives, and constraints.
Psychology	Scientific investigations concerning human needs, perceptions, and emotional factors.
Sociology	Study of interrelationships within and among human groups in society.
Anthropology	Cultural variations and discoverable patterns of behavior from history and environment.

the emphasis on organization behavior in the 1970s, yet, second, new demands by society on management have continually expanded the scope of management to include new streams of thought, e.g., the present attention to the environment, legal and ethical issues, and information systems.

The objective of this small volume is to summarize the vast, complex field of management and to encourage the reader to seek more depth in other books. However, the 1980s witnessed the publication of many small books with the opposite objective—to state the heart of management in a single set of cliches. Such titles as *The One-Minute Manager* and a sequel, *The 59 Second Manager*, have been purchased in large quantities. The prime reason for the success of these popular management books is that the American public became interested in the field when the Japanese and other nationalities demonstrated that other management ideas were needed by American managers.

This increased interest in improving management is a most favorable sign for the future. But one of the greatest threats to this improvement is the reduction of the subject to platitudes and homilies. As management literature expands in the 1980s the reader must show discretion to ensure that future improvements are built on a solid foundation. This chapter has provided the background needed to understand the complex ideas from which this improved management will evolve.

REFERENCES

FILIPETTI, GEORGE, *Industrial Management in Transition.* Homewood, Ill.: Richard D. Irwin, Inc., 1949.

GEORGE, CLAUDE S., *The History of Management Thought,* 2nd ed. Englewood Cliffs, N.J.: Prentice-Hall, Inc., 1972.

MERRILL, HARWOOD, ed., *Classics in Management.* New York: American Management Association, 1960.

METCALF, HENRY C. and L. URWICK, eds., *Dynamic Administration.* New York and London: Management Publications Trust, Ltd., 1941.

URWICK, L., ed., *The Golden Book of Management.* London: Ryerson Press, Newman Neame, Ltd., 1956.

WREN, DANIEL, *The Evolution of Management Theory.* New York: Ronald Press, 1972.

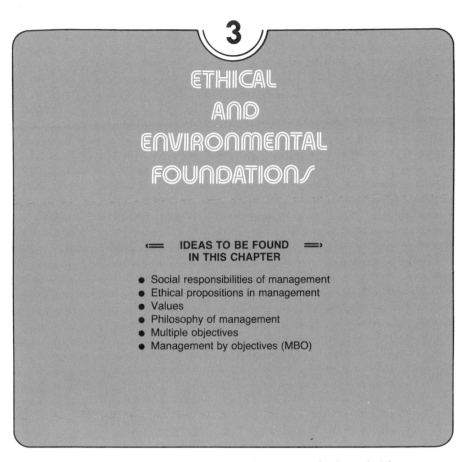

3

ETHICAL AND ENVIRONMENTAL FOUNDATIONS

⟸ **IDEAS TO BE FOUND** ⟹
IN THIS CHAPTER

- Social responsibilities of management
- Ethical propositions in management
- Values
- Philosophy of management
- Multiple objectives
- Management by objectives (MBO)

The emergence of management as a distinct and identifiable activity has had an important impact on the society within which it developed. So, too, society, with its institutions, customs, and value systems, has molded the foundations upon which management has formed its framework of thought. In recent years, the attention of businessmen, philosophers, scientists, and the general public has been directed to issues concerning responsibilities of management, ethical and legal practices of managers, and the entire set of value systems of the business community. In this chapter, we shall consider the cultural setting within which managers make decisions and the moral framework for their philosophies of management. We then point out the fundamental role of objectives in a firm.

MANAGEMENT AND SOCIETY

Management first evolved as the part of an economic system that allocated the resources of land, labor, and capital in a way to maximize material returns to satisfy the wants of human beings. Its primary orientation is still economic; yet, as a result of its increasing importance in society, it has become a social institution. Its decisions and actions now have widespread impact on other social institutions, and, therefore, management cannot escape social issues.

The growth of the large corporation, with its professional managers, has changed the nature of society through its effect on competitive forces and the ownership of private property. With its increased power in society, it has been forced to concern itself with the nature of its social responsibilities. Management must make decisions involving moral issues and must adapt itself to the social forces that affect it.

Among the many social institutions that have affected the value systems of management, the following four are particularly important: (1) the family, (2) the educational system, (3) the church, and (4) the government.

Within the patterns of values formed by these institutions, the executive must resolve issues of social responsibility. Consumerism with its emerging spokesmen and new laws, environmentalists with their increased emphasis on pollution and on threats to health and the quality of life, and political disclosures of Watergate, activities of the CIA, and bribery of executives by multinational firms forced increased attention on managers' social responsibility. Legally, executives are representatives of stockholders or a governmental agency; yet they have responsibilities to employees, consumers, suppliers, and the general public. Conflicts of ethical concepts necessarily develop.

Four schools of thought relative to social responsibility offer a framework for managers in viewing social responsibility. (1) *Profit maximization as socially desirable:* Many agree with Milton Friedman and Theodore Levitt that executives can make their best contribution to society if they focus on profit maximization. This school argues that if managers attempt "to do good" for society they will do a poor job in performing the role for which they are best fitted and will usurp the responsibility of government and social institutions which have clear roles in promoting public welfare. (2) *No long-run conflict between corporate and social responsibility:* A second school argues that the executive finds that he must assume responsibility for community and social development because his organization's profits depend upon such activities as aid to education, community development, and social welfare. In short, the executive should be socially responsible because it pays! (3) *Improvement of one's own organizational behavior best leads to social betterment:* This third school focuses on social improvements *within* one's own organization through attention to motivation, leadership, communications, power equalization, and worker satisfaction. The emphasis in this school is on a social consciousness within the organization where the manager can be effective in achieving improvements. (4) *Management as trustee:* The fourth school represents the opposite extreme from the profit maximizer; it takes the view that managers should act voluntarily as trustees of the public interest. In this view, large corporations have such increased power that their responsibilities transcend the boundaries of their own organizations. The strategic position of these large organizations requires special consciousness of social obligations. Regardless of which school is followed, the manager must develop some strategy concerning (1) how his company will adjust to external factors and (2) what impact his organization will have on its environment.

The social issues faced by modern managers are numerous and complex. Here we can list only a few as a sample to indicate the scope of subjects requiring managerial policies.

1. Policies regarding racial discrimination in its employment practices. For example, how should a firm attempt to comply with laws and court decisions on civil rights?

2. The position of multinational companies concerning divestment in South Africa because of apartheid. For example, should General Motors apply Sullivan principles in continuing South African operations to help black employment or should it divest as proposed by such people as Nobel Prize winner Bishop Tutu?

3. The willingness by business to accept "voluntary" restraints. For example, in helping the country meet its balance of payments problems, how far should management go in voluntarily restricting its overseas investment?

4. Adjustments by management to controls over exports to certain countries. For example, what guides can be established to comply with public policy concerning sale of goods to countries that have been designated as unfriendly or enemies?

5. Recognition of responsibilities to developing countries. For example, how should a large company conduct itself in small developing countries in which large purchases of raw materials have a large impact on the economic and social development of those countries?

6. Policies toward support of educational institutions. For example, should a corporation contribute to public and private educational institutions when the return on the "investment" is only indirect?

7. Involvement of management personnel in political campaigns and organizations. For example, should a corporation seek to cement ties with a particular political party?
8. Marketing policies promoting products that create health, safety, and other social problems. For example, should corporation executives be concerned with overuse or misuse of its products to ultimate social detriment—as with tobacco, liquor, drugs, weapons, and so on?
9. Operating policies that impose social costs. For example, should manufacturing operations aim at minimizing costs to the firm when they increase the costs to society in greater air pollution, water pollution, urban congestion, or unemployment?
10. Involvement in the community and in the family life of employees. For example, should management become involved in community planning, marital counseling, or religious activities?
11. Policies of providing opportunities for women in roles traditionally unavailable to them in the past.

The orientation of management has broadened in the last several decades. Initially, scientific managers focused at the shop level on how to operate efficiently. Later, the focus was on organization behavior at all levels within the organizations. More recently the scope has broadened from **micro-management** (operations within the organization) to **macro-management** (interactions between the organization and its environment). Thus a manager must develop understanding of matters affecting numerous social issues such as those listed above. Furthermore, a manager in modern society must develop some philosophical foundation for his own value system.

VALUE SYSTEMS AND MANAGEMENT

Management is confronted with two general types of propositions: those of a factual nature, which accurately describe the observable world, and those of an ethical nature, which assert that one course of action is better than another. According to this classification, a **factual proposition** can be tested and proved to be *true* or *false*, but an **ethical proposition** can only be asserted to be *good* or *bad*. Ethical matters pertain to what conditions "ought to be." The ethical elements of a proposition are subject to varying opinions and value judgments. To date, no philosophical system has been developed that can be called a "science of ethics." The problem is that there is no way to *prove* ultimate values. Value systems can be constructed only if we assume what is good; for example, one school of thought may assume that "happiness" is an ultimate good, and another school may assume that custom and tradition determine "right."

Management must meet problems involving varying mixtures of factual and ethical elements. A useful approach is to segregate the factual elements from the ethical ones and to use different methods for handling each group. A great part of the remainder of this book involves methods by which the factual elements can be analyzed. In this section, we concentrate on the ethical elements.[1]

Chester I. Barnard has described **moral behavior** as "governed by beliefs or feelings of what is right or wrong regardless of self-interest or immediate consequences of a decision to do or not to do specific things under particular conditions."[2] The difficulty concerning moral propositions is that varying standards may be used. A number of the generally accepted virtues, such as happiness, lawfulness, consistency, integrity, and loyalty, may in a specific situation conflict with one another. For example, a manager who attempts to use integrity and loyalty as his standards may experience conflict if he discovers wrongdoing on the part of a superior. Should he remain loyal to his superior, or should he maintain his integrity? Managers typically face moral dilemmas in their decisions and actions. Wayne A. R. Leys illustrates the moral conflicts faced by management in a diagram (see Figure 3–1) in which moral standards surround action but in which the standard at one arrow conflicts with the standard at the opposite arrow.

Two approaches to moral questions will illustrate some philosophical treatments of what is good or what "ought to be." One theological approach considers that certain ultimate values are matters of **natural law**. Under this view, certain actions are always wrong because they break some basic intuitive law. If one of these laws is "Thou shalt not kill," then a strict interpretation of this law would make killing wrong under all conditions. Self-defense, capital punishment, abortion, or "killing for what is right" would be considered to be wrong because they violate the natural law. An opposing viewpoint is often referred to as **situational ethics**. Under this approach, the question of whether an action is right or wrong depends upon the total situation in which the action occurs. This view holds that an action under one set of circumstances and in one environment would be right, whereas the same action under another set of circumstances and

---

[1] Also, most recent advances in the behavioral sciences have been **descriptive** (studying what *is*) while managerial policies and strategies require a **normative** orientation (determining what *should* be).

[2] Chester I. Barnard, "Elementary Conditions of Business Morals," *California Management Review*, vol. I, no. 1 (1958), p. 4.

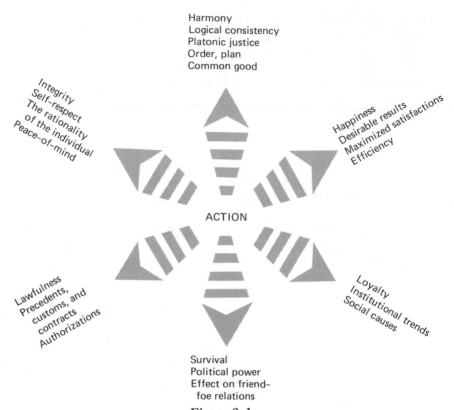

Harmony
Logical consistency
Platonic justice
Order, plan
Common good

Integrity
Self-respect
The rationality
of the individual
Peace-of-mind

Happiness
Desirable results
Maximized satisfactions
Efficiency

ACTION

Lawfulness
Precedents,
customs, and
contracts
Authorizations

Loyalty
Institutional trends
Social causes

Survival
Political power
Effect on friend–
foe relations

Figure 3–1
Conflict of Six Kinds of Moral Values

From Wayne A. R. Leys, "The Value Framework of Decision Making" in Sidney Mailick and Edward H. Van Ness, eds., *Concepts and Issues in Administrative Behavior* (Englewood Cliffs, N.J.: Prentice-Hall, Inc., 1962).

in another environment would be wrong. In an organization, a subordinate may face a situation in which his superior orders him to do something that is for the good of the organization but that may conflict with the interests of others to whom the subordinate has a responsibility. Does an order by a superior absolve the subordinate of blame, in the event that an action is detrimental to society or is outright illegal? Managers often must face dilemmas of this type.

David Riesman describes changes in societies by distinguishing three types of men according to their source of moral direction: (1) the tradition-directed type, (2) the inner-directed type, and (3) other-directed type. The *tradition-directed* type conforms to the culture and social order in which he lives. Society presents unchanging relationships that are accepted as right. In this society, little effort is directed toward changing the status quo, because it is considered wrong to break traditions. The *inner-directed* man receives his source of direction early in life from his elders and develops a "psychological gyroscope" that keeps him on his moral course. If he should get off course, he tends to feel guilt. The *other-directed* man receives his source of direction from his contemporaries and changes his concepts of what is right through a socialized sensitivity to the actions of others. Riesman describes the change in direction from the tradition-directed type of the Middle Ages, to the transitional inner-directed type of the nineteenth century, to the other-directed type of modern man.[3]

Closely related to Riesman's thinking, yet more directly pertinent to management's moral dilemma, is William H. Whyte's description of the **organization man**.[4] Whyte sees a major shift in American ideology, from the rugged individualism of the nineteenth century to the social orientation of the twentieth century. He describes this shift as a change in ethics, from what Max Weber called the Protestant Ethic to what Whyte calls the Social Ethic. The **Protestant Ethic** emphasized the quest for individual salvation through individual efforts, thrift, and competitive forces. The **Social Ethic** emphasizes that moral good is determined by pressures of society against the individual. Recent social issues, such as sexual permissiveness, the public right to information, and the personal right to privacy, raise many problems for practicing managers.

The philosophical background for managers is, of course, much too vast to cover in a short summary. Nevertheless, a study of management without a recognition of its cultural and philosophical heritage would be particularly naive. The enlightened manager of the late twentieth century should consider the vast quantity of literature that has developed over the past 3000 years. From an understanding of the provocative comments by leading philosophers and reflections by current practitioners in management, the individual manager must develop his philosophy of management for his own particular firm.

In developing a value system, managers experience conflicts of values. They need first to identify the possible causes of these conflicts. Three groups of causes have been classified: (1) differing sources of values—a diety, man's reasoning, and society, (2) differing values of individuals and organizations, and (3) differing cultural goals and values.

A primary source of managerial values is a religion. They may be based on the Moslem, Hindu, Jewish, Christian, or another religion.

---

[3] David Riesman, *The Lonely Crowd* (New Haven, Conn.: Yale University Press, 1950).

[4] William H. Whyte, *The Organization Man* (New York: Simon and Schuster, Inc., 1956).

Within each religion, we find differing and conflicting values. For example, within Christianity, vastly different creeds provide the basis for managerial action. During the 1980s many denominations have faced the complex problem of determining the position of their church and capitalism (e.g., the Roman Catholic Church's pastoral letter entitled "Catholic Social Teaching and the U.S. Economy and church committees on economic justice). Any discussion of the essentials of management must first consider religion as a source of values.

Human beings and organizations can provide the source of their own values. Too often the study of management tends to concentrate on facts and data with little attention given to the relation of basic values to managerial techniques.

A most important third source of values for management is the cultural setting. With the increasing interrelationships among nations in business, managers have become acutely aware that the cultural assumptions of managerial practices have an impact on managerial concepts. In the 1980s American managers are looking carefully at Japanese management practices because they appear to be so successful. From studies it is evident that the Japanese cultural underpinnings are strong and clearcut. Likewise, a concise statement of cultural assumptions of American management would seem to be desirable in the chapters on managerial essentials. Table 3–1 presents six basic assumptions of American management as stated by William H. Newman, a leading management writer. Although the American culture is continually changing, and thus its managerial values are changing, Newman's six assumptions can provide a first approximation of the relevant assumptions for the twenty-first century.

PHILOSOPHY OF MANAGEMENT

Executives in a specific firm operate with some type of philosophy, regardless of whether they have studied their philosophical heritage. Furthermore, they may not consider consciously the broad structure of ideas that influence their decisions, let alone make explicit the elements of this philosophy to others. If they attempt to write down the basic elements, their statements tend to appear vague and general. Even though it may be difficult to verbalize these basic ideas, the attempt to understand the moral issues involved in managerial activities provides a broad framework that gives meaning to day-to-day actions.

Philosophies differ among firms. One philosophy might be good for Firm A but not useful to Firm B. In this connection **philosophy of**

Table 3–1
Cultural Assumptions of American Management*

Basic Assumption	Related Beliefs	Managerial Function involved
Master of Destiny Viewpoint	Confidence in self-determination Rewards for hard work Obligation to fulfill commitments Time is a critical factor	Planning
Independent Enterprise—an Instrument for Social Action	Enterprise—a separate social institution Right to dissolve by either party Avoidance of conflict of interest	Organizing
Personnel Selection based on Merit	Appointment of best man Removal of "second raters" Opportunity for upward mobility Freedom for horizontal mobility Reconciling authority with egalitarian principles	Staffing
Decisions Based on Objective Analysis	Factual, rational support Need for dependable data Availability of data Freedom of expression	Decision making
Shared Decision Making	Faith in employee potential Attitudes toward work Competition in getting ahead	Leadership style
Never-ending Quest for Improvement	Normalcy of change Changing the status quo Importance of results Need for constructive evaluation	Communicating and controlling

* William H. Newman, "Cultural Assumptions Underlying U.S. Management Concepts," in Joseph L. Massie and Jan Luytjes, *Management in an International Context* (New York: Harper and Row, Publishers, Inc., 1972), pp. 327–52.

management refers to those general concepts and integrated attitudes that are fundamental to the cooperation of a social group. These concepts and attitudes evolve into the particular way in which the firm perceives itself. Generally, the philosophy of a given firm can be learned only through close and continuous association with it. It is uniquely determined for the individual firm and is affected by a group of factors that, together, may be called the concept of the firm. The concept of the firm is the total of how the firm got where it is, the place it occupies in the industry, its strengths and weaknesses, the viewpoints of its managers, and its relationship to social and political institutions.

THE ROLE OF OBJECTIVES IN MANAGEMENT

Human beings attempt to be purposive; that is, they try to act in a manner that will enable them to reach certain goals. **Rational behavior** can be defined in terms of whether actions are conducive to the achievement of predetermined goals. To the extent that management is rational, it directs its actions toward objectives. The realization of objectives is the target toward which decisions and actions are oriented.

Personal versus Organizational Objectives

Individual members of a cooperative group have their own personal ideas of what results they want to achieve. The needs of individuals are important as bases for their motivation. People will cooperate as long as the goals of a group are consistent with their ideas of their own goals. The individual has many goals: some tend to conflict; some are more important to him than others; some are short run and some are long run.

A cooperative group must maintain a set of objectives that is common to the members of the group. The organizational objectives are nonpersonal; yet they must remain consistent with the personal objectives of individuals in the organization. If an individual is to accept organizational objectives, he must feel that achieving the organizational goals will satisfy, or at least not conflict with, his own personal goals. Although an organization is composed of a number of different persons, each with his own set of goals, organization goals must serve as common denominators for the entire group. Some organizational goals will conflict with the goals of the individual; however, an individual usually has a wide "zone of indifference" and will continue to cooperate unless he becomes convinced that the conflict is fundamental.

Hierarchy of Objectives

Organizational objectives give direction to the activities of the group and serve as media by which multiple interests are channeled into joint effort. Some are ultimate and broad objectives of the firm as a whole; some serve as intermediate goals or subgoals for the entire organization; some are specific and relate to short-term aims. Moreover, there is a hierarchy of objectives in an organization: at the top, the entire organization aims in a given direction; each department, in turn, directs its efforts toward its own sets of goals; each subdivision of each department has its own meaningful aims. Each of the subgoals should be consistent with, and contribute toward, the goals of the next higher level. For example, it is generally assumed that a corporation has the broad objective of maximizing profit. To aid in achieving that overall goal, it is necessary to define more meaningful subgoals for individual departments. The marketing department may have goals in terms of a certain increase in total sales and its subdivisions may be given goals in definite geographical areas or in specific product lines. The production department may state its goals in terms of minimizing production costs, and its subdivisions may be given subgoals for particular types of costs. Other departments in turn have goals redefined for them so that they can visualize exactly their part in striving for the company's broad goal of maximizing profits.

Although economists have assumed, for analytical reasons, that profit making is *the* goal of a business enterprise, in fact management has many objectives. All these objectives form hierarchies for cooperative action; yet organizational goals often tend to conflict. For example, growth may be considered an objective that is measured in terms of sales, market share, acquisition of assets, and so on. At times, growth may be achieved by accepting new orders that are "unprofitable," for the sake of achieving a competitive edge over another firm. Management should be conscious of this conflict so that it can make basic decisions as to which goals are considered most important. In times of poor business conditions, the mere survival of the firm may be a most important goal. Profitable business may be turned down if acceptance would mean that the finances of the firm would be strained to the extent of bankruptcy. If the corporation attains a dominant position in an industry, an important goal may be the minimization of attack by the Department of Justice on antitrust grounds. The management of a firm may set as its goals the retention of present personnel and the minimization of the chance of a proxy fight by a group of stockholders. Stability of operations and security of jobs for employees may be additional objectives. Finally, service to the government and society may be not only a public relations statement but also an actual basic goal of the organization.

With an understanding of the historical basis for the management field, a clearcut definition of the concept in terms of its functions, an overview of the moral and ethical underpinnings of management, and a first approximation of the environmental and cultural factors, we conclude this introduction and move into part 2 which is a more detailed description of the techniques available for performing the managerial functions.

REFERENCES

BAUMHART, RAYMOND, *Ethics in Business*. New York: Holt, Rinehart & Winston, 1968.

BUCHHOLZ, ROGENE A., *Essentials of Public Policy for Management*. Englewood Cliffs, N.J.: Prentice-Hall, Inc., 1985.

CHEIT, EARL F., ed., *The Business Establishment*. New York: John Wiley & Sons, Inc., 1964.

DAVIS, KEITH and ROBERT L. BLOMSTROM, *Business and Society: Environment and Responsibility* (revised). New York: McGraw-Hill Book Company, Inc., 1975.

EELLS, RICHARD and CLARENCE WALTON, *Conceptual Foundations of Business*, 3rd ed. Homewood, Ill.: Richard D. Irwin, Inc., 1974.

GALBRAITH, JOHN K., *The New Industrial State*. Boston: Houghton Mifflin Co., 1971.

KUHN, JAMES W. and IVAR BERG, eds., *Values in a Business Society: Issues and Analyses*. New York: Harcourt Brace Jonanovich, 1968.

SELEKMAN, BENJAMIN M., *A Moral Philosophy for Management*. New York: McGraw-Hill Book Company, Inc. 1959.

WALTON, CLARENCE, *Ethos and the Executive*. Englewood Cliffs, N.J.: Prentice-Hall Inc., 1969.

4

DECISION MAKING

⟸ **IDEAS TO BE FOUND** ⟹
IN THIS CHAPTER

- Steps in the decision-making process
- Decision making by groups
- Techniques for aid in decision making
- Stochastic methods—payoff tables and decision trees
- Simulation
- Breakeven analysis and charts
- Direct costing
- Marginal income analysis

Most managers' duties involve making decisions of one kind or another. The other six functions could be discussed under the broad heading of decision making; therefore, we shall begin our survey of managerial functions with this activity. A manager is oriented toward making decisions rather than toward performing the actions personally; the actions are carried out by others. Thus a manager can be viewed as a specialist in the art of decision making.

In this chapter we outline the rational process of decision making by individuals. We then evaluate the types of decisions often made by groups and state the basic guidelines for use of committees in decision making. The last section of the chapter describes the most generally used techniques for aiding in the decision-making process in business firms. These techniques have been refined by economists, accountants, and specialists in quantitative methods.

DECISION MAKING BY INDIVIDUALS All human beings make decisions that affect their own actions. Managers are chiefly concerned with making decisions that will influence the actions of others. Thus, the decision-making process of management is affected by the environment of the decision makers and the role that they assume.

The product of the process is a **decision** that can be defined as a course of action consciously chosen from available alternatives for the purpose of achieving a desired result. Three ideas are important in this definition. First, a decision involves a *choice*; if there is but one possible course of action, no decision is possible. Second, a decision involves mental processes at the conscious level. The logical aspects are important; yet, emotional, nonrational, and subconscious factors do influence the process. Third, a decision is purposive; it is made to facilitate the attainment of some objective.

In the last several decades, research on the decision-making process has indicated that decision behavior is quite complex and variable; any summary of this behavior should be viewed as a first approximation of "the real thing." However, for convenience, the decision-making process may be described in five steps:

1. A good decision depends on the maker's being consciously aware of the factors that set the stage for the decision. Past actions and decisions provide the structure for current decisions. The environment of the maker determines many factors that must be accepted as being out of the control of the maker. Predetermined objectives provide the focus for a current decision. Many decisions seem to be simple at first glance merely because the maker fails to comprehend the number of factors that impinge on the situation. Broad education and experience may tend to complicate the task of decision making by increasing awareness of the number of factors involved. Confusion is not uncommon *nor* unhealthy at this stage; however, the decision maker must recognize the impossibility of considering all the facts and the need to develop a selective approach for keeping the most important and relevant facts in mind. The decision maker's mind may be saturated with facts about the situation and yet, by concentrating on the key aspects, avoid factual indigestion. It is at this stage that creative ability is put to the test. If time is available, the decision maker may find that allowing the facts to "simmer" for a while will provide opportunities for sudden insights. This gestation period can be planned and directed so that the decision maker will increase the probability of recognizing an idea when it does come to mind. This first step in decision making

too often is neglected; however, no group of high-powered techniques will substitute for an attempt to lay a good foundation for *understanding the situation*.

2. A good decision is dependent upon the *recognition of the right problem*. Too often, a decision maker is so intent on jumping to the right answer as to fail to look first for the right question. If current operations appear to be proceeding nicely, the good manager will not relax and assume that there are no problems. One of a manager's key duties is to search for problems. In this search, however, it is important to avoid creating problems or consuming time in handling insignificant problems.

The proper definition of the right problem depends on use of the concept of the **limiting factor**. Out of the maze of problems and facts, the manager seeks to frame an understanding of the problem by seeking a definition that will strike at the heart of the issue and provide residual answers to lesser problems. A key problem has the characteristic of being closely related to a series of other problems. The most damaging proof of a poor decision is to change the factor that has received attention, only to find that the problem remains.

The search for the correct questions in decision making depends upon the ethical problem of determining the end to be sought. A decision is rational if it selects means that lead to desired ends. It is useful, therefore, to try to differentiate between means and ends; yet, in reality, an end for one decision is a means for another. For example, one may wish to select a job (means) to obtain money (end), yet want the money (means) to buy a new auto (end). The auto, in turn, becomes a means for transportation or prestige (end), and so forth. This continuous process, viewed as a **means-end chain**, is a pattern showing the hierarchy of ends that, at any level, serve as instruments for attaining an end at the next higher level.

3. *Search for and analysis of available alternatives* and their probable consequences is the step most subject to logical and systematic treatment. Various disciplines offer many ideas of practical help to the manager, such as mathematical models, the theory of probability, and the economist's concept of incremental revenue and cost.

The use of logic is the key to this step. The study of logic involves the way in which the human mind passes from premises to propositions based on the premises. A **premise** is a statement of the relationship between a cause and a consequence. The process of decision making involves the consideration of a number of these "if we do A, then B will result" statements. If we classify the consequences into "desired" and "undesired," we then can develop some framework in which the premise can be weighed.

The premise is the fundamental unit of consideration in decision making. First, it is desirable to recognize the premises upon which an approach is based. Concealed premises may provide traps for reasoning. Second, we need to test the validity of our premises. We must anticipate whether the consequence will actually follow from the cause. Third, we should distinguish between value premises and factual premises. The test of the validity of a factual premise is observable and measurable; a value premise can only be asserted to be valid. If this distinction can be made clearly, we can concentrate objectively on handling the factual premises and consciously on recognizing the value judgments upon which the decision will rest. Every executive must make value judgments that are open to errors not subject to scientific study. One manner of handling these judgment errors is to recognize their existence and to understand the probable biases. Goals can be ranked by the decision maker and included in the conscious determination of alternatives and consequences. The good executive will not stop with a consideration of factual premises but will recognize that the job requires using value premises. Such an executive will attempt "to get the feel of the situation," that is, to make value premises in order to deliberately assess them.

This step of searching and analyzing alternatives and consequences is often delegated to staff executives. The staff concentrates on providing a framework of explicit premises that the line executive uses in selecting the best solution. One writer refers to this step as the design stage of decision making. No framework can possibly include *all* premises; therefore, any framework will tend to lead toward certain conclusions. Studies of the optimum number of alternatives that can be handled by a human being show that usually more than seven alternatives tend to confuse rather than help. Some individuals have the mental capacity to handle ten alternatives; others should break problems into the simplest form of two alternatives—"do or don't do." It may be desirable to include among the alternatives such possibilities as postponing action or leaving action to someone else.

4. Even in the best-designed framework of alternatives-consequences, the crucial step remains—the *selection of the solution.* At this stage, the ranking of preferences is important. The executive who must make decisions quickly may wish for the best solution but may settle for only a satisfactory one; often the theoretically best decision may be only slightly better than a number of satisfactory ones. It may be feasible to maintain a large "zone of indifference," with no need for spending additional time to find the "best." In fact, the cost of refining the decision-making process so that the

"best" can be determined is in itself a factor in determining the "best."

5. Finally, a decision must be *accepted by the organization*. The entire process is directed toward securing action. If others are affected, the decision must be communicated to them; they must be motivated to implement the decision; furthermore, control provides information for future decisions.

These five steps form a framework for the decision-making process; however, the techniques used in the process may vary, depending upon the type of executive decision making employed. Two types of decisions can be distinguished: (1) by initiation and (2) by approval. In the first type, the maker originates the process; in the latter, the decision maker receives recommendations that are approved, disapproved, or sent back for further study. The qualities needed by executives in initiating decisions are different from those needed in approving recommendations. When decision by approval is used, group interactions become more important; however, most management decisions involve some degree of interchange among different managers, and so we now turn to decision making by groups.

DECISION MAKING BY GROUPS

In a cooperative endeavor, one person may appear to have *made* the decision but in fact may have performed only one step in the process. Executives usually make decisions in a social environment. *A* may provide a fact; *B* may provide a premise; *C* may provide a value judgment; *D* may supply one complete alternative; *E* may supply a second alternative. Even if all are not present at the time of the final choice, each has had a definite part in the process. In fact, organization may be viewed as an interrelationship of decision centers. Cooperative decision making is a process by which a group attempts to develop a composite organization mind.

In large firms facing complex problems, decisions emerge from a series of meetings in which executives jointly approach problems. These group meetings may be called conferences, committees, boards, task forces, or merely staff meetings.

A **committee** may be defined as any group interacting in regard to a common, explicit purpose with formal authority delegated from an appointing executive. Some of the disagreement among managers about the use of committees is a result of a failure to discriminate among the purposes to which a committee can be assigned. Thus a critical factor in successful use of committees is the explicit statement by the appointing authority as to its expected functions. In making this statement the appointing authority should identify which of the following **purposes of committees** he is assigning in each case:

1. For fact-finding, investigation, and *collecting information.*
2. To avoid the appearance of arbitrary decisions and to *secure support* for a position.
3. To *make a decision*—a choice among alternatives.
4. To *negotiate* between conflicting positions taken by opposing interests.
5. To *stimulate* human beings to think creatively, to generate ideas, and to reinforce thoughts advanced by others.
6. To *distribute* information—to brief members of an organization on plans and facts.
7. To *provide representation* for important elements of an organization.
8. To *coordinate* different parts and subgroups of an organization toward common, overall goals.
9. To *train* inexperienced personnel through participation in groups with experienced members.

As the reader will notice in considering the above purposes, committees may be involved in any or all of the basic five steps of the decision process. Furthermore, formal committees constitute only one of many possible forms of group decision making. As a result the manager must develop an understanding of these possibilities in order to answer satisfactorily several important questions:

1. Should group decision making be used extensively in the organization? At what stages?
2. What types of problems are best tackled by groups?
3. If groups are used, how should the meetings be conducted?

Operating executives usually have strong opinions on the answers to these questions; however, these opinions range all the way from outlawing any idea of group decision making to continual use of groups in all steps.

Whether to use a committee or some other group method of decision making is a question that can be approached by looking at the following advantages:

1. A decision can be approached from different viewpoints by individual specialists on a committee.
2. Coordination of activities of separate departments can be attained through joint interactions in meetings.
3. Motivation of individual members to carry out a decision may

be increased by the feeling of participation in the decision-making process.

4. Committees provide a means by which executives can be trained in decision making.
5. Committees permit representation of different interest groups.
6. Group discussion is one method of creative thinking; a fragmentary idea by one member may create a chain reaction in the minds of others present.

The disadvantages of committees, however, are:

1. Considering the value of the time of each individual member (as measured by his salary), committees are costly.
2. The length of time required to make a decision by a committee makes its use inadvisable if a decision must be made promptly.
3. Group action may lead to compromise and indecision.
4. A superior line executive present at a meeting may make the decision individually, with subordinates attempting to appear competent by proposing ideas they believe will make a good impression.
5. Committee decisions may be reached by a method in which no one is held responsible for a decision; "buck passing" may result.

Some problems lend themselves better to committee action than do others. Any decision requiring deliberation by a group of specialists tends to encourage the committee approach. Often the conclusions of a committee are said to be advisory, the actual decision being made by a single line officer. In practice, if the members have maintained close contact with the appointing authority, the "advisory" committee report becomes the action basis for the decision.

A decision involving implementation by several departments requires some means by which the departments become involved in the decision making. Committees are means by which each department can obtain the benefit of comments from other departments. The joint decision made in a committee tends to be a balanced decision that takes into account interactions of different viewpoints. Planning decisions lend themselves to committee work, whereas implementation of orders tends to be clearer when made by a single line executive. Committees are extremely weak if forceful, immediate action is needed.

Many criticisms of committee activities are not inherent in the committee concept but result from a lack of thought about how to handle a group in the process of making a decision. Typically, if advance thought is given to a meeting, the chairman often assumes that Robert's Rules of Order will provide the "best way" to handle the meeting. The business executive tends to conduct meetings formally when the meeting involves high-level executives. Often the result is that the meeting does not engage in actual decision making but merely supplies information about a final report of a decision that has been made previously (either by a single member or by an informal group that had met prior to the formal meeting). Because group interactions are time-consuming, business executives make use of formal devices, such as agenda for the meeting, minutes of the secretary, and motions and votes on motions, to expedite the business of the group.

Research on small groups has indicated several **principles of group participation** that provide guides for group interaction.[1]

1. The physical layout, size of group, and general atmosphere are important factors determining the effectiveness of problem solving. For example, a meeting located in the boss's office will be entirely different from one held in a "neutral" conference room. If the committee has only three members, it may not have enough "interaction"; if the committee has thirty members, it is not possible for each member to participate freely.

2. Threat reduction is an important objective in the planning for group action so that the group will shift from interpersonal problems to group goals. Any tendency to put a member "on the spot" or to force him to "take sides" will increase the debating society feeling and will result in an increase of tension.

3. The best group leadership is performed by the entire group and is not the job of the "chairperson," "secretary," or other formal leader. A group that functions well tends to function informally, with no single person providing all the leadership. Leadership may shift, and different types of leaders may evolve. One member may serve as the social leader, another may serve as "questioner," another may act as "clarifier" or "summarizer," and so forth.

4. Goals should be explicitly formulated by the group. The group should refrain from being "fenced in" by predetermined rules. The objective is to increase the involvement of each member in the decision-making process.

5. An agenda should be formulated by the group but should be changed as new goals develop from new needs. Preplanning for meetings should retain *flexibility* so that the group maintains its ability to meet issues as it perceives them.

[1] J. R. Gibb, G. N. Platts, and L. F. Miller, *Dynamics of Participative Groups* (St. Louis, Mo.: Swift and Co., 1959).

6. The decision-making process should continue until the group formulates a solution upon which it can form a *consensus*. If the group action results in a minority opinion, the group has failed to maximize its effectiveness. In a group that emphasizes this principle, there is no formal voting. Discussion continues until no one in the group can add any improvements to the solution.
7. Any group should be made aware of the *interaction process* by which the group arrives at solutions. In this manner, the skill of being a member of a group becomes a distinguishable skill that the executive can develop. This principle leads to the idea that group actions are important subjects for study; continual evaluations should be made of group processes.

Note that these principles were derived from research in the 1950s in the United States; however, not many American firms seriously attempted to apply them until recently. But with the obvious success of their practice in Japan, American firms are eager to try Japanese approaches, especially quality circles and the stress on seeking consensus. The Japanese **ringi system** of decision making has received less attention. This approach, which involves the horizontal participation by a number of middle managers prior to consideration by top management, represents a device for knitting together as many people as possible in decision making.

In 1985, prior to the construction of the new Saturn plant in Tennessee, General Motors Corporation reached an agreement with the United Automobile Workers union that radically changed organization structure and joint decision processes with management and labor. All levels involve committees with both management and labor participants. At the top is a strategic advisory committee composed of middle management joint committees, business units, work unit modes as well as a work unit of 6 to 15 workers led by an elected UAW counselor. After 30 years practicing managers are recognizing the value of group-decision processes and many of the principles outlined above. The immediate cause for this change was the desire to reduce the several thousand dollar cost advantage held by the Japanese in the production of small cars.

Decisions vary as to their complexity and importance, whether they are made primarily by individuals or by groups. The more complex and important a decision, the greater the need for useful decision rules. The complexity of a decision increases as the number of variables to be considered increases, as the degree of uncertainty increases, and as more value judgments are required. The importance of a decision increases when more decisions are dependent on it, when more subordinates are involved, and when the financial consequences are more critical.

**TECHNIQUES FOR AIDING
DECISION MAKING** Decisions can be greatly improved, whether made individually or in groups, by employing a number of techniques of analysis developed over the last five decades by economists, statisticians, accountants, and mathematicians. In this section we shall introduce four of the most useful and fundamental analytical techniques. In Chapters 10 through 17, we will add to this tool bag for decision makers.

We start with techniques that help managerial decision making under conditions of risks. Usually, the manager faces uncertainty and risks and thus this introduction applies generally to most decision situations. We then move to probably the most basic and simplest technique—the breakeven analysis. Finally, we offer a short introduction into two theoretical approaches developed by accountants and economists—direct costing and marginal analysis.

**Stochastic
Methods** In many management decisions, *the probability* of the occurrence of an event can be assumed to be known, even when a particular outcome is unpredictable. Under these conditions of risk, stochastic methods will be useful. Actually, stochastic methods merely systematize the thinking about assumptions, facts, and goals that is involved in decisions under conditions of risk.

Three steps are basic to formalizing the factors to be considered in a decision involving probabilities: (1) The decision maker should first lay out, in tabular form, all the possible *actions* that seem reasonable to consider and all the possible *outcomes* of these actions. (2) The decision maker must then state in quantitative form a "probability distribution" projecting chances of each outcome that might result from each act. In this step, it may only be possible to assign probabilities that are reasonable estimates. The key to this step is to state explicitly the various probabilities that might be attached to each act-outcome situation. (3) Finally, the decision maker must use some quantitative yardstick of value (usually dollars) that measures the value of each outcome. It is then possible to calculate an average of the outcome-values weighted by the assigned probabilities; the result is called the **expected monetary value**.

To illustrate the use of these steps, suppose that a store manager must decide whether to stock Brand A or Brand B. Either brand can be stocked, but not both. If A is stocked and it is a success, the manager can make $200, but if it is a failure, there can be a loss of $500. If Brand B is stocked and it is a success, the manager can make $400, but if it is a failure, there can be a loss of $300. Which brand should be stocked? Without some idea of the probabilities of success and failure of these brands, the manager's thinking cannot be quantified. But assume that the manager's feelings about the probabilities of each outcome are:

Probability of	Brand A	Brand B
Success	.80	.50
Failure	.20	.50

Payoff Table   The store manager can present the above information in tabular form, showing the conditional values for each **strategy** (choice of brand) under each **state of nature** (the combination of uncontrollable factors, such as demand, that determine success or failure). The simplest payoff table is illustrated in Table 4–1 (as the first step in stating strategies and possible outcomes.

With the information in Table 4–1, the store manager can use subjective estimates of risks assumed above and multiply the conditional values by their probability of occurrence. This calculation will result in *expected values*. Table 4–2 shows the expected value payoffs, using the assumed payoff in Table 4–1 and the above feelings about the probability of success for Brands A and B.

From the expected value payoff table, the store manager can determine the total expected value for each strategy by obtaining the sum of the expected values for each state of nature. If Brand A is stocked, the total expected value is $60 ($160–$100); if Brand B is stocked, the total expected value is $50 ($200–$150); therefore, under the assumptions in this case, the store manager would decide to stock Brand A, because its total expected value is $10 more than if Brand B were stocked. Obviously, if the total expected value for stocking each brand had been negative, the manager would decide not to stock either, because there would probably be a loss under either strategy.

Table 4–1
Payoff Table

	State of Nature (Demand)	
Strategy	Success	Failure
Stock Brand A	$200	−$500
Stock Brand B	$400	−$300

Table 4–2
Expected Value Payoff Table

| | State of Nature | |
Strategy	Success	Failure
Stock Brand A	$200 × .80 = $160	−$500 × .20 = −$100
Stock Brand B	$400 × .50 = $200	−$300 × .50 = −$150

Decision Trees   In order to examine problems of this type better, a *tree diagram* is useful. With it, extremely complex problems can be analyzed. A tree diagram shows each choice situation together with each payoff and each probability. A tree diagram for the problem of the choice of brands appears in Figure 4–1.

To interpret the tree in Figure 4–1 we would start at the origin or trunk of the tree. If we choose Brand A we have an 80 percent chance of making $200 and a 20 percent chance of losing $500. Our expected value is $60. If we choose Brand B we have a 50 percent chance of mak-

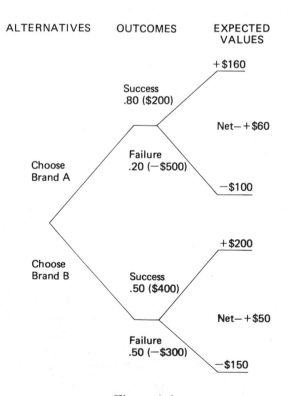

Figure 4–1
Tree Diagram

ing $400 and a 50 percent chance of losing $300. Our expected profit is $50. If we can choose only one product, we would pick Brand A.

The manager should be aware of the possibility of using such a technique but must also interpret the results correctly. It is altogether possible that in the problem of the choice of brands, the manager will lose money. It is important to remember that an expected monetary profit of $60 does not mean an assured profit of $60. It merely means that if this decision is made many times, on the average there would be $60 profit if the choice was Brand A and on the average there would be $50 profit each time the choice was Brand B. If Brand A is stocked only once, there may be a loss of $500, but the chances of a greater profit are better by choosing Brand A.

With the help of a person specialized in stochastic model-building, some of the manager's most pressing problems are capable of analysis. The prerequisite, however, is for the manager to be able to state beliefs in a concise manner (in terms of probabilities) so that the model builder can handle the factors mathematically.

Simulation Techniques Often, when a management problem is too complex to be answered by a series of mathematical equations, it is possible to simulate the probable outcomes before taking action. In this way, the manager may rapidly try out on paper (or with a computer) the results of proposed actions before the actions are taken. By trying out several policies, it is possible to determine which one has the best chance of providing the optimum result.

The idea of randomness represented by random numbers is at the heart of simulation. **Random numbers** are numbers, each of which has the same chance of being selected. Tables of random numbers are now readily available.

One type of simulation is used in queueing problems, ones in which the need for personnel or equipment varies over a time period but the determination of the peak demands cannot be estimated because the occurrence is random or due to chance. With simulation, the manager can try out available strategies as they might result in different outcomes, depending upon probabilities from a table of random numbers. For example, the store manager may wish to determine the work schedules for three salespeople to serve customers and to decide whether to add a fourth salesperson. The problem arises from not knowing when customers may appear in the store. Experience may indicate the probabilities that at some hours of the day all three salespeople will be serving customers, but that at other times the salespeople will be idle. In simulating the traffic for a day, the manager may wish to use subjective probabilities for those times in which there are no data from experience; but even if there are no experience data, it is still possible to simulate an activity by using random numbers.

In practice, simulation is carried out by electronic computers. In seconds, a computer can perform thousands of simulation trials and at the same time compile all costs. At the present time, inventory decision rules are commonly tested on computers. The executive specifies such things as reorder points and order quantities, and the computer generates the total cost for, say, five years. Then the executive specifies a different reorder point and order quantity and the computer determines the costs of that policy over the same period of time. After many different policies are put through the series of simulation runs, the best policy can be selected.

Breakeven Analysis

The simplest approach for showing the relationship of revenue to cost is the breakeven chart. Revenue and cost can be studied by directing attention to: (1) total revenue and total cost, (2) average revenue and average cost per unit of output, and (3) changes in revenue and cost. Breakeven analysis directs attention to the first of these. Breakeven analysis implies that at some point in the operations total revenue equals total cost—the breakeven point. This analysis can be handled algebraically or graphically; however, in all cases, the first step is to classify costs into at least two types—fixed and variable.

Distinction Between Fixed and Variable Costs

The manager has long recognized that, during a given period of time, some costs are subject to change as the rate of production changes and other costs will continue unchanged. If the time period is extremely short—say, one minute—all costs will remain unchanged or fixed. If the time period is very long—say, ten years—all costs will be subject to change. Generally, it is useful to use a time period, which economists call the **short run**, in which it is possible to vary the rate of production but which is so short that the capacity or scale of operations cannot be changed. In this period, some costs will be **variable** as a result of a change in rate of operations (for example, materials and direct labor) but other costs will be **fixed** (that is, will remain constant regardless of the quantity of output). The manager continually is faced with decisions in which the classification of total costs into variable and fixed costs will help focus attention to the correct costs.

The distinction between total fixed and total variable costs stresses that only variable costs will increase with an increase in the production rate of output. However, it should be clear that when average cost *per unit* is considered, fixed cost per unit of output will *decline* as volume increases—the constant fixed costs are spread over more units of output. Variable costs per unit of output may increase proportionally with an increase in output (which will be the assumption in the breakeven charts in this chapter), or they may decrease per unit of output (for example, if quantity discounts are significant), or they may increase per unit of output (if the quantity of materials is very short and thus price increases as output increases). In most industries, variable costs per unit can reasonably be assumed to be constant, and thus total variable costs will appear as a straight line (linear) when plotted against various quantities of output.

The process of classifying costs into fixed and variable costs is a necessary first step in breakeven analysis. At times, this process is complicated by the fact that the types of costs being classified may be partly fixed and partly variable (semi-fixed costs). For example, electrical current may be used partly for lighting the plant (fixed) and also for running machines that may be turned off if output declines (variable). In such cases, additional breakdowns of costs may be necessary in order to segregate fixed from variable. If there is no basis for additional breakdowns, the manager may resort to using judgment (or analysis of past experience) and to considering some fraction of the type of costs as fixed and the other fraction as variable. For example, if it appears that maintenance costs are partly fixed and partly variable, the manager may take some percentage of maintenance costs as fixed and some percentage as variable. In any case, a clear distinction between fixed and variable costs must be made in order to secure the value of breakeven analysis.

Construction of a Breakeven Chart The cost-volume-profit relationship can best be visualized by charting the variables. A **breakeven chart** is a graphical representation of the relationship between costs and revenue *at a given time*. Figure 4–2 is one form in which the chart typically appears. Fixed costs also may be drawn below variable costs, in which case the fixed-cost line will be horizontal with the X axis.

The simplest breakeven chart makes use of straight lines that represent revenue, variable costs, and total costs. The construction of this chart requires only that the costs and revenue be known at two points (volumes of output), because only two points are required to draw a straight line. The points at the Y intercept (left-hand side of chart) are given by definition: Revenue line will start at zero at zero volume; variable costs also will start at zero at zero volume; fixed costs

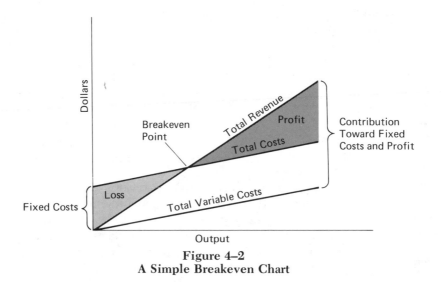

Figure 4–2
A Simple Breakeven Chart

will be a given level on the Y axis because, by definition, they would continue even if there were no production. Cost and revenue data at an actual volume level provide the basis for the necessary second point. All other points on the lines are the result of the assumption of linear relationships for both revenue and costs.

This simple analytical device is very useful if interpreted properly but can cause trouble if certain assumptions, upon which it is based, are forgotten. These assumptions are:

1. The linear revenue line indicates an assumption that the price at which any quantity of the output can be sold is fixed and does not change with output. (For example, points along the line merely indicate that Price P [$6.00 per unit] is multiplied by the number of items sold Q [100 units] to obtain Revenue R [$600].)

2. Variable costs vary proportionally with output.

3. The product mix (the percentage of each of the several types of products produced) remains constant.

4. The relationship is for a given point in time (and thus volumes, other than the ones used in the construction of the chart, are merely assumed values).

5. Fixed\costs and variable costs are clearly distinguishable.

Interpretations The value of the breakeven chart is
of a in the simple and straightforward
Breakeven Chart manner in which it illustrates
some important economic concepts. One obvious observation is that

profits do not appear, if any costs are fixed, until a given volume of output is reached. Once the breakeven point is reached, profits appear and increase at a faster rate than do total costs.

The idea of **contribution toward fixed costs and profit** is clearly indicated in Figure 4–2. We can simply state that a decision to produce extra volume first depends upon whether the revenue will at least cover *variable costs*, provide extra funds to help cover fixed costs, and add to profits. This point appears so simple, in the interpretation of this breakeven chart, that the reader may feel that there is nothing profound about the idea. Further deliberation on the question will indicate that this idea can be one of the most useful concepts for a manager to understand thoroughly.

Numerous applications of breakeven charts superimpose different charts (one useful way is by drawing with a grease pencil on acetate) over the basic chart. Each chart that is superimposed can graphically represent the effect of changing a single assumption. For example, if the problem is to determine the effect of an increase in price on profits per unit, a new revenue line (dashed line) will be drawn with a greater slope. If costs remain unchanged, the breakeven point will be at a lower volume and profits will increase (see Figure 4–3a). In a similar manner, a new chart that assumes an increase in fixed costs (possibly from the purchase of a new machine) will indicate the effect on the breakeven point and profits (see Figure 4–3b). In Figure 4–3c, the dashed lines indicate a prospective increase in variable cost (because a basic raw material has increased in price). In Figure 4–3d, the "stairstep" is caused by an increase in fixed cost at some volume of output because it is necessary to add a second shift with extra supervision or because there is an increase in light and heat. The manager will be able to visualize the effect of many possible decisions before actually making them, by using a breakeven chart.

Several formulas for computing the breakeven point make it possible to compute the exact value without making a chart. The formulas also aid in understanding the relationships of fixed and variable costs and revenue, because the formulas are merely common-sense expressions, in symbols, of assumed relationships. The formulas are:

$$\text{Breakeven Point} = \frac{\text{Total Fixed Cost}}{1 - \dfrac{\text{Variable Cost}}{\text{Sales}}} \quad \text{or} \quad \frac{\text{Total Fixed Cost}}{\text{Profit Margin as \%}}$$

$$\text{Sales} = \text{Fixed Costs} + \text{Variable Costs as a \% of Sales}$$

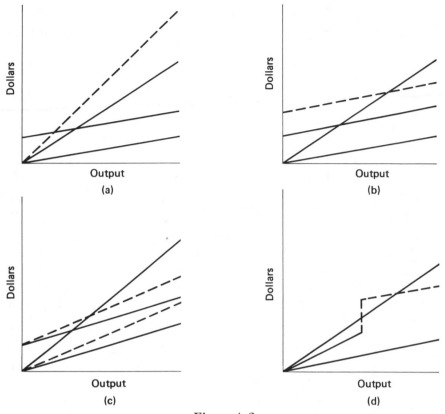

Figure 4–3
Interpretation Using Breakeven Charts

The Incremental Concept The manager can obtain accounting information designed to aid
him in deciding between alternative courses of action in two ways: (1)
The routinized collection of relevant data for certain types of anticipated decisions is called **programmed analysis**; (2) **nonprogrammed
analysis** develops special cost information for specific decisions. The
relevent cost information for decision making should pertain to those
costs that will be different under alternative actions not yet taken.
Thus the central idea in accounting for decision making, whether it be
by programmed or nonprogrammed methods, is the incremental
concept; that is, the analysis of *changes* in total costs and in total
revenues.

Direct costing, or variable costing, is a product-costing technique
that identifies only variable costs with products. All fixed costs are

charged against revenue from the accounting period in which they are incurred and do not become a part of product costs for inventory valuation purposes.

The arbitrary allocation of fixed costs to products, called **absorption costing**, can result in confusion in some decisions. For example, the full cost of a product includes fixed-cost allocations and requires a special analysis to determine the increase in total costs if sales of that product increase. Direct costing attempts to eliminate the confusion by avoiding allocations and by presenting cost information that corresponds closely to incremental costs. The manager derives several benefits from direct costing: (1) cost-profit-volume relationships required for profit planning are obtained from regular acccounting reports; (2) profit for a period varies with sales rather than with production; (3) relative appraisals of products are not obscured by allocations of common costs; and (4) incremental cost information for pricing and other product-oriented decisions is readily available.

Management systematically receives the type of data needed for short-run decisions involving changes in volume (variable costs) as well as the data needed for long-run decisions (variable costs and escapable fixed costs). **Marginal income analysis** is an attempt to measure the contribution of each segment to common fixed costs (fixed costs not applicable to any particular segment) and profits. No attempt is made to allocate common fixed costs or to require that each segment carry its "share of overhead." Rather, the relevant criterion is the ratio of marginal balance to the investment employed in the segment.

This discussion of decision making will help you as we continue in the next chapter with more details on two additional managerial functions: organizing and staffing.

REFERENCES

ANDERSON, DAVID R., D. J. SWEENEY, and T. R. WILLIAMS, *Essentials of Management Science Applications to Decision Making*. St. Paul, Minn.: West Publishing Co., 1978.

CHURCHMAN, C. WEST, *Prediction and Optimal Decision*. Englewood Cliffs, N.J.: Prentice-Hall, Inc., 1961.

EBERT, RONALD J. and TERRENCE R. MITCHELL, *Organizational Decision Processes, Concepts and Analysis*. New York: Crane, Russak, and Company, 1975.

JONES, M. H., *Executive Decision Making*, rev. ed. Homewood, Ill.: Richard D. Irwin, Inc., 1962.

MOORE, P. G. and H. THOMAS, *The Anatomy of Decisions*. Middlesex, England: Penguin Books, 1976.

SIMON, HERBERT A., *The New Science of Management Decision*. New York: Harper & Row, Publishers, Inc., 1960.

SIMON, H. A., *Administrative Behavior*, 3rd ed. New York: The Macmillan Company, 1976.

SPRAGUE, R. H., JR., and E. D. CARLSON, *Building Effective Decision Support Systems*. Englewood Cliffs, N.J.: Prentice-Hall, 1982.

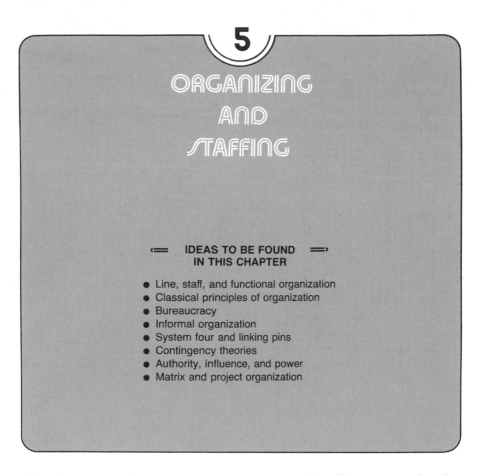

5

ORGANIZING AND STAFFING

Two functions of management, organizing and staffing, are so closely related that they are often discussed together without any distinction between them. **Organizing** focuses attention on the structure and process of allocating jobs so that common objectives can be achieved; **staffing** pertains to the people in the jobs. In other words, organizing is job-oriented; staffing is worker-oriented. Organization deals not only with both organizing and staffing but also with the *relationship* between the two.

Problems of organization have confronted men ever since they started to work together on the simplest projects. The increasing dependence of people on one another and the concentration of people have increased the importance of organization in modern society. The development of organization theory, therefore, has received greater attention in recent years than ever before. The early pioneers of management thought concentrated on the organizing function and developed a theory which *prescribed* the manner in which jobs should be grouped in the structure. This theory will be called the **classical theory of organization**. More recently, students in the behavioral sciences have focused attention on interactions in organizations. The latter group has concentrated on *describing* how human beings actually work together. **Organization Behavior (O.B.)** concerns individuals in organizations.

In recent years, the trend has been to concentrate on scientific research in organization behavior and to describe organization as a system of human relationships. The concepts resulting from this research comprise **modern organization theory**.

Organization has been defined in many ways, depending on the viewpoint from which the subject was observed. Today, numerous approaches to problems of organization exist, chiefly because different assumptions have been made and different definitions used. For our purpose, **organization** will be defined as the structure and process by which a cooperative group of human beings allocates its tasks among its members, identifies relationships, and integrates its activities toward common objectives. It will be observed that this definition involves the structure of tasks (organizing), the placement of human beings in the structure (staffing), and the integration of the two functions into a human system of activities.

CLASSICAL THEORY OF ORGANIZATION

The classical theory of organization contributes provocative observations about the *design* of a formal structure of organization and the manner in which *specialization* can be applied in the organizing process. The foundation for this approach is in the proposition that planning of positions and departments should precede consideration of the particular individuals who might fill the positions. Although this proposition made it possible to state a group of principles about organization structure, there has been little empirical verification of the assumed human characteristics and the assumed manner in which human beings interact in social groups. The chief contributions of traditional theory include (1) a clear definition of types of formal organization, (2) certain generalizations that offer first approximations for planning an organization structure, and (3) limited models for organizing activities.

Types of Formal Organization

Traditionally, organization has been analyzed as a structure of authority relationships. **Authority** was defined as the right to act. In this legal sense, authority flows down in an organization. For example, an industrial chief executive delegates authority to lower levels in his organization and is viewed as receiving his authority from the Board of Directors, which receives authority from stockholders, from the government, and ultimately from the people (in a democracy).

Three types of organization are classified by the nature of authority: line, staff, and functional. **Line organization** is the simplest, most direct type, in which each position has general authority over lower positions in the hierarchy in the accomplishment of the main operations of the firm. **Staff organization** is purely advisory (either generalist or specialist) to the line structure, with no authority to place recommendations into action. Functional organization has developed from the increasing complexity of operations and the need for a great number of specialists for aiding line positions. **Functional organization** permits a specialist in a given area to enforce his directives within a limited and clearly defined scope of authority. Staff becomes desirable when the line needs advisory help; yet, in effect, it complicates the supervision problem faced by the line manager. Functional organization decreases the line manager's problem because it permits orders to flow directly to lower levels without attention to routine technical problems by the line positions.

Line organization is the backbone of hierachy; staff and functional organization merely supplement the line. In an actual organization, a single position might serve as line, staff, and functional at the same time but for different phases of activities. For example, the chief accountant in a business firm might give tax and accounting advice (staff) to the chief line officer, supervise his own accounting department of one hundred people (line), and set specific accounting procedures for lower levels with his own specialist authority (functional). In fact, the value of the distinction among the three types of organization is in focusing attention on the different types of authority assigned to individual executives. The determination of the particular use of these types will depend upon the situation in which the manager finds himself (see Table 5–1).

Classical Principles of Organization Traditional organization theorists developed certain generalizations which they considered to be principles of organization. These principles are useful first approximations, or guides for thought, in the organizing function. They provide a simple group of intuitive statements that provoke thought by both operating managers and researchers in an organization. The most important of these principles are (1) unity of command, (2) exception principle, (3) span of control, (4) scalar principle, (5) departmentation, and (6) decentralization.

Table 5–1
Comparison of Line, Staff, and Functional Organization

Line Organization

Advantages
1. Maintains simplicity
2. Makes clear division of authority
3. Encourages speedy action

Disadvantages
1. Neglects specialists in planning
2. Overworks key people
3. Depends upon retention of a few key people

Staff Organization

Advantages
1. Enables specialists to give expert advice
2. Frees the line executive of detailed analysis
3. Affords young specialists a means of training

Disadvantages
1. Confuses organization if functions are not clear
2. Reduces power experts to place recommendations into action
3. Tends toward centralizaton of organization

Functional Organization

Advantages
1. Relieves line executives of routine, specialized decisions
2. Provides framework for applying expert knowledge
3. Relieves pressure of need for large numbers of well-rounded executives

Disadvantages
1. Makes relationships more complex
2. Makes limits of authority of each specialist a difficult coordination problem
3. Tends toward centralizaiton of organization

Unity of Command   One of the traditional principles of organization, generally referred to as **unity of command**, states that no member of an organization should report to more than one superior on any single function. This principle appeals to common sense in a pure line organization, in which each superior has general authority; however, it becomes a complex problem in actual cases in which some form of staff and/or functional organization is used. In practice, instructions may be received from several sources without loss of productivity. The central problem is to avoid conflict in orders from different people relating to the same subject. One should recognize immediately that the actions of a subordinate may be *influenced* by many persons who are not recognized in the formal hierarchy of authority. The principle of unity of command may be useful in the planning of an organization if it is interpreted as a tendency toward the simplification of relationships between superior and subordinate; it is not realistic if it is interpreted as an immutable law that would eliminate useful relationships among executives.

Exception Principle   A second principle, called the **exception principle**, states that recurring decisions should be handled in a routine manner by lower-level managers, whereas problems involving unusual matters should be referred to higher levels. This principle emphasizes that executives at the top levels of an organization have limited time and capacity and should refrain from becoming bogged down in routine details that can be handled as well by subordinates. Thus, it is an important concept concerning the delegation of authority in an organization.

The exception principle can be very useful to an executive by focusing attention on those matters that should receive attention first. It is applicable at all levels and, if kept in mind, can help the inexperienced executive compensate for a human tendency to concentrate on the concrete, immediate, and detailed problems at the expense of the more fundamental, difficult, and abstract issues. At the same time, attention to the principle can help the lower-level managers understand exactly what they are expected to do.

The principle has remained important in modern theory because of the distinction it makes between programmed and nonprogrammed decisions. **Programmed decisions** are those that are repetitive and routine and that can be handled by a definite procedure. **Nonprogrammed decisions** involve new, one-shot, and unstructured elements that require tailored handling by superiors. Programmed decisions may be easily delegated; nonprogrammed decisions usually need the attention of the superior in handling "exceptions."

Span of Control   A third traditional principle involves the **span of control** of a manager and states that there is a limit to the number of subordinates that one superior should supervise. Often this principle is stated in terms of the exact number of subordinates that should report to a superior and thus has become highly controversial. The determination of the optimum number depends on many factors in a given organization and should always be tied directly to the question of the number of levels in the hierarchy. If it appears that a small span of control for each manager is desirable, then the number of necessary levels will be larger than would be the case with a larger span of control. The organization with more levels will be "tall," whereas the organization with a larger span of control will be "flat."

Span of control focuses attention on the basic fact that any human being has limitations. First, one has limited *time available* for one's activities. Second, one has limited *available energy* and must depend on others to supplement one's energy. Third, the number of subjects to which a manager can give *attention* is limited. These limitations not only support the concept of span of control but indicate that the optimum span of control varies among individuals. Also, the span of control under one set of physical conditions will differ from the span under another set. For example, the problems of a military commander fighting in the desert differ from the problems of a commander fighting in the jungle. Improving communication devices may make a larger span of control desirable. The dispersion of necessary information may change the optimum span.

Span of control refers to the number of people that one person can supervise directly. A related, but broader and possibly more useful, idea is the **span of managerial responsibility**. It refers to the number of people whom one superior can assist, teach, and help to reach the objectives of their own jobs—that is, the number who have *access* to the superior. The span of responsibility probably can be larger than the span of control.

The span of control principle does not resolve the conflict between the advantages of a "tall" organization versus those of the "flat." It is evident that as the number of levels increases, the number of channels through which orders must flow increases. Questions of span of control and number of levels must be handled concurrently in any decision about the structure of an organization.

Scalar Principle   A fourth traditional principle, called the **scalar principle**, states that authority and responsibility should flow in a clear unbroken line from the highest executive to the lowest. The military stresses this idea under the term *chain of command*. One writer describes this vertical relationship as a job-task pyramid. The principle simply states that an organization is a hierarchy. The importance and usefulness of the principle is evident whenever the line is severed. The splintering of one organization into two or more results from a permanent breach of this principle.

Departmentation   The manner in which activities should be divided and formed into specialized groups usually is referred to as **departmentation**. The purpose of departmentation is to specialize activites, simplify the tasks of managers, and maintain control. Three common types of departmentation are: geographical, commodity, and functional. Often, different types are used at different levels of the organization structure. For example, Figure 5–1 illus-

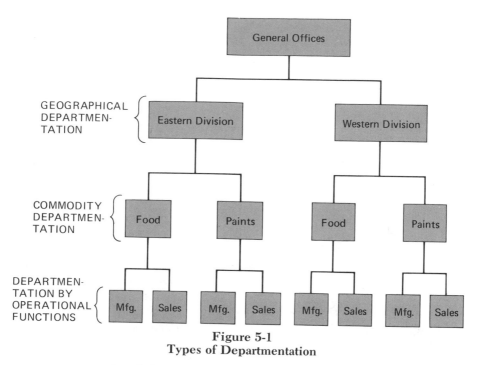

Figure 5-1
Types of Departmentation

trates geographical departmentation at the top level, commodity at the second level, and functional at the third.

No single formula for departmentation applies to all situations. The following criteria may help the organization planner:

1. Similar activities may be grouped together, based upon likeness of personal qualifications or common purpose, for example, medical and dental personnel.
2. An activity may be grouped with other activities with which it is used, for example, safety with production.
3. Functions may be assigned to that executive who is most interested in performing them well.
4. Activities may be grouped to encourage competition among departments or to avoid friction among departments.
5. If it is difficult to make definite distinctions between two activities, they may be grouped together.
6. Certain functions require close coordination and, if separated, would increase problems of higher-level managers; in this case, such functions should be grouped together.

Decentralization   The concept of decentralization has been an important organizing principle, especially in large corporations. However, the concept has been confused by the use of the term to describe different ideas. Often it refers to operations at different geographical locations. In this sense, decentralization describes physical characteristics of a company but does not indicate the type of organization structure used.

Decentralization, as an organizing concept, refers to the process of pushing decision making to lower levels of the organization. It is closely related to the delegation of authority to the broader base of executives who are at the lower levels of the hierarchy. Decentralization is a matter of degree. Basic decisions and policies must receive attention at the top levels. Although delegation is generally recognized as an important art by most operating executives, in practice delegation involves significant costs and risks. Two important considerations determine the degree of decentralization desirable in a given situation. First, the amount of skills and competence possessed by subordinate executives influences the success of any program of decentralization. Executives must be developed who can adequately handle the decisions delegated to them. Second, the distribution of the necessary information to points of decision is critical to any delegation process. Unless an executive has sufficient information available for a decision, he will have little chance to make a good decision.

Decentralization is not universally good. It may be preferable for Firm A but disastrous for Firm B. If speed in making decisions is important, decentralization of decisions may be desirable. Divisionalization along product lines has proved to be desirable for many large multiproduct firms.

Bureaucracy

The traditional theory of organization has received systematic treatment by many thinkers in management (see Table 2–1). Max Weber[1] stands out as developer of a model of formal organization structure. Weber, in his historical study of social behavior, noticed three influences on organizational behavior: (1) the traditional taboos of society, (2) personal leadership of the great men (which he called charisma), and (3) the concept of bureaucracy. The characteristic of the third influence has been the subject of study by social scientists and offers a model of a formal theory of organization.

Bureaucracy, as used by Weber, does not have the opprobrious meaning that it has in general usage. It has a technical meaning and identifies the following basic characteristics of a formal model:

---

[1] Max Weber, *The Theory of Social and Economic Organization* (New York: Oxford University Press, 1947).

1. Regular activities aimed at organization goals are distributed as fixed official duties.
2. Organization follows the principles of hierarchy.
3. Operations are governed by a consistent system of abstract rules that are applied to individual cases.
4. The ideal official operates as a formalistic impersonality without emotion.
5. Employment in the organization is based on technical qualifications and is not subject to arbitrary termination.
6. From a purely technical point of view, bureaucracy attains the highest degree of efficiency.

Bureaucracy concentrates on a rational structure with universal applications in social institutions. Although Weber has been criticized as being too autocratic, his concept of bureaucracy has had great impact on classical thinking about formal organization.

Assumptions of the Classical Theory of Organizing The classical theory of organizing remains important because it offers explicit guidelines for many present organizations. Yet it has been attacked by many writers because, in spite of its efficiency, it has led to social dissatisfaction. Douglas McGregor referred to it as Theory X and identified the assumptions about human nature implicitly made by the principles which he used as the foundation for his criticism.[2]

1. Members of an organization are unable to work out relations among their positions without thorough guidance and planning.
2. Some members are aggressive and will trespass on the domain of others unless clear boundaries are drawn.
3. Members are reluctant to assume responsibilities unless assigned a definite task.
4. Members generally prefer the security of a definite task to the freedom of a vaguely defined one.
5. Members are prone to conflict.
6. Justice is more certain if the enterprise is organized on an objective, impersonal basis.

[2] Douglas McGregor, *The Human Side of Enterprise* (New York: McGraw-Hill Book Company, Inc., 1960), pp. 33–35, 45–49.

HUMAN AND PARTICIPATIVE THEORIES OF ORGANIZING The classical theory of organization has met increasing opposition starting with the human relations proponents in the 1950s and the behavioralists in the 1960s and 1970s. McGregor proposed an alternative theory based on different assumptions about human nature. The assumptions of his Theory Y are:

1. The expenditure of physical and mental effort in work is as natural as play or rest.
2. People will exercise self-direction and self-control toward objectives to which they are committed.
3. The average individual learns not only to accept but to seek responsibility.
4. The human capacity of imagination, ingenuity, and creativity is widely distributed among individuals.
5. In modern industrial life the intellectual potentialities of the average human being are only partially utilized.

Although McGregor did not focus on organizational design, R. Likert and others have proposed structural recommendations that are consistent with the Theory Y assumptions.

Likert developed a theory of organizing which he called **System 4**.[3] His System 4 theory is built on three concepts:

1. *Principle of Supportive Relationships:* The process of organization must ensure a maximum probability that in all interactions and relationships each member will view the experience as supportive and one which builds and maintains a sense of personal worth and importance.
2. *Linking Pins:* The charting of hierachical relationships should provide "linking pins" among groups (not individuals), and these relationships should be overlapping (not in a tight chain of command). Management should deliberately endeavor to build effective groups, linking them in an overall organization by means of people who hold overlapping group membership, i.e., a manager at each level participates in groups of higher-level managers and joins lower-level managers in participating as a group.
3. *Performance Goals:* Goals describe the interrelationships of the organization better than job descriptions and charts of flow of formal authority.

[3] Rensis Likert, *The Human Organization* (New York: McGraw-Hill Book Company, Inc., 1967).

These assumptions and concepts of the participative theories of organizing yield propositions that conflict with those of classical theories. Both claim universality. The participative theories are less mechanistic, less impersonal, and less formal. They focus on human face-to-face relationships with allegedly greater satisfaction and productivity. Some participative theories propose an extreme view of "shared leadership." According to this view, no sharp distinction should be made between leadership and membership in a group. Diffusion of leadership should be encouraged. Members should share in setting goals. Groups should be continually in the process of self-examination, self-training, and the flexible reallocation of roles. Concepts of participative theories have been applied with remarkable success. With the clear lines drawn between the classical and participative theories, the manager needs guidance as to which theory to use.

The manager's choice of organizing theories depends upon several factors:

1. One's assumptions about human nature.
2. The preference, personality, and educational background of the organizer.
3. The technology and environment faced by the specific organization.

For these reasons, modern organizing concepts have evolved into a group of contingency theories.

CONTINGENCY THEORIES OF ORGANIZING

Managerial practitioners and empirical researchers have developed new approaches to organizational design that help the manager make rational choices both in situations where classical concepts are relevant and in those where the participative theories are preferable. Thus the contingency approach to organizational structure emphasizes that the proper approach is to refrain from choosing one of the two universal theories on an all-or-nothing basis but to adapt certain ideas from both to the situation. The contingency approach has identified four groups of factors important in a manager's choice: (1) the nature of the people in the organization, (2) the type of task and technology, (3) the environment within which the organization operates, and (4) the degree of change and uncertainty faced by the organization. Most studies are directed to the latter three factors.

Task and
Technology Determinants
of Structure

Rapid changes in technology such as computer controls, machine-paced production, and increased use of indirect labor have increased the need for flexible structures. Structures compatible with dynamic technology differ from the structures that work in stable situations.

Results of research by Joan Woodward and her associates in Great Britain offer more specific elements indicating the relationship of technology and structure. Woodward classified production technology into three types: (1) small-batch, job-order production; (2) mass production using assembly lines; and (3) continuous process production, such as used in oil and chemical manufacture. She found that the more successful firms using each of these three technological processes had different structures. Span of control of both the chief executive and first-line supervisors varied with the type of technology, as did the ratio of direct to indirect workers and the ratio of line operators to staff workers. The flexibility gained by participative approaches indicated that for job-order production and for continuous-process production System 4 type organization was more successful; yet for assembly-line processes the more successful firms used classical and bureaucratic guidelines.

Based on Woodward's pioneering research and follow-up studies, the modern approach to organization design is to adapt the structure to the different technological processes. Using this approach, a single company may have different structures depending upon the processes of different parts of the company. The result is that the overall structure is more complex, using ideas from each of the pure, or universal, prescriptions.

Environment's Impact
on
Organization Design

The industrial environment is a second determinant of organization structure. A firm in one industry may find one type of structure to be best, while a firm in a different industry may find a different type to be suitable. Early work by Paul Lawrence and Jay Lorsch led to the identification of different characteristics of the industrial environment that affect the suitable structure for a firm operating within that environment. They identified three classes of environments related to the sales, production, and R & D functions: market, technical-economic, and scientific. Each of these environments may vary as to (1) the rate of change experienced in the industry, (2) the degree of uncertainty of information about the situation, and (3) the length of the feedback time in which results become known.

Lawrence and Lorsch studied three industries: plastics, food, and containers. Initial focus was on the plastics industry, with its diverse and dynamic environment. The food and container industries were then added to provide comparison with more stable industries. Using three concepts—*differentiation* (differing orientations of functional departments), *integration* (the unity of efforts among subsystems), and *environment* (all factors outside the boundaries of the entity under consideration)—Lawrence and Lorsch found that the best structures of organization differed among different departments and industries, since each structure made accommodations to the demands for differentiation and integration in the light of the environment. For example, different structures were successful in each of the plastics, food, and container industries. Furthermore, within the plastics industry, the companies used different structural approaches for different departments. The production departments were more formalized along the lines of classical theories; the sales departments used some participative concepts and were less formally organized; the research and development departments focused primarily on the flexibility of participative approaches.

Most recently, comparative research across national boundaries has indicated that organization structures differ as they are affected by moral values, political systems, stages of economic development, educational systems, and culture. In adjusting to the multiple environments, multinational firms have developed complex overall structures that permit variations for subsidiaries operating in different external environments.

Although some contingency theories have yet to identify and measure the effect of other specific variables on organization design, the current approach is to recognize that many environmental factors have a significant impact. Thus, the earlier trend to search for a single universal theory has given way to a search for the individual environmental variables that must be considered.

Effect of Change and Uncertainty on Organization Design

No organization design remains unchanged. People change, technology changes, environment changes, and the organization itself matures. Thus, even a manager who has discovered an optimum structure for a given technology and environmental setting must continually modify the structure to fit new stages in the organization's growth. Case studies have always indicated that an entrepreneur of a small firm tends to minimize formal organization structure and to operate in a manner consistent with participative theories. Upon developing a larger and more complex organization, this entrepreneur reaches a stage that requires hiring professional managers and formalizing their relationships on the basis of classical concepts. Later, upon diversification into varied industries, concepts of System 4 become more relevant.

Organization design tends to change as the characteristics of the economy and society change. In less developed societies, the supply of educated managers is scarce, reducing the possibilities of delegating authority to trained supervisors and developing skilled staffs of specialists. The classical approaches serve as the basis for structural decisions. As the workforce becomes more specialized and educated and subordinates develop aspirations for more involvement, demands for participative approaches increase. Thus structural guidelines must change to accommodate these aspirations. Transfers of structural concepts from one environmental setting to another therefore depend upon a careful study of the characteristics of both environments.

Contingency approaches to organization design are rapidly expanding. Empirical research is providing additional factors to be considered in adapting structure to the needs of the organization. Practitioners with little sophistication in design have experimented with unique approaches that have been successful. The result is that the subject of design has moved from a routine application of simple concepts to a challenging matching of designs to new technologies and environments.

CONCEPTS FUNDAMENTAL TO ORGANIZING

Certain basic concepts for organizing are important to all of the preceding theories. Authority, influence, power, identification, loyalties, and responsibility are six terms that have special meanings in the thinking of organizing. Furthermore, economists' assumptions used by economists about the economic man have evolved into a behavioral assumption commonly referred to as **administrative man**. These concepts provide additional foundations for organizational design.

Probably one of the most important and controversial contributions of modern theory involves the concept of authority. Barnard and Simon proposed an **acceptance theory of authority**, which states the view that a communication carries authority only if the receiver accepts it. This theory upset the traditional assumption that authority invariably flows from the top of a hierarchy. The apparent conflict in concepts of authority has resulted in two schools of thought on the subject. The conflict is not necessarily great, however, if one recognizes that the acceptance theory contributes a new perspective to the subject. One approach to reconciling the two theories would be to consider that a right to act which is delegated from the top must be met with the willingness and capacity to act which flows from below.

Several concepts related to authority are often confused with it. Persons with little or no authority may influence others through comments, advice, or suggestions, or by expediting, or blocking, the flow of information. For example, the secretary of a chief executive may have no authority over subordinates in the organization but may have great influence. **Influence** implies a voluntary, and even unconscious, manner of affecting the actions of others through persuasion, suggestion, and other methods. Organization can be described by determining the flow of influences in the decision-making process.

While the concept of authority remained important from its emphasis in classical theory and influence received special attention in participative approaches, the concept of power has only recently been emphasized. **Authority** is the right to act as indicated in the organizational hierarchy; **influence** is the effect of one person on the behavior of others. **Power** is the potential force that others perceive a person to possess that gives the capacity to influence actions of others. Power, then, is a psychological force that identifies the potential of a person as perceived by others. The design of structure helps to identify one's authority and the interrelationship for influencing others, but power is a more general term that includes other sources of potential force in the organization. For example, a person may be low in the hierarchy of authority and yet have significant power as a result of personal characeristics, associations with family or political connections, expert knowledge or strategic duties, or physical location at a particular time. Thus recognition of power centers is essential to effective organization design.

Still another concept useful in understanding organizations relates to the manner in which individuals decide to participate in an organization by accepting its goals as theirs. This concept is referred to as **identification** with the organization. The idea is that *self-involvement* of an individual is most important in organizational activities. At the time of a decision, this identification of the individual with the group enables the individual to accept the premises provided by the organization without the necessity of continually reappraising all the value judgments important in the situation.

Loyalties to an organization strengthen the tie of relationships between the individual and the organization. Loyalties help coordinate decisions by assuring that the members of an organization will act in a predictable pattern. Problems involving loyalties develop when the individual feels torn among the goals of different groups. At times the loyalty toward a narrow group—say, a particular department of a company—may conflict with the loyalty toward the broader group, the company.

Responsibility has always been an important concept in organization and usually refers to the obligation or duty of a person to act. Barnard, however, stressed the importance of **responsibility**, in broader terms, as the power of a personal code of morals to control the conduct of an individual. Organization behavior is affected by the entire moral framework of those within the organization. Effective organizational activities depend upon some common moral foundation.

The approach to organization depends upon the assumptions that one makes concerning the type of people who operate in an organization. Are they primarily rational beings? Do they try to maximize absolutely? Do they, by nature, like to fit into organizations, or do they naturally have conflicts with organizations?

The economist makes the assumption that people are economic, that they strive to maximize profits, and that they act rationally and intelligently toward their goals. The psychologist points out that people have emotions and often respond in non-rational ways. Organization theorists assume that the administrative man tries to be rational and that he attempts to find a satisfactory solution that may not necessarily be the optimum. Administrative man thus tries to act rationally, although conscious of limitations and tendencies to act in a non-rational manner.

EVOLVING ORGANIZATION DESIGNS

At the beginning of this chapter we outlined three classical types of organization: line, staff, and functional. Later, we have seen that decisions on structure depend upon many factors, including one's assumptions of the nature of man, differing technology, and varieties of environments. The result is that new designs have evolved; designs using a matrix approach, project organization, and grid organizations. This section will summarize these developments to indicate current responses to the theories and concepts discussed earlier.

The **matrix approach to organization** concentrates on three crucial variables: (1) the intrinsic properties of the task along a continuum from repetitive to unique, (2) the personality (norms and aspirations) and the competence (expertise) of the personnel within a unit, and (3) the institutional and/or historical circumstances associated with the unit. This approach identifies subsystems of a complex organization, each with its appropriate strategy of planning, control, rewards, and boundary negotiations. These subsystems are viewed along a continuum from dependence on hierarchical concepts to autonomous units or projects.

Based upon five observable characteristics of an organization— group structure, group roles, group processes, group style, and group norms—one recommendation of organizational design strategies provides the following guidelines: (1) a routine situation that deals with a task requiring similar or repetitive solutions, calling for Taylor's functional specialists in the design; (2) the engineering situation that deals with nonrepetitive solutions by personnel who are professionally educated, calling for professional staffs in the structure to advise line managers; (3) the craft situation that deals with uniquely different but repetitively processed outputs, calling for a flexible and person-oriented structure; (4) the heuristic situation that deals with unique and nonrepetitive tasks with output ill-defined, calling for a flexible and group design with considerable participation.

Project organization is one that can be tailored to a particular mission or project, to coordinate actions toward the completion of the project while retaining the advantages of functional specialists. Whereas the classical approach is built around authority centers and the participative approach is built around people, project organization is designed to meet the demands of a particular job. A functional specialist can be lent for a particular project and answer to the project manager as in a line organization. When the project is finished, however, the specialist returns to the functional department, thus retaining relationships with others in the specialty.

Project organization has been adopted to fit a number of widely differing situations, from building contractors and advertising agencies to accounting and consulting firms. Its suitability to modern complex projects makes it particularly valuable in meeting modern needs while retaining the stability of functional specialists. The structure accommodates the formal ideas of classical thinking, together with the team and participative ideas.

With the rapid development of multinational firms, a third design has evolved that uses the matrix approach. Multinational firms typically have used one of three bases for developing their design: grouping functional specialists such as production, marketing, and finance together; geographical groupings by continents or regions; product groupings with similar products in distinct divisions which operate globally. The problem in using any one of these is that there are rational advantages for each and yet each has definite shortcomings. For example, if geographical divisions are used as the primary basis for top-level organization, each division must have duplicate product specialists and functional specialists. Coordination suffers, and duplication of specialists raises costs. Several multinational firms, including General Electric, have experimented with **grid organization**. This design attempts to assign responsibilities on one of the above three bases, such as product divisions, while retaining geographical responsibilities under a collateral group of departments and attempting to provide functional specialization in a third set of departments. The result is, of course, a complex and overlapping flow of authority down in the organization, with resultant coordinating problems. However, the grid organization recognizes that multinational firms must attempt to maintain a consistent global approach while at the same time encouraging adaptability to differing national environmental situations.

As a result of the rapid technological breakthroughs in the 1980s and the industrial competition by an increasing number of developed and developing countries, a new organizational design for the 1990s is evolving—a *dynamic network* structure. At this stage of the evolution, a small central organization, which serves as a switchboard for contacting other companies (often in other countries) to perform crucial functions in which local suppliers have special advantages, directs operations on a contract basis. The evolution of this organizational design is most evident in the electronics, textile, and automotive industries where American firms retain marketing, research, and financial control while moving manufacturing overseas where production costs are lower. Promises of this organizational design are its flexibility, its adaptability to change, and its focus on those functions in which the organization has clear advantages. Its weaknesses are the loss of control by the central organization, the instability of dynamic shifts in operations, and the potential competitive threats of present contractors moving into the market with their own dynamic networks.

**STAFFING—
HUMAN RESOURCE
ADMINISTRATION**
Any organizational structure requires a variety of people, and the supply of people consists of differing types. The **staffing function** includes the process by which the right person is placed in the right organizational position. **Human resource administration** involves matching the jobs and people through preparation of specifications necessary for positions, appraising the performance of personnel, training and retraining of people to fit the needs of the organizational positions, and developing methods by which people will respond with maximum effort and increased satisfaction. Often the organization structure includes a special functional department to administer the program. This often is called the personnel or industrial relations department.

The functional aspects of **personnel management** include recruitment of personnel, placement of personnel in the proper positions in the structure, training and development of personnel to suit the needs of the organization, and service activities directly related to the welfare of personnel.

Formal routines and techniques have been developed for the rationalization of the personnel functions. Interviewing techniques have received considerable attention. The development and standardization of tests to measure aptitude, achievement, and personality have provided management with additional tools for providing objectivity in the process. **Job evaluation** has remained an important process in its use of job descriptions, job specifications, and job analysis. **Merit rating** systems have formalized procedures of evaluation of performance in a specific job for purposes of pay increases and promotions.

After the needs of the organization are determined through establishing a rational job structure by means of detailed job descriptions and analysis of facts about the jobs, staffing involves locating suitable people to fit the jobs. Recruitment of personnel involves the use of several general techniques, including (1) personal data sheets or resumes; (2) batteries of tests measuring achievement, aptitude, proficiency, personality, and interests; and (3) interviews with the screened prospective candidates. These techniques are described in specialized literature on personnel management.[4]

After the personnel are hired, the staffing function shifts to administering the human assets of the organization by planning and implementing a system of performance appraisal. Concurrent with this appraisal is the development of a compensation system which will reward the personnel in an equitable and feasible manner.

As a result of demands of the organization for continual improvement of qualifications, the staffing function devotes a large portion of its efforts to special programs of training and development. These efforts include use of orientation sessions, apprentice training, programmed instruction, formal short courses administered by the organization, and support of continuing education offered by educational institutions.

Human resource administration, furthermore, deals with handling grievances and the resolution of conflicts of personnel in their

---

[4] For a concise summary of these techniques, see Joseph L. Massie and John Douglas, *Managing: A Contemporary Introduction*, 4th ed. (Englewood Cliffs, N.J.: Prentice-Hall, Inc., 1985).

performance of duties. Suggestions systems, grievance procedures in conjunction with union representatives in organized plants, and improved participation of employees are techniques available for this part of the function.

Manpower planning and forecasting future needs of the organization have received increased attention. Systems by which replacements are trained for each position are often elaborate. For example, many firms use a threefold approach to planning for each position: development of the present occupant of the position, a trained replacement who can take over immediately if needed, and a third person who is being trained for the position and who can be available within a specified period of time.

REFERENCES

BARNARD, CHESTER I., *The Functions of the Executive*. Cambridge, Mass.: Harvard University Press, 1938.

CHANDLER, A., *Strategy and Structure*. Cambridge, Mass.: The M.I.T. Press, 1962.

DALE, ERNEST, *Planning and Developing the Company Organization Structure*. New York: American Management Association, 1952.

LAWRENCE, P. and J. LORSCH, *Organization and Environment*. Boston: Division of Research, Graduate School of Business, Harvard University, 1967.

LIKERT, RENSIS, *New Patterns of Management*. New York: McGraw-Hill Book Company, Inc., 1961.

MARCH, JAMES G., *Handbook of Organizations*. Chicago: Rand McNally & Company, 1965.

———AND HERBERT A. SIMON, *Organizations*. New York: John Wiley & Sons, Inc., 1958.

MINTZBERG, HENRY, *The Structuring of Organizations*. Englewood Cliffs, N. J.: Prentice-Hall, Inc., 1979.

———, *Structuring in Fives*. Englewood Cliffs, N.J.: Prentice-Hall, Inc., 1983.

PERROW, C., *Organization Analysis: A Sociological View*. Belmont, Calif.: Wadsworth Publishing Co., 1970.

SIMON, HERBERT A., *Administrative Behavior*, 2nd ed. New York: The Macmillan Company, 1957.

THOMPSON, J. D., ed., *Approaches to Organizational Design*. Pittsburgh: University of Pittsburgh Press, 1966.

VOUGH, CLAIR F., *Tapping the Human Resource: A Strategy for Productivity*. New York: AMACOM, 1975.

WOODWARD, JOAN, *Industrial Organization: Theory and Practice*. London: Oxford University Press, 1965.

6

PLANNING AND STRATEGIC MANAGEMENT

⟵ **IDEAS TO BE FOUND** ⟶
IN THIS CHAPTER

- Nature of planning
- A Model for planning
- Budgeting—a basic planning technique
- Forecasting techniques
- Components of strategic management
- The role of policy
- Time management—planning a manager's own time

Planning is the process by which a manager looks to the future and discovers alternative courses of action. This chapter outlines those essentials of planning that serve as common threads of thought throughout any discussion of management. Some techniques and applications will be discussed in later chapters.

**IMPORTANCE
AND NATURE
OF PLANNING**

The planning function has received increased attention as organizations have grown and management theory has developed. The need for planning becomes more obvious as persons and organizations develop an awareness of the precise nature of their objectives. Therefore, the first stage of any type of planning is the conscious and explicit statement of the ultimate objectives.

Planning pervades management. Plans from the view of the top levels of an organization may be overall and broad or they may be the detailed day-to-day type, important to the individual employee. Planning at all levels of an organization is desirable.

Planning is that function of management in which a conscious choice of patterns of influence is determined for decision makers so that the many decisions will be coordinated for some period of time and will be directed toward the chosen broad goals. The process of planning may begin with a vague hunch or an element of intuition on the part of an individual or a group; yet, good managers will visualize quickly a clear pattern for handling current thought about future actions. In planning for group action, this pattern must provide a reference for all members of the group. Each member need not understand all the details of all related plans, but must comprehend how that member's own detailed plans fit into the general overall plan.

A **plan** is a predetermined course of action. Plans may be tailored to a specific project, or they may be established as standing plans for any future actions. If prospective actions appear to be routine, standard operating procedures have the advantages of economizing on thought processes and making control more uniform. Checklists, developed after considerable detailed study of a routine set of actions, can serve as a predetermined pattern, which will insure correct future action with a minimum of rethinking on the part of the operator. Emergency fire plans and the detailed countdown program in missile firing are illustrations of standard procedures.

Planning not only involves predetermining a course of action to be taken, relative to a known event, but includes mentally searching for possibilities of future problems that might appear. Techniques of handling uncertainty are extremely valuable. If the probability of the occurrence of several events is great enough, alternative plans might be developed. The economics of alternative uses of the managers' time governs the extent to which alternative plans are desirable. A small business, with limited resources, may devote less time to detailed planning than will a large firm, with its planning staff.

Plans become premises for decisions to be made in the future. Planning provides frames of reference for decisions of individuals in an organization. Policies, as guides to decisions and actions, depend upon the deliberate planning of future possibilities.

The increased importance of planning in a business enterprise is the direct result of the changing environment in which the enterprise operates. The modern manager must continually anticipate changes which will require discarding old ways and adopting new ones. Thus, the need for planning results from various changes in the environment. The aspects of this changing environment are:

1. Changes in technology.
2. Changes in government policy.

3. Changes in overall economic activity, including prices, employment of labor, raw materials, etc.
4. Changes in the nature of competition.
5. Changes in social norms and attitudes.

A MODEL FOR PLANNING

Scientific managers, starting with Taylor, have advocated that the planning function be separated from actual performance. Because line executives have limited time available, the function tends to be delegated to specialists. This delegation helps to set aside time for planning and avoids continual "fighting of fires," caused by the failure to think in advance. However, the use of planning specialists increases the need for means by which a set of plans by one group of specialists can be coordinated with plans set by another group of specialists.

The planning process can be viewed systematically as composed of five elements. Each of these elements may be handled by different groups of people, as indicated in the following outline of the model:

1. *Setting Primary and Intermediate Goals.* The primary goals are affected by the personal values of the top management. The principal goal setters in a business firm are the board of directors, president, executive committees, and stockholders. The intermediate goals help to clarify the primary goals and are usually set by vice-presidents, general managers and functional specialists. Examples of intermediate goals are diversification of a product line, concentration on production of a limited line of products, reasonable prices, volume production, and so on.
2. *Search for Opportunities.* The search or scanning element is primarily a data-collecting function in which a group of specialists directs its attention toward discovering in the environment opportunities for the firm's activities. This element includes forecasting events in the future and identifying changes in demand, competition, technology, finances, and industrial structure. The principal searchers are market researchers, economic forecasters, research and development scientists, and other technical specialists who influence planning.
3. *Formulators of Plans.* The formulators of plans usually are grouped together and consider themselves as *the* planners, since it is they who translate or convert the opportunities discovered through search into strategies and policies which are directed toward the primary and intermediate goals. Formulators in a firm are generally called planners, program developers, or assistants to the line manager.

4. *Target Setters.* In the implementation of plans there is the indispensible group of people who influence the carrying out of the plans and thus are in a position subtly to change elements of the plan or to ignore certain parts. The target setters are usually the line or operational managers who translate the broader plans into specific and detailed quantities and times for the many decision makers and workers. This stage of planning involves all levels of management and ultimately has an impact on the workers in planning their own activities.

5. *Followup of Plan.* Unless there is a mechanism in a planning model to check whether the actual performance is related to the estimated activities, planning can result in considerable thought without any direct results. Operating the plan involves continual checks to determine whether the plan actually results in performance consistent with the original previous thinking.

The element of *time* must be considered in planning. First, it takes time to prepare plans. The complexity of the subject planned and the techniques used affect this time. Broad plans, involving a number of specialists and departments, need extra time for coordination. Second, the length of time between the preparation of plans and the beginning of implementation, often called lead time, may be significant. For example, in the automobile industry, the lead time for designing a new model is determined by other departments' need for completed designs before starting to plan for the raw material supply, purchase of new tools, and so on. Third, the time needed to place the plan into full effect is important, because the speed of implementation may affect the degree of details covered in the original preparation. Fourth, the length of the time period a manager attempts to plan for is a big question. Long-range plans may cover ten to twenty years; short-range plans may be for the next month or year.

The *cost* of planning necessarily affects the degree of specific details to be covered, the completeness of factors to be considered, the formality of necessary approval, and the amount of data to be studied. If there is little information available upon which to base plans, it may be economical to postpone planning until immediately before action is necessary. In other words, a master plan sets a pattern by which other plans can be developed quickly at a later date.

Programming is a recent development that increases precision in planning. A **program** is an explicit statement of steps to be taken in order to achieve an objective. The development of a program requires that the programmer anticipate the what, who, how, and when of action. The existence of a program enables the planner to test its workability prior to its actual use. With existing computers, a program can be checked out and operating conditions can be *simulated*. In this way, difficulties that may develop can be carefully considered in advance of actual implementation of the program.

Because planning is assumed to be a rational process of human beings, it is important to be aware of some of the psychological hazards that might be encountered. Several hazards are: (1) The imagination of a human being is conditioned by past experiences. Plans are usually confined to assumptions based upon past experiences of the planner. (2) Often, assumptions used in a plan are mistaken for "facts." If there is not enough time available to validate facts, assumptions can be made, but the planner should not confuse assumptions with facts. (3) Human beings are often reluctant to accept the unpleasant. If planning uncovers disagreeable factors, the planner should concentrate on accepting them and adjusting the planning accordingly. (4) The popularity of the humorous statement of **Murphy's Law**—i.e., if anything *can* go wrong, it *will* go wrong—has an interesting impact on planning processes, for it is possible to build into the plans adjustments for the probability that things will not work out as planned.

USEFUL GENERALIZATIONS OF PLANNING

Certain generalizations of planning may be useful guides for the manager:

1. A plan should be directed toward well-defined *objectives*. Unless plans help lead toward well-understood goals, performance in the future cannot result in purposive effort.
2. Plans made by different specialists should be *coordinated* through adequate communications among specialists. For example, a sales planning specialist must transmit to the production planners estimates of the amount of products that can be sold in order to balance production with sales.
3. Planning is a *prerequisite* to other functions of management. We shall see, in the next section, that the concept of control is meaningless without planning. Moreover, each of the other functions depends upon thinking in advance of execution.
4. Adaptation of plans to current actions demands continual *redrafting* of plans. If a firm makes a long-range plan covering ten years in the future, it should reconsider periodically—say, yearly—making changes warranted by new developments and extending the plan to cover the new ten-year period. This has been called the principle of navigational change, in which the analogy of tacking a sailing vessel is used. The firm continually "tacks" (shifts back and forth) to take advantage of immediate opportunities, yet gradually gets closer to its ultimate destination.

5. Planning pervades the hierarchy of an organization. Planning at lower levels tends to be detailed and for short periods in the future; planning at higher levels tends to be general and for long periods of time.

6. A manager should relate the degree of *commitment* of his resources to the need for definite plans. If a firm plans to construct a new building, which will tie up funds for an extended period of time, it should make its plans in some detail and for the time period in which the funds will be tied up. The "firmness" of a contract might indicate the degree of commitment. Options in a contract, short-term leasing, and buying rather than making one's products are some of the techniques that may be used to decrease the degree of commitment of resources and thus to decrease the need for detailed plans.

7. Plans should retain *flexibility*. Planning tends to preset a rigid course of action unless change is incorporated in plans. Alternative courses of action will help provide flexibility, though often only at extra cost.

FORECASTING TECHNIQUES

Each manager must identify explicitly how future conditions will affect operations. The conditions in the external environment are outside one's control, but they must be estimated so that the organization can quickly adapt to changes that are occurring rapidly.

If one wishes to forecast general economic conditions, the following components of the gross national product (GNP) provide a framework for the approach: consumer purchases (including durable consumer goods, nondurable consumer goods, services); private investment expenditures (construction, durable equipment, inventory buildup); government expenditures (federal, state, and local spending); and net exports or imports (the difference between imports and exports). Using the GNP model, one can make general estimates of specific values for each of these components, and with the help of published forecasts, the manager can arrive at an estimate of general economic conditions.

The demand for the industry can be viewed as consisting of such components as sales of products to new customers, sales of additional products to old customers, replacement sales for products that have worn out, and sales affected by recent technological developments.

A number of approaches for specific forecasting are available as follows:

1. *Quantitative time series analysis.* A study of past data such as monthly sales or shipments made.

2. *Derived forecasts.* If we can discover another phenomenon that

has been forecasted by a government agency or expert, and this phenomenon is closely associated with the variable that we need to predict, a forecast can be derived from these other estimates.

3. *Causal models.* If an underlying cause for the variable can be determined, the forecast can be handled mathematically and produce quite accurate results. For example, one might find that sales are the direct result of the number of contacts by salespeople and predict that from every five contacts, one sale will result.

4. *Survey of plans and attitudes.* The University of Michigan has, for a number of years, been successful in using statistical samples of consumers for determining their plans and attitudes about purchasing in the future.

5. *Brainstorming.* On the assumption that two heads—or more—are better than one, one method for predicting the future is to assemble a group of people with knowledge and interest in a specific problem and encourage free flow of creative comments. The conditions required for these **brainstorming** sessions are important: (a) No participant may criticize any idea, regardless of how farfetched it might be; (b) each participant is encouraged to supplement the comments of others and to provide inputs for future estimates; (c) after recording the comments during the meeting, a manager may then construct a forecast built on the variety of ideas from the group.

6. *Delphi Method.* The judgment of experts is sometimes the best and most feasible method of forecasting. The Rand Corporation developed the **Delphi Method** as a means of forecasting by seeking expert opinions. The method contrasts with brainstorming in securing independent judgments by having experts complete a detailed questionnaire *independently* and without knowledge of the responses of other experts.

7. *Contingent forecasting scenarios.* One approach for handling the lack of precision in forecasting is contingent forecasting and planning. At the heart of this approach is the development of several scenarios, each scenario providing a different set of assumptions about future events. The **scenario** describes a logical sequence of events that might occur in the future.

COMPONENTS OF STRATEGIC MANAGEMENT

To meet the challenges of modern society, more and more organizations are concentrating on formal approaches and concepts for planning their long-range progress. Specifically, these challenges result from (1) the increasing rate of changes, (2) the complexity of managers' jobs, (3) the increasing importance of fitting the organization into its external environment, and (4) the increasing lag between the preparation of plans and their implementation in the future. Prospective managers will find that their duties directly involve four components of strategic management: goals, mission, strategies, and policies.[1]

Goals of Organizations

Goals of organizations are the general and ultimate ends toward which they are aimed. Different organizations have different goals. A private business firm views operating at a profit as its goal. If it doesn't reach this goal in the long run, it will not survive. Yet organizations have multiple goals, and business firms are no exception.

Mission of Organizations

Once the goals are identified, the strategic planner seeks to answer the question, What activities should the organization perform in order to reach its goals? The mission of an organization is the specific and well-defined roles and activities on which the organization elects to concentrate its efforts; it determines the scope of planned activities. The degrees of specialization and diversification are issues that affect the mission of the organization.

Strategy of Organizations

With a clear understanding of where it is headed (goals) and what scope of activities it will engage in (mission), management needs to select the routes and common threads of its approach for its decisions. Management has many alternative routes and directions available for reaching its goals. The choice of a mission is itself a strategic choice, but in addition, management must seek an appropriate group of guidelines for laying out the route for performing its mission.

Strategy consists of the common threads of thought for facing risks and uncertainty, seizing the opportunities presented by the environment, and using the distinctive competences of the resources of the organization. Strategies must be tailored to the specific situation in which an organization finds itself. A strategy that has been successful for one company may not be good for another. In fact, if a competitor successfully uses one strategy, it may mean that another organization should adopt a different one so as to take advantage of

[1] The terminology of the field, historically referred to as *business policy*, is continually undergoing change; however, these four components are usually included in the rigorous discussions of the subject. See Milton Leontiades, "The Confusing Words of Business Policy," *Academy of Management Review*, 7, no. 1 (January 1982), pp. 45–48.

unfilled niches in society. And the strategy of a large firm may differ from that of a small firm.

Good strategic planning depends as much on identifying the critical questions as on attempting to answer them.

The following questions offer a guide to the basic determinants of a good strategy:

1. Opportunities available in the market?
2. "Distinctive competences" held by the firm?
3. Constraints of the environment including governmental regu-lations, technological developments, changes in consumer life styles, and cyclical economic considerations?
4. Personal aspirations and interests of owners?
5. Society's ethical, political, and cultural framework?

In short, goals answer: Where are we going? Mission answers: What are we doing? Strategies answer: In what direction are we headed and what routes have we selected? Policies provide guides for getting there. We turn now to more on policy.

Nature of
Policy Decisions

Policy is an understanding by members of a group that makes the actions of each member of the group in a given set of circumstances more predictable to other members. A policy is a guide for making decisions. If a decision provides help for decisions in other situations, it is said to be a **policy decision**, because it sets a precedent and provides some guide for decision making in the future. Policy decisions provide a range of freedom within which subordinates can make single-shot decisions. Table 6–1 clarifies the meaning of policy by defining related terms that should not be confused with it.

An important characteristic of policy is that it provides a guide and a framework for subordinates' decisions. Therefore, strong and clear policies encourage the delegation of decision making; they do not predetermine decisions. For example, top management might establish a financial policy that subordinates must obtain approval for all expenditures over $500. This clear policy would eliminate subor-dinates' decisions involving large sums of money, but it also clearly states the range (0–$500) in which subordinates may make their own decisions without worrying about whether they have the right to make them. Good policies provide definite and clear direction by top management and at the same time allow subordinates to make their own decisions within clearly stated limits.

The usual source of policies is the top management of the firm.

Table 6–1
Policy and Related Terms

Policy:	An understanding by members of a group that makes the actions of each member more predictable to other members. Policy is a guide for making decisions.
Rule:	A statement of precisely what is to be done (or not done) in the same way every time, with no permitted deviation. Rules allow no range for decision making; policy encourages decision making by offering guides.
Law:	A statement of an order that is invariable under given conditions. Laws are rigid statements by external authority, providing a framework for policy formulation.
Procedure:	A system that describes, in detail, the steps to be taken in order to accomplish a job. Procedures emphasize details; policies concentrate on basic general approaches.

Policies may (1) *originate* at the top by executive deliberation, (2) be *imposed* from outside the firm by a trade association or the government, (3) be formulated on *appeal* from a subordinate as a result of a specific problem not covered by previously set policies, or (4) be *implied* from consistent actions of subordinates and known by top management but not explicitly stated. Policies may apply to the entire firm or they may relate to only one department. Generally, policy decisions are considered to be the more important decisions of a firm; yet many important decisions have no policy implications. For example, a decision to build a $10 million plant would be important, but it would not set a precedent or be a general guide to future decisions.

A good policy has the following characteristics:

1. It is related to an objective of the firm and is explained to all persons to whom it is to apply.
2. It is stated in understandable words and placed in writing.
3. It prescribes limits and yardsticks for future action.
4. It is subject to change but relatively stable.
5. It is reasonable and capable of being accomplished.
6. It allows for discretion and interpretation by those responsible for carrying it out.

Many firms require that policies not only be in writing but also be organized in a policy manual. This practice helps keep subordinates informed of policies that apply to a given situation. Of course, if a policy has been formulated but has not come to the attention of a subordinate, it cannot be effective. An oral policy can be generally known and applied, but it runs the risk of being overlooked or misinterpreted.

Policies are important to management, but they have the following limitations:

1. They are formulated by top management to relieve subordinates of the necessity of rethinking the factors upon which the policy was based. In short, a policy eliminates thinking about repetitive matters. If subordinates develop the habit of referring to company policy as the only reason for their actions, they may use policies as crutches and defeat the intent of the policies.
2. Policies provide stability and direction to the action of members of the firm; yet, if a policy remains in existence long after conditions have changed, it can have the effect of opposing progress.
3. If policies are not stated in broad and definite terms, they may tend to encourage subordinates to avoid responsibility for their own decisions.

Policy Issues

Business problems are often discussed in terms of current policy issues. A policy that works for one firm may not work for another. Some business policies apply to the entire company and may cover long periods of time. Several general policies receiving attention in recent years are:

Diversification

Large companies often guide their activities into many different lines of business to avoid having all their eggs in one basket. Among other reasons, diversification is employed to: insulate the company against violent fluctuations in the sales of a single product; give the company growing room (in those cases in which the current share of the market in one industry is looked upon with disfavor by the Justice Department); follow up discoveries made in a research and development program which provide new knowledge in areas not previously considered to be of company interest.

Many companies decide against a diversification policy. They reason that diversification can lead a company into areas in which they have little knowledge or experience and in which competitors have strong advantages.

Vertical Integration

Some companies strive to operate at all stages of production, from the raw material to final sales to consumers. An integration policy gives more security to the source of supply for raw materials and more control over the quality of parts and supplies used in production. In some industries, such as oil and steel, the manufacturing processes dictate that a single company handle the product at different stages in order to attain economical operations.

Search for Niches   A firm may concentrate on looking for those areas of operation that are overlooked by its competition. This policy stresses the development of those operations in which the firm has a comparative advantage and avoids trying to "beat a competitor in his own backyard."

Departmental policies may apply to personnel matters, marketing guides, financial questions, or any other operational phase of the business. The following are several illustrations of some personnel policies.

Nepotism   Should the company avoid hiring persons who are closely related to present employees? The purpose of an antinepotism policy is to curb favoritism; however, should a company refuse to hire the best applicant for a job because she is the daughter of a man working in another plant of the same company?

Racial Discrimination   A current policy issue involves the manner in which the company views the hiring of different races and nationalities. Such policies are directly affected by the social customs and legal decisions of the time. Affirmative action programs have focused on elimination of racial discrimination.

Mandatory Retirement at   The increase in the length of hu-
u Given Age   man life has caused the retirement policy issue to receive increased attention. A mandatory retirement policy has the advantage of providing openings for aggressive young people and of preventing older people from remaining on their jobs past the age at which they are effective. On the other hand, individuals differ as to their physical and mental capacities at a given chronological age; some men at age 70 can provide great service to a company, whereas others, at the same age, are quite feeble. Federal laws have restricted the use of the policy of mandatory retirement.

BUDGETING—
A BASIC PLANNING
TECHNIQUE   Business budgets are the principal financial means by which the manager can formalize and express a plan. Moreover, once budgets are established they serve as a control technique by setting predetermined criteria against which managers can compare actual results. In addition, the budgeting process serves as a tool for coordinating the activities of various functions and operating segments of the firm.

Figure 6–1 shows that comprehensive budgeting consists of a number of budgets with the sales budget, based upon a sales forecast, usually serving as the starting point in the process. The production

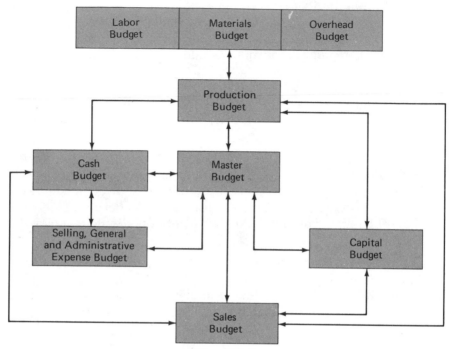

Figure 6–1
The Interdependence and Coordinating Nature of the Various
Budget Types as Indicated by the Connecting Arrows

budget is based on the sales budget, and all others are, in turn, constructed on consistent assumptions concerning the future.

Responsibility for preparing and coordinating the budgets usually rests on the controller or some other staff executive; however, budgets must reflect joint planning of all operating segments. Budget committees, composed of responsible operating heads, usually make the planning decisions, because budgets established with the cooperation and understanding of all principal parties will be better understood and accepted as guides for future activities.

The period of time for which a budget will be made is the first issue for management to resolve. Two factors provide a range for the length of time: first, it should be short enough to permit the making of fairly accurate predictions; second, it should be long enough to raise significant problems of policy, strategy, and procedure. A number of factors can affect the length of the budget period: (1) the availability of factual information, (2) the stability of the market faced by the firm, (3) the rate of technological progress, (4) the seasonal characteristics of the industry, (5) the length of the production cycle, (6) the customary credit extension time for customers, and (7) delivery times of both raw materials and finished products. In addition, the budget period must coincide with the accounting period so that comparisons between actual results and budget amounts can be made routinely.

A budget for a stated future period of time that does not make allowance for cost changes due to possible changes in output is a **fixed budget**. A **flexible budget** shows expected costs of production at various levels of production. The prerequisite for flexible budgeting is the separation of fixed and variable costs. Once the flexible budget is formalized and reports are flowing to management, opportunities for analysis are opened. The advantages of flexible budgets are: (1) cost variations due to output changes are indicated; (2) the segregation of fixed and variable costs is useful for other management functions; and (3) standard costing (an important control technique) is more easily implemented.

The information provided by budgets enables managers to prepare *pro forma* (estimated) balance sheets and income statements. Financial results and commitments can be anticipated. Such estimates enable the manager to approach the future with less hesitancy than would be true otherwise.

TIME MANAGEMENT— A TECHNIQUE FOR PLANNING USE OF MANAGER'S OWN TIME

We've seen that managers provide plans for others by setting strategies, policies, and procedures, yet experience demonstrates that managers tend to devote insufficient time to this important function. One writer has described the tendency to neglect planning as a basic law of human nature as "Gresham's Law of Planning"—daily attention to operations and actions tends to drive out attention to planning. This tendency is a direct result of the pressures faced by managers to get the job done in the present and the manager's feeling that time is not available to do everything. In short, managers need to plan the use of their own time. We, therefore, conclude this chapter with a technique to help managers find time to plan.

Although Taylor's scientific managers developed time-study techniques early, as we saw in Chapter 2, the focus until the last decade was on setting time standards for subordinates; little attention was given to the management of time of managers themselves. **Time management** is a technique for allocation of the manager's own time through setting goals, assigning priorities, identifying and eliminating time wasters, and use of managerial techniques to reach goals efficiently.

Time management has emerged as a useful planning technique because (1) it deals with a very critical element—manager's time; (2) it is a technique by which each manager is challenged to use his or her time more efficiently and avoids the directive approach of attempting to set time standards for others without their participation in making their own time allocations; and (3) it is a general-purpose technique for systematizing one's own efficiency without undue sophistication.

The technique of time management involves four clear phases: First, the detailed *recording* of one's own use of available time during a representative period; second, an *analysis* of the detailed times classified into meaningful types and identification of underlying characteristics of one's time usage; third, deliberation and setting of *priorities* while evaluating one's critical responsibilities that determine how one's time *should* be spent; and finally, *implementing* the planned use of time in the light of the priorities one has set forth.

The actual collection of the time data involves a minute-by-minute record of activities during a representative period of time of several weeks. Collection of the data can employ sampling techniques, electronic recording (several types of instruments are now available), or a simple but detailed log of all activities in which you are engaged during the day over the period of a month. Since a log can be constructed easily and is similar to a typical appointment book or other existing memo of plans, this method of collection is the most feasible for collecting time data.

Here are a few guides for planning the collection of actual times spent:

1. Account for all types of activities, no matter how apparently trivial or unimportant.
2. Record the time of each activity immediately upon completion.
3. Make records wherever you go and at all times.
4. Use symbols to reduce time required for recording, and make records of all activities, including interruptions.
5. Be specific, use the smallest unit of time feasible, and break down a long period into its relevant parts (for example, a long interview, telephone call, or meeting may include important components that should be analyzed separately).

REFERENCES

BYARS, LLOYD L., *Strategic Management: Planning and Implementation.* New York: Harper and Row, Publishers, Inc., 1984.

COMERFORD, ROBERT A. and DENNIS W. CALLAGHAN, *Strategic Management: Text, Tools, and Cases.* Boston: Kent Publishing Co. 1985.

GLUECK, WILLIAM F. and LAWRENCE R. JAUCH, *Business Policy and Strategic Management*, 4th ed. New York: McGraw-Hill Book Company, Inc., 1984.

MCNICHOLS, THOMAS J., *Policymaking and Executive Action*, 6th ed. New York: McGraw-Hill Book Company, Inc., 1983.

PEARCE, JOHN A. and RICHARD B. ROBINSON, JR., *Strategic Management*. Homewood, Ill.: Richard D. Irwin. Inc. 1982.

SCHELLENBERGER, ROBERT E. and GLENN BOSEMAND, *Policy Formulation and Strategy Management*, 2nd ed. New York: John Wiley & Sons, Inc., 1982.

SHARPLIN, ARTHUR, *Strategic Management*. New York: McGraw-Hill Book Company, Inc., 1985.

SMITH, GARRY D., DANNY R. ARNOLD, and BOBBY G. BIZZELL, *Business Strategy and Policy*. Boston: Houghton Mifflin Company, 1985.

THOMPSON, A. A. and A. J. STRICKLAND, *Strategy and Policy*, 3rd. ed. Plano, Tex.: Business Publications, Inc., 1984.

WHEELEN, THOMAS L. and J. DAVID HUNGER, *Strategic Management and Business Policy*. Reading, Mass.: Addison-Wesley Publishing Company, 1983.

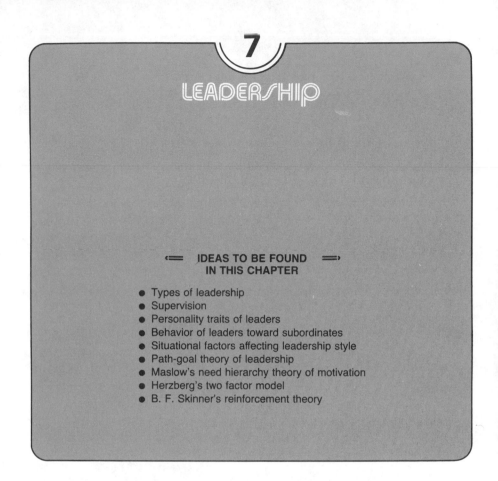

7

LEADERSHIP

**IDEAS TO BE FOUND
IN THIS CHAPTER**

- Types of leadership
- Supervision
- Personality traits of leaders
- Behavior of leaders toward subordinates
- Situational factors affecting leadership style
- Path-goal theory of leadership
- Maslow's need hierarchy theory of motivation
- Herzberg's two factor model
- B. F. Skinner's reinforcement theory

Leadership is the heart of the managerial process, because it is involved with initiating action. Other terms identifying the same idea are directing, executing, supervising, ordering, and guiding. Whatever term is used, the idea is to put into effect the decisions, plans, and programs that have previously been worked out for achieving the goals of the group.

ELEMENTS OF LEADERSHIP

Leadership concerns the total manner in which a manager influences actions of subordinates. First, it includes the issuing of orders that are clear, complete, and within the capabilities of subordinates to accomplish. Second, it implies a continual training activity in which subordinates are given instructions to enable them to carry out the particular assignment in the existing situation. Third, it necessarily involves the motivation of workers to try to meet the expectations of the manager. Fourth, it consists of maintaining discipline and rewarding those who perform properly. In short, leading is the final action of a manager in getting others to act after all preparations have been completed.

The manner in which activities are directed depends upon the manager's own personal *traits* and the *situation* involved. In leadership, more than any other function, the manager must determine an approach alone, after surveying the possibilities that are open. Each manager will do well to act as an individual and not to try to act as others act or to proceed according to the textbook. Moreover, a manager will be involved in various situations calling for different approaches. If subordinates are unskilled and need detailed instructions, the manager may find the direct, simple order advisable. If the subordinates are highly educated persons in a research activity, a permissive and consultative approach may be advisable. In cases of emergency, the manager may assume a "take charge" role and give short, clear authoritative commands, whereas if action is not pressing, a deliberate and analytical attitude may be appropriate.

TYPES OF LEADERSHIP

A large amount of research has been directed toward finding the characteristic types of leaders that are most effective. Much of this research has been carried out in the behavioral sciences. Different leadership types have been identified and provide a framework for a manager in selecting an approach to directing. For some time the types of leadership were grouped under four headings: (1) the dictatorial leader, (2) the benevolent-autocratic leader, (3) the democratic leader, and (4) the lassiez-faire leader.

The dictatorial leader accomplishes tasks through fear of penalties, and maintains a highly critical and negative attitude in relations with subordinates. As boss, such a person expects subordinates to perform well or be subject to punishment or replacement. At times, this approach apparently is effective in the short run, but it does not provide a solid foundation for continued performance, because it does not provide lasting satisfaction for those being led.

The benevolent-autocratic leader assumes a paternalistic role which forces subordinates to rely on the leader for their satisfactions. If this type of leadership is to be successful, the leader must be an exceptionally strong and wise individual who, by force of personality, generates respect and allegiance. The satisfactions of the subordinates of this type of leader depend solely on the good will of their superior. Because this leader makes decisions without the participation of others, subordinates have little chance to develop leadership qualities. This type results in dependency on the continued presence of the leader, and work deteriorates when that person is absent.

Democratic leaders depend not only on their own capabilities but encourage consultation with subordinates. Subordinates are invited to participate in planning, decision making, and organizing. They tend to venture on their own initiative and to communicate freely with their fellow subordinates. This type of leadership results in a cooperative spirit and the development of managerial abilities on the part of subordinates. Satisfaction is gained through a feeling of group accomplishment.

The laissez-faire leader depends completely on subordinates to establish their own goals and to make their own decisions. This leader assumes the role of just another member of the group. Under these conditions members of the group are permitted to act individually and, therefore, may easily head in different directions.

The manager, in developing an individual style of leadership, need not be limited to choices from among the above four classes. Robert Tannenbaum has argued that the style a manager chooses depends upon three groups of forces: (1) forces in the manager, e.g., the manager's value system, confidence in subordinates, inclinations, and feeling of security in an uncertain situation; (2) forces in the subordinate, e.g., subordinates' expectations; and (3) forces in the situation, e.g., type of organization, the nature of the problems, and the pressure of time. Given these forces, leadership behavior can be viewed along a continuum from "boss-centered" to "subordinate-centered" leadership. Moving from the boss-centered to subordinate-centered, one can observe the following styles:

1. The manager makes the decision and announces it.
2. The manager "sells" the decision.
3. The manager presents ideas, invites questions.
4. The manager presents a tentative decision subject to change.
5. The manager presents the problem.
6. The manager defines the limits and requests the group to make a decision.
7. The manager permits the group to make decisions within prescribed limits.

Leadership styles depend upon which set of assumptions about human behavior the manager uses. In Chapter 5 we have seen that Douglas McGregor summarizes two sets which he calls Theory X and

Y assumptions.[1] Blake and Mouton[2] have developed a **managerial grid** which cross-classifies managerial styles according to the degree to which the manager exhibits concern for subordinates (which they call consideration) and concern for production (which they call initiating structure). For example, on this grid a 9,9 style indicates high concern for employees and high emphasis on production.

The current approach to leadership styles is to emphasize the contingency approach, that is, to attempt to adapt a particular style to the situation faced by the leader. Most current works view leadership styles along a continuum from extreme employee orientation to extreme task orientation. Fred Fiedler,[3] probably the most influential theorist and researcher, recognizes that leadership effectiveness is multidimensional and that the style used in practice depends upon the situation. He identifies three situational factors as important determinants: (1) leader-member relations (the degree of confidence and loyalty of members in regard to the leader), (2) task structure (the degree to which tasks are routinized), and (3) position power (the amount of formal authority and support by upper management held by the leader).

Practicing managers can be helped by analyzing the above approaches to leadership styles; however, they must develop their own viewpoint after considering their own assumptions and inclinations and adapting them to each situation.

The traits, skills, and approaches of leadership are essential considerations in the leading function. No amount of analyzing, talking, thinking, and preparing will substitute for executive action.

Supervision   The directing function includes all processes for initiating action. A part of this function is called **supervision** when the manager is in direct physical contact with nonmanagers. Supervision literally means overseeing and thus implies that there is face-to-face contact. All levels of management usually are engaged in some face-to-face contact with subordinates, even if only with a private secretary, but the lowest managers have as their primary duty the supervision of workers in basic operations. This level is composed of supervisors, foremen, and section bosses.

In simple line organizations, the supervisor must perform all the

[1] For further information, see Douglas McGregor, *The Human Side of Enterprise* (New York: McGraw-Hill Book Company, Inc., 1960), pp. 33–35, 45–49.

[2] Robert R. Blake and Jane S. Mouton, *The Managerial Grid* (Houston: Gulf Publishing Company, 1964).

[3] Fred Fiedler, *A Theory of Leadership Effectiveness* (New York: McGraw-Hill Book Company, Inc., 1967).

functions of management. Even in highly functional organizations in which planning, controlling, organizing, communicating, staffing, and decision making are handled by specialists, the supervisor will contribute to these functions, even if only in a small way. For example, in a highly developed control system, using mechanical and electronic devices as well as inspectors and other specialists, the supervisor retains the residual control function of personally seeing that performance is accomplished in line with predetermined criteria. Moreover, the supervisor is the key person on the spot when corrective action must be taken.

It is often said that the most critical element in the management of a firm is the supervisor. This remains true even in cases where many staff departments are available for help. Therefore, the training of supervisors continues to be a most important problem for management. Numerous approaches have been used successfully in training programs for supervisors, including special schools, experience on the job, and individual reading plans. In terms of numbers of persons, supervisor training is the biggest challenge to management education.

The importance of the supervisor's position is increased by the uniqueness of this position in the management hierarchy. It is the major link between management and actual operations. The supervisor's task is made more difficult by the fact that to the individual worker the supervisor *is* the management. Having daily contact with the workers and interpreting company policies place the supervisor in a strategic position, as an important medium through which the workers can communicate with top management. Any failure on the part of a supervisor to represent workers to management may cause the workers to seek supplemental channels.

RESEARCH ON LEADERSHIP

The primary emphasis of early research on leadership was psychological in nature and focused on the *traits* or personality characteristics typically found among successful leaders. Such researchers began a long task of "laundry-listing" all conceivable personal characteristics of so-caled "great" leaders. Such compilations included the following kinds of characteristics:

Age	Extroversion
Maturity	Verbal skills
Intelligence	Prestige
Physical bearing	Attractiveness
Height	Charisma
Education	Popularity
Decisiveness	Aggressiveness

The problem with these early efforts was that they left too many questions about leadership unanswered. For example, is there any optimal combination of traits that is most critical in determining one's success as a leader? In what ways do such characteristics influence one's ability to lead? Are these characteristics that one can learn, or must one be born with them? Although such qualities might have fit popular stereotypes characterizing popular leaders or great personalities, their citation did little to expand our knowledge about the *process* of leadership.

It was not until a sociological view of the problem was combined with the psychological approach that headway was made in understanding leadership. Characteristic of these efforts was work carried out by researchers at Ohio State University in the 1950s. They recognized that leadership involves an interpersonal *relationship* between a leader and subordinates. Furthermore, the most critical element in this relationship is the *behavior* of the leader toward the subordinates.

This realization led them to focus their research efforts on the set of behaviors or actions that constituted leader behavior. Their basic approach was to isolate and measure the dimensions underlying leader behavior that could be used to define leadership; it was an empirical approach. A questionnaire was designed, with over 100 specific kinds of acts or behaviors a manager might engage in while supervising the work of others. The leader's subordinates were asked to use the questionnaire to describe the leader's behavior. The following is an illustration of the kinds of questions contained in the instrument that has come to be known as the **Leader Behavior Description Questionnaire** (LBDQ).

The subordinate indicates the degree to which each of the following statements describes the actions of the supervisor:

Refuses to give in when people disagree with him
Is easy to understand
Refuses to explain his actions
Encourages overtime work
Tries out his new ideas
Assigns people under him to specific tasks

Subsequent analysis of several thousand subordinates' responses to such questions consistently yielded two dimensions or factors that underlie subordinates' descriptions of their leaders: **Consideration** and **Initiating Structure**. In other words, the actions a leader takes regarding subordinates tend to cluster in one of these two major kinds of leader activities. Consideration is the extent to which the leader's behavior toward subordinates is characterized by mutual trust, mutual respect, support for subordinates' ideas, a climate of rapport, and two-way communication. A low score on consideration reflects an impersonal way of dealing with subordinates.

Initiating Structure, on the other hand, is the extent to which a leader defines and structures his role and those of subordinates. A high score reflects a leader who is likely to play a very active role in directing, planning, and scheduling the group's activities. Initiating Structure and Consideration have come to refer to kinds of leadership behavior that constitute a leader's **style**, the way the person influences subordinates.

As so often happens with attractive models, the work of the Ohio State researchers was prematurely applied by others as a set of **normative prescriptions** for leaders to follow, rather than being used as a model to be tested further in order to enhance our understanding of leadership. Many entrepreneurs traveled the country assessing supervisors on their measures of initiating structure and consideration. For some reason, they presumed that the ideal leader is one who is high on both leadership dimensions.

For a fee, they would then provide two kinds of services: (1) diagnose a particular leader's style, using this two-dimension framework; and (2) propose changes (usually involving expensive training programs) in leadership style that should lead to improved leader effectiveness.

In all this entrepreneurial flurry two major questions went unanswered: (1) How do we know when a leader is effective? and (2) What factors determine whether or not a given style of leadership behavior will be effective? Reliable answers to the first question remain the subject of continuing research. The problem is that the goals of a leader are many, and each constitutes a valid dimension of leader effectiveness. At the very least, we can say that the following are elements of leader effectiveness: (a) individual effectiveness of subordinates in accomplishing their tasks, (b) the morale or satisfaction of subordinates, (c) the productivity or efficiency of groups of subordinates in accomplishing their tasks, (d) the quality of products or services generated by subordinate groups.

Fortunately, research on what constitutes the most effective leadership style became the topic of serious research efforts during the 1970s. Two such efforts deserve our particular attention: (1) the work of Fred Fiedler and (2) the path-goal theory of leadership.

Building upon the results of the Ohio State studies, Fiedler reasoned, that there was probably no single best leader style to fit all work situations. His research has identified three major situational factors that determine the appropriateness of a given style of leadership:

Table 7–1
Summary of Research Findings Regarding Fiedler's Theory

Situational factor			
Leader-member relations	Task structure	Position power	Most effective leadership style
Good	Structured	Strong	Task-oriented
Good	Structured	Weak	Task-oriented
Good	Unstructured	Strong	Task-oriented
Good	Unstructured	Weak	Employer-oriented
Moderately poor	Unstructured	Strong	Employee-oriented
Moderately poor	Structured	Weak	Employee-oriented
Moderately poor	Structured	Strong	Employee-oriented
Moderately poor	Unstructured	Weak	Task-oriented

1. *Leader-member relations*: the quality of the leader's relations with subordinates, the confidence they have in the leader, and their loyalty. It is generally measured by asking the leader to rate the atmosphere of the group on a numbr of dimensions.
2. *Task structure*: the degree to which the work tasks are routinized. This is generally measured by asking observers to rate the degree of routine observed in carrying out assigned tasks.
3. *Position power*: the amount of formal authority vested in the leader's formal position, including the degree of control over rewards and the degree to which upper management supports the leader in the use of authority.

Fiedler collapsed the original Ohio State dimensions into a single dimension of leader style with employee-oriented behaviors (high consideration) at one extreme and task-oriented behaviors (high initiating structure) at the other extreme. His research (as well as that of subsequent investigtors) has found that the most successful style of leader behavior depends upon the situation defined by the three conditions just listed. These contingencies are summarized in Table 7–1. A task-oriented style, for example, appears to be most effective where leader member relations are good and the task is structured. A task-oriented style is best, furthermore, when leader-member relations are good, the task is unstructured, and the leader's position power is strong. Under similar conditions, however, if the leader's position power is weak, an employee-oriented style is more effective. An examination of Table 7–1 will reveal the varying situational conditions under which two entirely different styles of leader behavior can be equally effective.

The major importance of Fiedler's work lies in the discovery that the situation surrounding the leadership role has a critical bearing upon the success of any given leadership style. Subsequent management students have credited Fiedler with introducing a **contingency** or **situational** approach to the study of leadership.

A second theory of leader effectiveness also concentrates on contingencies as they influence the effectiveness of various leader behavior styles. According to the work of Robert J. House and his colleagues, leaders can choose the degree to which they engage in four kinds of leader behaviors:

1. *Instrumental Behavior*: very similar to Initiating Structure, consisting of planning, organizing, controlling, and coordinating subordinates closely in their tasks;
2. *Supportive Behavior*: very similar to Consideration, consisting of displaying concern for the interests, needs, and well-being of subordinates;
3. *Participative Behavior*: characterized by sharing information and an emphasis on consultation with subordinates;
4. *Achievement-Oriented Behavior*: setting challenging goals, expecting subordinates to perform at the highest level, and continually seeking improvement in performance.

This model has been labeled a **Path-Goal Theory** of leadership effectiveness, because it proposes that a leader's choice of these behaviors should be premised upon a goal of increasing personal payoffs to subordinates for work-goal attainment, and making the path to these payoffs as free of obstacles as possible. The path-goal model, furthermore, is a contingency model, in that it posits that the appropriate mix of such leader behaviors depends on two major sets of factors: (a) the individuals being supervised, and (b) the characteristics of the work environment.

Individual characteristics influencing the impact of leader behaviors include: (1) Ability—the greater the employee's perceived level of ability to accomplish a task, the less the individual will accept direction or instrumental behavior on the part of the leader. (2) Locus of control—this is the degree to which employees believe they have control over what happens to them. Those who believe that they have a great deal of control over what happens to them are said to react more favorably to a participative leader, and others would prefer a more directive leader. (3) Needs and motives—the particular set of needs that are felt strongly by an employee will affect the impact of a particular set of leader behaviors on that person's performance. People with a high need for autonomy will probably react negatively to instrumental kinds of leader behavior.

A number of organizational characteristics, in addition to subordinates', are also proposed by path-goal theory as influences on the effectiveness of leader behavior. Specifically, three broad groups of work environment properties have been studied: (1) subordinates' tasks—the degree of structure involved in work operations; (2) the work group—informal work group norms and cohesiveness; and (3) organizational factors—stress levels in the work situation, situations involving high uncertainty, and the degree to which rules, procedures, and policies govern an employee's work.

A full explication of contingency leadership theories is beyond the scope of this chapter. It is important, however, to note that present research on the topic of leadership is just now beginning to yield an understanding of the complexities of leadership phenomena. The practice of leadershp involves elements of the leader's own personality and behavior, complex relationships beween the leader and subordinates, informal group characteristics, and a variety of characteristics of the formal environment within which work activities are carried out. Any formula, then, that proposes to make one an effective leader by adopting a single ideal leader style is hopelessly wrong, and anyone purporting to sell such a formula is no more of a help than were the snake oil salesmen of 70 or more years ago.

LEADERSHIP AND MOTIVATING WORKERS

The very concept of leadership—inducing others to work toward an objective—raises a fundamental question in management: How can people be led to perform at higher levels of productivity? The manager as a leader must seek some theory or model for motivating others.

Several theories have received a great deal of attention. We shall summarize one that is built on assumptions of man's basic nature and one that is focused on the human environment. Both classifications offer guidelines for managers to induce others to perform. Of course, all of these theories come from psychologists.

Maslow's Need Hierarchy Theory

Abraham Maslow's principal argument is that employee needs emerge in a hierarchical fashion; lower-order needs are experienced first and must be satisfied by the work environment before higher-order needs are perceived. The implication is that rewards of higher-order needs will have no incentive effect upon employee motivation until lower-order needs are satisfied. Maslow labeled this phenomenon the concept of **prepotency of needs**.

Maslow's hierarchy is illustrated in Figure 7–1. From lowest to highest, the needs are defined as:

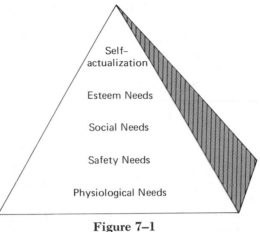

Figure 7–1
Maslow's Need Hierarchy

Physiological needs: These include hunger, sex, thirst;

Safety needs: These represent the need to be free of bodily threat;

Social needs: These represent the need to love and be loved. They include affection, friendship, affiliation;

Esteem needs: These include an employee's need for self-respect and respect from others;

Self-actualization: This need has never adequately been defined either by Maslow or subsequent theorists. In an existential sense, the term refers to becoming all that one chooses and is capable of becoming.

Most industrial psychologists agree that Maslow identified several classes of needs that are important sources of work motivation. The theory has been faulted, however, over the prepotency issue. Very few management theorists believe anymore that a strict ordering exists in the sequence in which needs are felt (except, possibly, for physiological and safety needs). Perhaps the most important managerial implication emerging from Maslow's work is that most employees experience a variety of needs motivating them to come to work and perform at a given level of effort. It is important for a manager to consider each employee's unique profile of felt needs when explaining his or her response to the organization.

Herzberg's
Two Factor Model   A second famous statement of employee needs was made by Frederick Herzberg and his associates. Herzberg is credited with a **two-factor** model of motives that

(like Maslow's) was adequate in describing the content of work motives but failed to describe adequately their impact on work behavior and performance. Herzberg and his associates analyzed the content of interviews carried out with approximately 200 employees about their jobs. Respondents were asked to think of times when they felt particularly good and particularly bad about their jobs, and to describe the conditions leading to these feelings in as much detail as possible.

An analysis of these interviews led Herzberg to propose that the conditions leading to positive feelings about the job were fundamentally different from those leading to negative feelings. The former were called satisfiers and the latter were labeled dissatisfiers. He inferred from these findings that needs were discontinuous as far as their impact on motivation and performance is concerned. Positive work motivation (factors leading to enhanced performance) would only be influenced by **satisfiers** (e.g., the satisfaction of achievement needs, recognition, advancement, the work itself, personal growth). Later theorists agreeing with Herzberg considered these factors **intrinsic** because they exist primarily within the context of the work being carried out.

Dissatisfiers, according to Herzberg, could only lead to dissatisfaction with the job, and therefore could not positively motivate job performance. Dissatisfiers include such factors as company policy and administration, technical supervision, interpersonal relations with supervisors and peers, salary, job security, work conditions, and status. Later theorists referred to these elements as **extrinsic factors**, because they exist outside the context of the immediate work being performed on the job.

As was the case with Maslow, Herzberg's ideas gave us an interesting and useful framework for considering a variety of needs and rewards that are important to employee motivation. His model, however, has failed as an accurate statement of the process by which these needs influence behavior and performance. Few serious students of management today accept the notion of a discontinuity between satisfiers and dissatisfiers. These constitute two opposite ends of the same continuum, and both have measurable impacts on employee motivation and performance.

B. F. Skinner's Behavioralist-Reinforcement Model

B. F. Skinner has made a valuable contribution to our understanding of reinforcement as a powerful managerial tool for controlling and shaping patterns of employee behavior. Two generalizations about reinforcemnt emerge from his work. First, the timing or *scheduling* of reinforcements is at least as important as the absolute level of re-inforcement. He has demonstrated, for example, that intermittent rein-forcement (rewarding the desired behavior only part of the time) is more effective than constant reinforcement (rewarding the desired behavior each time that it occurs). Second, Skinner has demonstrated a vital distinction between the notion of *reinforcement* on one hand, and that of *punishment* on the other:

> Reinforcement can be positive or negative. Positive reinforcement is the presentation of an attractive stimulus following the desired behavior. Negative reinforcement is the *removal* of an aversive or unpleasant stimulus following the desired response.
>
> Punishment, on the other hand, consists of *removing* a pleasant event following an undesired behavior or *presenting* an aversive or unpleasant stimulus following an undesired response.

Note the important differences between reinforcement and pun-ishment. According to strict Skinnerian logic, behavior can only be positively influenced and learned under conditions of reinforcement (positive or negative). The reason for this is that reinforcement focuses upon the desired behavior, and therefore gives the employee a great deal of information. Punishment, in contrast, can only serve to disrupt an undesired behavior. It carries no informational content about the desired behavior. Under conditions of punishment, the employee only knows that whatever he or she is doing is wrong.

The behaviorist-reinforcement model has two major qualities associated with it. First, it has been developed and thoroughly tested in a rigorous scientific fashion. Generalizations made from it to applied settings are on firm theoretical and empirical ground. Second, much of the content of the model lends itself directly to one of the most cogent and pressing concerns of managers: how does one influence the behavior and performance of others? This model is only now influencing the applied field of management. We should expect to see a great deal more influence and application of the model in future years.

Motivation theories that promise new breakthroughs have emerged in the last several decades. Psychologists and academics have refined the topic with expectancy theories, equity theories, and other proposals. This book continually attempts to restrict its coverage to those topics that have been applied in managerial situations and promise to be useful to the practicing manager. For this reason, we have reduced the coverage of motivation theories in this edition in an effort to refrain from merely providing a rigorous, academic exercise for specialists. Nevertheless, leaders continually evolve their own useful generalizations for inducing others to perform effectively.

REFERENCES

ARGYRIS, C., *Interpersonal Competence and Organizational Effectiveness.* Homewood, Ill.: Richard D. Irwin, Inc., 1962.

BLAKE, ROBERT R. and JANE S. MOUTON, *The Managerial Grid.* Houston, Texas: Gulf Publishing Company, 1964.

FIEDLER, FRED, *A Theory of Leadership Effectiveness.* New York: McGraw-Hill Book Company Inc., 1967.

HAYES, JAMES L., *Memos for Management Leadership.* New York: Amacom, 1983.

HERZBERG, FREDERICK, *Work and the Nature of Man.* New York: World Publishing Co., 1966.

HOUSE, ROBERT J., "A Path-Goal Theory of Leader Effectiveness," *Administrative Science Quarterly* (1971), pp. 301–332.

MASLOW, ABRAHAM, *Motivation and Personality,* New York: Harper and Row Publishers, Inc., 1954.

McGREGOR, DOUGLAS, *The Human Side of Enterprise.* New York: McGraw-Hill Book Company Inc., 1960.

ROETHLISBERGER, F. J. and W. J. DICKSON, *Management and the Worker.* Cambridge, Mass.: Harvard University Press, 1939.

STOGDILL, R. M., *Handbook of Leadership.* New York: Free Press, 1974.

TANNENBAUM, ROBERT and W. H. SCHMIDT, "How to Choose a Leadership Pattern," *Harvard Business Review*, 36, no. 2 (March–April 1958), pp. 95–101.

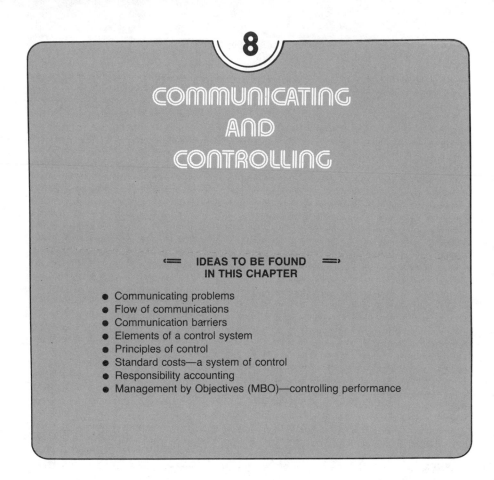

8

COMMUNICATING AND CONTROLLING

<== IDEAS TO BE FOUND ==>
IN THIS CHAPTER

- Communicating problems
- Flow of communications
- Communication barriers
- Elements of a control system
- Principles of control
- Standard costs—a system of control
- Responsibility accounting
- Management by Objectives (MBO)—controlling performance

Many writers do not identify the communicating function as a separate managerial process; all emphasize controlling as a distinguishable function. In this chapter we discuss both the communicating and controlling functions because they are, in fact, closely related. Both are also closely related to the emerging importance of managing information and computers, to be discussed in Chapter 9.

COMMUNICATING   Managers spend a major percentage of their time transmitting their ideas to others, orally and in writing. They most often use the symbols of their language but also employ mathematical symbols, codes, graphical devices, electronic impulses, and other media for expressing their ideas. Other managerial functions, especially controlling and organizing, involve communication problems. Communication serves as a linking process by which parts of a system are tied together. The subject has received the attention of many specialists, including the technical communications engineer, the linguist, the psychologist, the sociologist, and the organization theorists.

Communicating, as used in this book, is a managerial function because it represents a basic human characteristic required by all managers in performing their jobs. (In fact, all managerial functions involve the human element.) Today managing information is centered around computers and other non-human devices and thus is distinguished from communicating and other managerial functions. The interface between human beings and computers is an intriguing issue—for the present, we assume that managers will continue to manage computers rather than be managed by computers.

Types of Communication Problems All communication problems can be treated in three basic groups:

1. The technical problem of how accurately the symbols can be transmitted.
2. The semantic problem of how the symbols convey the desired meaning.
3. The effectiveness problem of how meaning effects the desired results.

Cybernetics has contributed new insights into answers to the first group of problems. The terms in this new discipline have precise meaning to the communications engineer but may be confusing to a manager. Several important distinctions made by the communications engineer will provide an introduction to this interesting subject and will hint at some fundamental ideas of use to a manager in transmitting messages.

In cybernetics, information has nothing to do with meaning (the subject of the second group of problems). It is a quantitative measure of the amount of order in a system and is related not to what you *do* say but what you *can* say about a matter. If a system is highly disorganized, a message can say a great deal. **Information** is a measure of one's freedom of choice when one selects a message. If there is no freedom of choice, there is no information. If "Q" is always followed by a "U" in a language, "U" is perfectly predictable and, therefore, no information is added. The more probable a message is, the less information it gives. If a subordinate always sends his superior the message "Things are fine," the superior can predict the message before he receives it and thus receives no information. The more disordered a situation is, the more information is required to describe it completely.

The idea of **noise** in information theory includes the undesirable uncertainties in the transmission process. "Snow" on televison, "static" on the radio, or any interference in the receipt of a message increases uncertainty. Redundancy is used to help combat noise and insure against mistakes. **Redundancy** is anything that makes the transmission more predictable. Redundancy provides some structure (the opposite of randomness) that will increase the probability that the message will be received. Because all transmission of messages is subject to the "loss of information" through noise, the sender of a message should always be conscious of the need for redundancy and the minimization of the number of times that the message is to be retransmitted.

The second group of communication problems involves the meaning that a message has to the receiver. A person may *say* one thing but the receiver may *hear* something different, even if the word sent and the word received are exactly the same. This is a matter of semantics. Securing understanding of a message is affected by a number of factors: (1) the similarity of past experiences of the sender and the receiver; (2) the environment in which the communication takes place; (3) the distinction between facts and opinions; (4) the degree of abstractness of the symbols used; and (5) the complexity of the phrases used. A manager must constantly check whether the *meaning* of his communications has been understood.

The third group of communication problems involves the effectiveness of the communication. Usually the more direct the communication, the more effective it will be. In an organization, the number of levels through which a communication travels affects the action that is finally taken. Thus, the communication problem increases as the size of the firm increases. Of course, effectiveness of communications depends upon both efficient transmission of messages and the understanding of their meaning. In the final analysis, the acceptance of the communication is the key to effectiveness.

Acceptance of a communication by the receiver is a psychological phenomenon depending on the needs and past experience of the receiver and the environment in which the communication takes place. We all tend to hear what we want to hear and to reject what we do not want to hear. A communication will be accepted if it does not seriously conflict with the receiver's own goals. Usually a person has a broad "zone of acceptance" and will accept communications even without agreeing with the entire message. A person who feels a part of a well-developed working team will tend to accept many communications without consciously questioning them.

Flow
of
Communications

Three types of communications in an organization can be classified by their flow: vertical, horizontal, and informal. In directing activities of subordinates, the manager issues orders to others further down in the hierarchy. Organization charts show the flow of authority and the channels through which this downward, vertical communication flows. Authority lines are important channels of communication, but they comprise only one type of channel. Control reports and memoranda flow back up through the levels of the hierarchy as subordinates are made accountable for their actions. This upward vertical flow of communications is the heart of a control system.

Horizontal channels provide means by which managers on the same level of an organization coordinate their activities without referring all matters to their superior. One writer has called this a "gang plank." His idea was that many matters can be handled on the same level of an organization, thereby speeding action while at the same time relieving superiors of unnecessary problems. Multiple copies of memoranda that flow to all positions needing the information increase coordination of effort.

Formal communications are planned to meet the specific needs of the organization; however, many communications are informal. The **grapevine** may be helpful for the attainment of organizational goals, but it also serves the social needs of the individuals in the organization. A manager can utilize the grapevine as a positive aid, but may also face problems of rumors, gossip, and other negative outlets of expressions by people in the organization. The grapevine cannot be destroyed; therefore, it should receive conscious attention. Informal channels may be superior for some organizational purposes. A "word" can be dropped at the proper time and may remedy a disciplinary problem without resort to a formal reprimand. Because the speed at which information flows through a grapevine is often astounding, management must seriously consider this third type of communication.

Communication may be viewed as a pattern of interconnecting lines, referred to as **networks**. We have already seen an example of one type of network in the illustration of feedback. Researchers have experimented with various structural patterns of communications in small groups. Figure 8–1 illustrates some possibilities. The simple, direct, one-direction network in Figure 8–1a tends to be speedier and less disorderly. The star, or circular, network in Figure 8–1b provides the individual with more choice of channels and offers more satisfaction; yet it tends to be slower, noisier, and, on first observation, more disorganized. The serial and radial network of Figure 8–1c insulates the chief from overt criticism by the lowest level and places the intermediate superior in a position of considerable power. Of course, there are many other networks that may be used. Analysis of communications networks offers a means by which a manager can study the

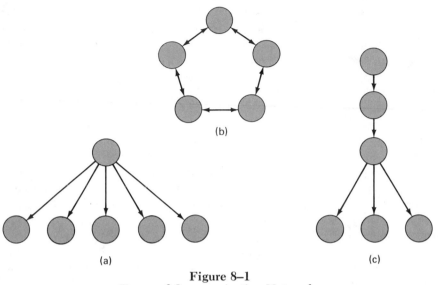

Figure 8–1
Types of Communication Networks

flow of communication and choose the type best adapted to a given situation.

Communication Barriers

Problems of communication directly retard the success of managers in the performance of their functions. If messages are poorly transmitted, or if the action is not effected, management cannot plan or control activities properly. The barriers to good communication require constant attention. Some of these barriers and remedies will now be considered.

Distortion may be a matter of noise in transmission or it may result from inadequacy of the words in carrying the precise ideas of the sender. If an accountant submits a report on "costs" to an economist, distortion may result because of differences in meanings of the word "costs." If the industrial engineer receives the report, he may get ideas entirely different from those of the accountant or economist. The financial manager will view "costs" as outgo of funds; the production manager may think of unit costs of the manufactured product; the marketing manager will think of costs as part of the total selling price; the industrial relations manager may view "costs" as a social factor of employment. Each of these specialists will tend to have different frames of reference within which to interpret a report.

An important means of overcoming the distortion barrier is to expand the horizons of each member of the management team so that each can understand the meaning in the minds of other members.

Another means is to use what the psychologist calls **empathy**—attempt to project oneself into the viewpoint of the other person. A major step in handling distortion is the development of an awareness that some degree of distortion always exists.

Filtering is a barrier to communication that takes the form of intentionally sifting the information so that the receiver will look favorably on the message. No one likes to admit mistakes to some one else, especially to the boss. The boss, on the other hand, wants to secure information about what is actually going on, especially those actions that need attention. If management is not careful, it may encourage a free flow of just those messages that provide little information. The remedies for filtering are a well-designed control system, the development of rapport with subordinates, listening to subordinates with an understanding attitude, reducing the fear of failure, and increasing the awareness of management to problems of subordinates.

Overloading of communication channels can cause the network to be jammed with irrelevant messages. Newer methods of processing and transmitting data have increased the number of communications which flow to executives. Managers can literally be buried in memoranda and reports with no hope of digging themselves out. The answer to this problem lies in monitoring the channels to clear messages in order of priority and importance. More messages do not necessarily mean more information. The communication system should provide for editing devices, or persons, to regulate the quality and quantity of communications with regard to sufficiency of information for decision centers.

Timing of communications can result in problems for management. Some types of messages need to be released so that everyone will receive them simultaneously. Other types of messages being transmitted should be timed sequentially so that receivers will not be confused by issues that are not important to them at the moment.

Routing of communications should provide sufficient information for a decision to be made by the proper persons. The route may determine the content of the message and the language in which it is stated. If official information is first received by the grapevine, or from persons outside the organization, the employee may be placed in an insecure position. If a supervisor receives information from subordinates, it signifies a short circuit in the line of communication from top management, and thus threatens the supervisor's status and authority. The answers to the problem are in the proper planning of a communication system and in the recognition of its human elements.

Determination of the flow of communications and recognition of the many barriers to good communication are basic to the communicating function. Communication networks, communication channels, and barriers to communication must continually receive attention.

NON-VERBAL COMMUNICATION

A very powerful means of communicating involves any activity not placed into words, neither orally nor in writing. Everyone is conscious of the power of a smile, a gesture, or a fist as a means of communicating. The cliche "Actions speak louder than words" illustrates the importance of non-verbal communication. While this method is important in all managerial situations, it becomes a major managerial problem when people communicate across cultural boundaries; therefore, we discuss this more fully in Chapter 13 when we deal with communicating internationally.

As we conclude this section on communicating, let us notice that non-verbal communication is truly a "silent language" and think of the many examples where it is even more important than words—how the daily presence of a CEO among workers can change the climate of the workplace, a glance across a room can carry important meaning, a pictorial greeting card with no words timely sent can convey much meaning. As we continue this discussion of the variety of means and issues of communicating, we turn to a very important special case that employs communication—controlling.

CONTROLLING

Many advancements in management are essentially improvements in the individual techniques of control. In this chapter, we state the factors common to any type of control.

Control is the process that measures current performance and guides it toward some predetermined goal. The essence of control lies in checking existing actions against some desired results determined in the planning process.

Essential Elements of Any Control System

The essential elements of any control system are:

1. A *predetermined* goal, plan, policy, standard, norm, decision rule, criterion, or yardstick.
2. A means for *measuring* current activity (quantitatively, if possible).
3. A means of *comparing* current activity with a criterion.
4. Some means of *correcting* the current activity to achieve the desired result.

The first element of a control system involves the answer to the question: What *should* be the results? This element forces attention on the future and what is desired or expected. The attempt to predict future events provides the basis for interpreting the meaning of events when they actually occur. Even poor prediction provides a framework for better understanding of current experience. The predetermined criterion may even be set arbitrarily. The goal may be judged by others to be bad. A useful control system does not evaluate the goodness of the goal; it merely provides a means by which activity can be directed toward an actual goal.

The predetermined criterion should be stated explicitly. For this reason, quantitative statements are usually preferable. In production management, physical units, such as ton-miles of freight, units per machine-hour, or pounds of scrappage per unit of output, may provide a simple and direct yardstick for operations. In financial management, dollar values serve as explicit statements of norms. Often, financial managers use past achievements of the firm as crude yardsticks for controlling current operations, for example, the record of the past twelve months. The assumption is that past performance was not too bad and that if it can be equalled or surpassed, the firm will not decline. Marketing managers often use such industry data as benchmarks against which the company can compare its own sales efforts. They also develop quotas based on market potential to serve as predetermined goals.

The second element in any control system is the measurement of actual performance. This step usually requires the greatest attention and expense, because records and reports must be devised to present information in a form that will fit the control system. Measurements of actual performance must be in units similar to those of the predetermined criterion. Prompt reporting of actual performance increases the value of a control system. Recent improvements in data processing increase the speed of reporting this data.

The degree of accuracy to which measurement is carried will depend upon the needs of the specific application. All measurement is accurate only to some limited degree. There are many instances in management when it is desirable to round a number to emphasize important magnitudes. Concern over small errors might overshadow major factors and confuse the interpreter. The ability of a good manager to strike quickly at the heart of the meaning of past performance is a most important factor in successful management.

Comparison of a criterion with actual performance indicates variations in activity. This key step adds meaning to the data provided by the control process. Because some variation can be expected in all activity, a critical question facing a manager is the determination of what amount of variation is large enough to be significant and worth attention. If limits of variation are not clear, the manager may waste time studying unimportant problems while failing to give sufficient time to pertinent issues.

The method of presenting comparisons of performance with the predetermined goal is an important question. The simplest and most direct method is usually the best. Graphical techniques provide means of visualizing important relationships, uncluttered by insignificant details. Anyone who has attempted to interpret large volumes of quantitative data will recognize the sense of futility that develops unless some simplified approach can be devised.

This third element of a control system involves the study of relationships. Such techniques as ratios, trends, mathematical equations, and charts help add meaning to the measurements of actual performance by showing the relation of actual experience to the predetermined criterion.

The purpose of comparing past performance with planned performance is not only to determine when a mistake has been made but to enable the manager to *predict* future problems. A good control system will provide information quickly so that trouble can be prevented. A good manager will not be lulled into inactivity by success, but will remain alert to controls that indicate the need for some present action that will eliminate future potential problems before they develop.

The fourth element of a control system is the action phase of making corrections. This fourth element may involve a decision not to take any action—if the performance is "under control."

Two basic types of error face the manager taking corrective action: (1) taking action when no action is needed and (2) failing to take action when some corrective action is needed. A good control system should provide some basis for helping the manager estimate the risks of making either of these types of error. Of course, the final test of a control system is whether correct action is taken at the correct time.

Principles of Control

Certain basic ideas are useful in the development of a control system. Applications of these principles will appear in Part 3.

1. *Strategic Point Control.* Optimum control can be achieved only if critical, key, or limiting points can be identified and close attention directed to adjustments at those points. An attempt to control all points tends to increase unnecessary efforts and to

decrease attention to important problems. This principle of control is closely related to the exception principle of organization. Both emphasize the discrimination between important and unimportant factors. Good control does not mean maximum control, for control is expensive. For example, the development of a good fire-control program in a forest depends upon the strategic placement of towers on hills. The haphazard addition of a large number of devices and people in the forest cannot yield an equal degree of control.

2. *Feedback*. The process of adjusting future actions on the basis of information about past performance is known as **feedback**. Although applications of the idea date back to controls on windmills, the fly-ball governor of Watt's steam engine, and the steering of steamships, recent developments in electronic hardware of automatic control have reinforced the importance of this principle. The electrical engineer refers to a **closed-loop system of feedback** when the information of actual performance is fed back to the source of energy by electrical or mechanical means in an endless chain. An **open-loop system of feedback** involves human intervention at some point in the flow. Management has many uses of the feedback principle in areas that, at first, appear to be unrelated.

3. *Flexible Control*. Any system of control must be responsive to changing conditions. Often, the importance of a control system demands that it be adaptable to new developments, including the failure of the control system itself. Plans may call for an automatic system to be backed up by a human system that would operate in an emergency; likewise, an automatic system may back up a human system.

4. *Organizational Suitability*. Controls should be tailored to fit the organization. The flow of information concerning current performance should correspond with the organizational structure employed. To be able to control overall operations, a superior must find a pattern that will provide control for individual parts. Budgets, quotas, and other techniques may be useful in controlling separate departments.

5. *Self-control*. Units may be planned to control themselves. If a department can have its own goals and control system, any of the detailed controls can be handled within the department. These subsystems of self-control can then be tied together by the overall control system.

6. *Direct Control*. Any control system should be designed to maintain direct contact between the controller and the controlled. Even when there are a number of control systems provided by staff specialists, the supervisor at the first level is still important because of having direct knowledge of performance.

7. *Human Factor*. Any control system involving people is affected by the psychological manner in which human beings view the system. A technically well-designed control system may fail because the human being reacts unfavorably to the system. For example, a dynamic and imaginative leader tends to resist control. Controls for such a person demand special attention to the human factor.

The essentials of any control system and the principles of control provide a sound basis for a manager; planning is a prerequisite for this important managerial function.

ILLUSTRATIONS OF CONTROL APPLICATIONS The essentials and principles of any control system provide the foundation for developing one's own style of applying them in personal life (controlling one's weight) or in managerial life. The number of broad applications by managers is almost as extensive as the entire topic of management: quality control, inventory control, financial control, marketing control, budgetary control, and so forth. With the limited space of this book, we obviously cannot give illustrations of all types of control. We offer three short examples: two in accounting control and one popular, general purpose technique, management by objectives. Later, in Part 3 you will find other examples.

Standard Costs **Standard costs** are predetermined costs developed from past experience, motion and time study, expected future manufacturing costs, or some combination of these. They contrast with *actual costs*, which are the amounts actually incurred in the manufacturing process.

In standard costing, the unit cost of a particular product would be computed as follows:

1. *Calculate Standard Labor Costs*. From a motion and time study it is found that the normal labor time required to produce one unit is four hours; the expected hourly wage cost for those workers responsible for its production is known to be $3.50. Thus, the standard labor cost is $14.00 (4 hours at $3.50 per hour).

2. *Calculate Standard Material Cost*. From a study of materials flow and handling, it is estimated that no more than ten pounds of raw materials should be used in the production of one unit; the expected cost of raw materials, given reasonably efficient purchasing, is $.80 per pound. Thus, the standard material cost is $8.00 (10 pounds at $.80 per pound).

3. *Calculate Standard Overhead Costs.* The unit overhead cost depends upon the expected (budgeted) production. A relationship is determined between expected overhead cost and some indicator of activity (usually a relation between overhead and labor costs). Thus, assuming that expected overhead is to be 80 percent of expected labor costs (as shown by the budget), the standard overhead is $11.20 (80 percent of $14.00).

4. *Add the Three Amounts.* In this example, the standard unit cost of a hypothetical product is:

Standard labor cost	$14.00
Standard material cost	8.00
Standard overhead cost	11.20
Standard unit cost	$33.20

As products are completed, the inventory of finished goods is charged with the standard costs of completely manufactured units. From the manager's point of view, the chief benefit of standard costing is the analysis of reasons for the difference between actual costs and standard costs.

The analysis of **manufacturing cost variances** (accounts that accumulate differences between actual and standard costs) is based on reports flowing routinely to management. As an example, assume that the actual labor cost for the preceding example is $16.00; the labor cost variance would be $2.00. There are two sources of the variance: (1) departure from the standard time and (2) departure from the standard wage cost. If the actual labor time is five hours (instead of the standard four) and the actual wage cost is $4.00 (instead of $3.50), management must determine the causes of the variation. Was a new man on the job? Is the standard time too tight? Did the supervisor use a higher paid person on the job than was supposed to be used? Material cost variances and overhead cost variances raise the same types of questions.

To summarize these steps in terms of the four essentials of any control system: The first three steps satisfy the first essential—setting a predetermined standard. The recording of the actual cost during operations is the second essential. The third essential, comparing standard costs and actual costs, results in "cost variances," i.e., comparisons. Finally, the manager must seek to explain the variances and to make corrections as needed.

Responsibility
Accounting

In **responsibility accounting**, costs are identified with those individuals who are responsible for their control. In determining costs *controllable* by a given manager, it is necessary to analyze each cost element separately. All variable costs cannot be assumed to be controllable, nor are all fixed costs *uncontrollable*. The authority of the person being considered must be recognized; thus, responsibility accounting classifications must fit the organization structure. Furthermore, a minimum of cost allocation should be employed; that is, consideration should be given only to those costs that are clearly influenced by a particular individual.

Closely related to the concept of responsibility accounting is the idea of **profit centers**. Here the concern is to assign responsibility for both revenue and expenses to a segment of a business. The establishment of profit centers requires the allocation of costs, revenues, and assets in order to evaluate the performance of a segment manager.

Management by Objectives (MBO)   A general purpose control involves a manager and subordinate agreeing on objectives for the subordinate (the predetermined standard), recording the success in actual performance, and then, at a review meeting between the two, comparing the agreed-on objectives with actual performance. The manager then has a number of options for handling any variances. This approach suggested by Peter Drucker,[1] and popularized by George Odiorne,[2] is **management by objectives (MBO)**.

In MBO, an executive must narrow the range of attention of each person in the organization to focus on *definite* and *measurable* results that have a clear meaning for each individual. Each part of an organization can contribute toward companywide objectives if it clearly sees its own specific goals and can determine, through measurement, how well it is doing. The selection of the proper factors to be measured is an important decision, because usually that which is measured is that which receives attention.

The key to MBO is the mutual relationships between the superior and the subordinate in setting realistic objectives for the subordinate. Odiorne suggests that this meeting should establish objectives in three major categories; routine objectives, problem-solving objectives, and innovative objectives. For each of these categories, agreement should be reached for three levels of achievement: pessimistic (absolute minimum), realistic (normally expected), and optimistic (ideal). In the last decade many organizations have developed elaborate processes for MBO, with varying degrees of

[1] Peter F. Drucker, *The Practice of Management* (New York: Harper and Row, Publishers, Inc., 1954).

[2] George Odiorne, *Management by Objectives* (New York: Pitman Publishing Co., 1965).

success. However, the basic idea of MBO is fundamental—clear targets should be set by superior and subordinate at all levels of the organization.

The overall objectives of a firm generally are established by top management; yet, it is desirable for each subordinate manager to have a voice in setting his own objectives. If each manager is to understand the relationship of his own organizational objectives to the broader objectives of the company, he will need to participate in the goal-setting process. If he is involved in establishing his objectives, he will feel that the objectives are proper once they are set and will tend to accept them more readily. In this way, each part of the organization will strive in a joint effort toward the recognized organizational objectives.

Objectives may be set as ideals or as realistic expectations. Whether the objective is idealistic or realistic, it should be stated in definite terms of results. The statement "reduce costs" sounds fine, but it is vague and lacks precision. Even if a manager is conscientious and sincerely strives toward this vague objective, he never knows whether he has reached "the objective." The statement "produce at costs 10 percent less than last year" is better because it states the specific results desired.

In this part—Functions in the Management Process—we have discussed the seven managerial functions which we saw are interrelated. In the final chapter of this part, we move to the subject of information systems. The rapid developments in managing information promises to strengthen the bond that ties the seven functions together.

REFERENCES

FLEMING, ALICE, *What to Say When You Don't Know What to Say*. New York: Scribner, 1982.

HALL, EDWARD, *The Silent Language*. New York: Doubleday, 1959.

LAWLER, E. E., "Control Systems in Organizations," *Industrial and Organizational Psychology*. Skokie, Ill.: Rand McNally, 1978.

MASSIE, JOSEPH L. and JOHN DOUGLAS, *Managing, A Contemporary Introduction*, 4th ed. Englewood Cliffs, N.J.: Prentice-Hall, Inc., 1985.

ROBBINS, STEPHEN P., *Essentials of Organization Behavior*. Englewood Cliffs, N.J.: Prentice-Hall, Inc., 1984.

TANNER, DEBORAH, *That's Not What I Meant*. New York: Morrow, 1986.

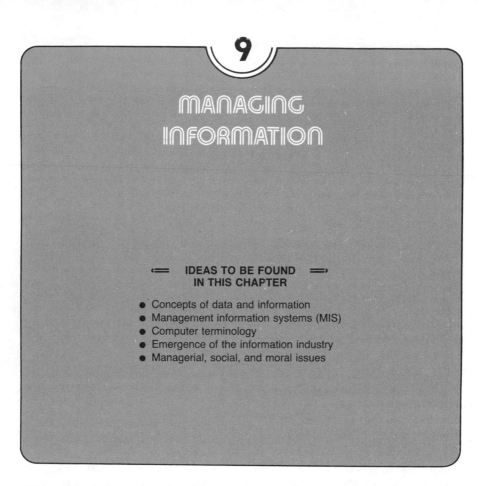

9

MANAGING INFORMATION

⟸ **IDEAS TO BE FOUND** ⟹
IN THIS CHAPTER

- Concepts of data and information
- Management information systems (MIS)
- Computer terminology
- Emergence of the information industry
- Managerial, social, and moral issues

Managing information has become a critical responsibility for managers in the last decades of the twentieth century. It is central to most of the manager's functions:

1. Decision making. This process depends on accurate information.
2. Organizing. The structures of organizations have been modified to adapt to the changes in the processing and flow of information.
3. Staffing. Today all employees should be trained in the operation of the nervons system of the organization—its information system.
4. Directing. Leadership styles have made adjustments to the immediate access to information—the terminal on the manager's desk.

The functions most affected by changes in the technology of information collection and distribution are probably planning and control. For these reasons, this chapter is included as a means of interrelating these functions with the rapidly changing technology for handling information.[1]

Information is power. This simple fact has been recognized since the birth of civilization. Military generals have always collected information about the enemy by means of reconnaissance probes, spies, and studies of their past activities in history and in the biographies of enemy leaders. Accountants have recorded and reported financial information for five centuries. F. W. Taylor and the early management writers searched for "the best way," "a fair day's work," and information to improve productivity. Throughout the process of collecting information, managers have tended to construct systems for collecting, recording, storing, and processing information to aid in reaching their objectives with special-purpose accounting systems, production systems, purchasing systems, filing systems, and so on. For decades the manual and mechanical methods used with these limited systems seemed to be adequate, since the available information was scarce and expensive to collect, transmit, process, store, and use.

This chapter will summarize: (1) the evolution of information systems; (2) the categories of information important to managers; (3) the five basic processes for dealing with information (especially valuable when computer hardware and software are employed in modern systems); (4) several fundamental concepts for developing an efficient and effective information system; (5) the design and implementation of a management information system (MIS); (6) definitions of a few important computer terms; (7) the emergence and rapid growth of an information industry; and, finally, (8) the chief issues and problems experienced in modern information systems. The key focus of this chapter is information, but it must include general computer terminology because increasingly all modern systems are computerized.

EVOLUTION OF INFORMATION SYSTEMS In the past twenty-five years, the "information explosion" has increased the need for managers to seek an optimum system for making use of this subtle and intangible power. Furthermore, with this explosion came the necessity for distinguishing between data and messages that were relevant to the managers' functions from those which would merely cause frustrations and confusion.

[1] This chapter contains sections from earlier editions of this book which were written by Dr. Martin Solomon, Director of Academic Computing, Ohio State University, Columbus, Ohio.

In the early stages of the development of computer hardware in the 1950s, the technology improved so rapidly that management had difficulty in appreciating the capabilities of the computer. However, simultaneously, information theory, then referred to as *cybernetics*, defined the components rigorously; operations research and *management science* developed mathematical and statistical models that offer a conceptual framework for handling information to meet explicit objectives of managers. The practitioners of management put the available computer hardware to work using languages. Thus, in the 1950s new jargon entered the English language as well as other languages. **Automation**, with its emphasis on electronic feedback, was viewed as the basis for the "second industrial revolution." **Electronic data processing**, with its emphasis on entry, processing, and output of data, quickly enabled managers to handle such routine activities as processing payrolls and accounts receivables.

Data processing has provided voluminous printouts of internal data, such as accounting and financial data, production schedules, inventories of raw materials, work in process and finished goods, sales by territory, products, and customers; and external, environmental data, such as marketing data of consumer demand, census of population, economic forecasts, population shifts, and reports of social conditions. With this explosion of data came the realization that managers might not need more data but what they *did* need was relevant, timely data.

Information theory provided the needed breakthrough by pointing out that data and information are not synonymous. **Data** are facts, statistics, opinions, or predictions classified on some basis for storage, processing, and retrieval. These data may be printed out as messages, but all data or messages may not be relevant to managers in the performance of their functions. **Information**, on the other hand, is data that are relevant to the needs of managers in performing their functions. A computer can store technically vast amounts of data— more than managers can comprehend or use. The semantic aspect provides meaning to the data so that managers can concentrate on the portion that will make them more effective. Messages that shed no new light on subjects of interest to the manager may be printed and transmitted. Some messages contain so much interference ("noise") that they jam the reception of pertinent information. In short, managers may be hindered by excess data and frustrated by meaningless messages, much as consumers are frustrated by junk mail. The rigorous definition of information is stated in terms of probabilities as we noted in Chapter 8. The more probable a message is, the less information it gives. Early uses of computers in data processing were primarily in handling large masses of routine activities, but they did not enable managers to distinguish relevant information from volumes of data with little meaning or of little interest to the receiver.

Computer technology has developed greater speeds, storage capacity, and improved methods of printing outputs so that managers are often inundated with data. But they needed better information, not more data. Furthermore, managers often installed computers merely because others were purchasing or renting computers and because it was the "in thing" to do. In short, they obtained equipment before they determined their needs.

This critical but realistic discussion of the evolution of information systems demonstrates the result of the rapid improvements in technology ahead and of the ability of human beings to make efficient and effective use of the improvements. It also serves to caution prospective managers that the expected technological improvements in the next decade might result in a repetition of past mistakes.

With a clear understanding of their needs for information, managers can then design systems for handling information specifically to aid them in performing their managerial functions. In summary, in order for managers to manage information they (1) must identify their specific and explicit needs, (2) design a system that will satisfy these needs, and (3) only then select the computer hardware to efficiently implement the system.

MANAGEMENT INFORMATION CATEGORIES

We turn now to an identification of the categories of management information needed by managers. These categories relate to types of information needed at different levels of organizations from top management to the first-line supervisors. Management information can be conveniently categorized into three main areas:

1. Strategic planning information.
2. Management control information.
3. Operational information.

Strategic planning information relates to the top management tasks of deciding on objectives of the organization, on the levels and the kinds of resources required to attain the objectives, and on the policies that govern the acquisition, use, and disposition of resources. Strategic planning depends heavily upon information external to the organization. When this is combined with internal data, management can make estimates of expected results. The specifics of this information are often unique and tailor-made to particular strategic problems.

Management control information sheds light on goal congruence; it helps managers take those actions which are in the best interests of the organization; it enables managers to see that resources are being used efficiently and effectively in meeting the organizational goals. Robert Anthony pinpoints three types of information needed for management control: costs by responsibility centers, direct program costs, and full program costs (including allocations for indirect costs). Management control information ties together various subactivities in a coherent way so that managers can gauge resource utilization and compare expected with actual results. Management control information is often interdepartmental, in that the inputs come from various organizational groups, cutting across established functional boundaries.

Operational information pertains to the day-to-day activities of the organization and helps assure that specific tasks are performed effectively and efficiently. It also includes the production of routine and necessary information, such as financial accounting, payrolls, personnel rosters, equipment inventories, and logistics. Operational information, such as scheduling work flow through a department or producing a payroll, generally originates in one department.

Systems for handling each of these categories differ as a result of the varying degrees to which the tasks can be well defined. Operational information can be well defined and easily reduced to a routine of a series of instructions, whereas strategic information is difficult to define; control information falls in between.

These three categories are useful when developing management information systems, because they identify the different types of needs of managers and because they point out a continuum from the well-defined information typical of operational information to the other extreme of ill-defined information characteristic of strategic planning information. This continuum is central to the problems of utilizing computers as the hardware in systems design. A well-defined body of information can be reduced to a series of written instructions; that is, it can be **programmed**. A programmed information system involves specific elements that remain unalterable and thus subject to straightforward calculation. For example, the usual payroll information can be reduced to a definite rate per hour multiplied by a number of hours worked. Some programmed information may be quite complicated, but as long as each element can be precisely defined, the result can be precise and calculable. Strategic planning information is more difficult to program but, as we shall see, recent developments in strategic planning and computer hardware make the computer of increasing value in strategy formulation.

INFORMATION PROCESSING COMPONENTS   The architecture of components of computers and their information interaction is a mirror of the functioning of the human physiological information system (nervous system).[2] Likewise the architecture of computer systems is basically similar to the structure of information as organizations commonly handle it in business. Human beings, business organizations, and computer systems can all be viewed as doing five things to data: (1) They receive data, they find things out—they **INPUT**; (2) They remember or write data down for reference—they **STORE**; (3) They compare, think about or manipulate data—they **PROCESS**; (4) They convey or send data to others—they **TRANSMIT**; and (5) They record and publish data in written form—they **OUTPUT**.

These five processes are basic to understanding information systems whether they are human nervous systems, organizational or managerial information systems, or computer systems. The similarity of the three types of information systems has become much clearer as computers have become more sophisticated. Medical doctors have long studied the human nervous system. Computer specialists developed their own jargon, which appeared foreign to doctors and managers. Not until the 1950s did managers recognize the need for management information systems as a specialized area. For a decade computer designers became functional specialists focusing on developing better **hardware technology** (the mechanical or electronic equipment) and **software** (sets of instructions that govern the operations and how the hardware runs). Managers either had to learn the technical computer concepts and jargon or delegate the design to computer equipment experts. However, the latter usually lacked an understanding of the needs of the manager and the resulting design failed to meet a manager's needs.

MANAGEMENT INFORMATION SYSTEMS (MIS) SUPPORT MANAGERIAL FUNCTIONS   Because information is power, managers have always managed information by some method. In the past, each operational department (finance, marketing, production, and personnel) maintained separate information systems to satisfy its particular needs. The problem was that each system collected, stored, and retrieved some of the same data. The data of each

---

[2] This discussion is based on the more complete treatment by the author in Joseph L. Massie and John Douglas, *Managing: A Contemporary Introduction*, 4th ed. (Englewood Cliffs, N.J.: Prentice-Hall, Inc., 1985).

department were not consistent or compatible, the systems were costly, and the information was inadequate.

The need for a comprehensive information system became evident. The result was the evolution of the concept of **management information systems (MIS)**. MIS can be defined generally as an integrated, structured complex of people, machines, and procedures for supplying relevant data (information) from both external and internal sources to aid managers in planning, staffing, communicating, controlling, and decision making. Increasingly, the concept has become dependent on a computer-based network of collecting, processing, storing, transmitting, and supplying outputs to the proper managers at the correct time.

The heart of the integration of information needed in MIS is a data base. A **data base** is an organized repository of the organization's information resources (internal and possibly containing some external data), including raw data and procedures. The idea is that the data base consists of most of the data available in the organization and can be accessed by different managers for their varied uses. One manager may access the data base for planning, another manager may need data for controlling, and generally all managers may need to access the data base for decision making.

The rapid technological developments and the availability of varied computer hardware have been accompanied by the improved availability of sophisticated software systems. This software has served as the interface between the complicated computer hardware and the nontechnical manager who needs the information contained in the computer. Yet managers still need to be knowledgeable of the improved potentials of new computer hardware and software, so that they can gain the maximum service from these electronic wizards.

One powerful, and probably more easily used, concept is that of **decision support systems** (DSS). Although DSS can be viewed as an application within MIS for supporting decisions, it has become more powerful and useful to managers because of the following developments:

> **Interactive computing**—a dialogue between the manager and the system through questions and responses
>
> **User-friendly** data-base languages and hardware
>
> **Distributed data processing**—where at least some portion of the computing function is decentralized via remote terminals

The manager's office of the future has been predicted to be built around executive terminals, or *work-stations*. These managerial work stations are multifunction, on-line terminals connected to a company-wide information network.

DESIGNING A MANAGEMENT INFORMATION SYSTEM

With the rapid development of computer technology, systems analysts conceptualized ideal and total information systems. It became clear, however, that information systems are easier to conceptualize than to implement. Failures developed from purchasing high technology hardware and attempting to make use of it without preliminary study. Successful MIS is the result of a deliberate step-by-step process, not a sudden leap. We shall outline these design stages and supply some guidelines for the design of a management information system.

The logical stages for developing an MIS are

1. System analysis. Make a preliminary survey and analyze the present system and its problems. This first step seeks to orient the system analyst concerning where the organization is relative to sufficient information before attempting to plan where it will go.
2. State explicitly the objectives for the new system. If these objectives are to be realistic, they must include standards for accuracy; the desired timeliness required, for example, hourly, daily, monthly, quarterly; the cost and the estimated budget; and the desired flexibility.
3. Construct a conceptual design. At this stage, the designer must discover the actual needs of each manager. It is here that tradeoffs among competing needs and budget resources are measured and agreed upon. The users and the designer should participate as a group at this point. One approach is to locate the **critical success factors** (CSF) or the limited areas for which information is needed if the organization is to be competitively successful. The design should satisfy the routine information requirements that each worker needs to perform a job.
4. Specify in detail how the system will work. In this stage the detailed requirements are outlined. Flow charts and process charts are useful to visualize the information needs. It is only at this stage that the organization is ready to start to select the computer hardware and the necessary capabilities. The software may either be selected from that commercially available or programs tailored to fit the needs of the organization may be developed.
5. Construct the integrated information system in every detail including computer programs and conduct pilot runs to debug the programs and procedures.
6. Test and implement. At this stage the new system is often introduced alongside the old system until the new system becomes

settled. Part of this stage is the continual evaluation of the system to meet new needs.

Some guidelines for successful design have evolved from past experiences:

1. The design of a management information system should be determined by the users—managers (including top management) and not delegated to a functional computer specialist, such as a director of computer services. The computer specialist may be a most valuable member of the design team for selecting the proper hardware and software and for programming the computer, but only the managers have the knowledge for determining exact information needs. Experience shows that even managers say that they want certain information, but later they will often not use or need what they originally said. What one perceives as a need is often changed by the acquisition of that "need." Only then does the person start to understand better the real needs. Thus, this guideline emphasizes "information needed," not just "information wanted."

2. All users of the information system should participate in the development of the new system. This participation is especially valuable to reduce resistance to change to computerized systems. Moreover, the user knows what information he or she needs, when it is needed, and how it will be used.

3. The costs of the system should be evaluated on a cost-benefits basis. In this evaluation it should be made clear that cost savings of information already offered is not the only benefit. Typically, the sophisticated computerized management information system supplies new, relevant, needed information not previously available to the managers.

4. The management information system should not merely increase the quantity of information. It should select, condense, and interpret information, so that managers receive only the required information.

5. Adequate training of all users should be provided during development and prior to final implementation, and written documentation should be made available for routine use by managers and others.

As we see in these design steps and guidelines, the subject of computer hardware and software typically arises. For this reason, managers need at least a minimum understanding of terms used by computer specialists. (A manager must remember that a little knowledge can be quite dangerous sometimes.) With this understanding the managers can better communicate not only with computer specialists but also with computers themselves.

TWO KEY CONCEPTS FOR MANAGERS IN COMPUTERIZING INFORMATION

Earlier editions of this book necessarily introduced elementary terms used by computer specialists. Today, computer terminology is defined effectively in manuals, seminars, and on TV, relieving the author from describing computers and enabling him to focus on information for management. Computer specialists use highly sophisticated concepts and their own professional version of English in advising managers on the use of computers. This chapter is directed to managers as an aid in stating their needs to computer specialists to gain advantage from technological developments in handling information.

Technology is a means to the end of improving management; the use of exotic new developments is not an end in itself. Too often managers have sought to attain the appearance of being modern by windowdressing with computers and adopting them prematurely. Fortunately, new developments in computer technology make it easier for managers to use the hardware. Two key concepts are fundamental:

User friendly is an increasing characteristic of computers—that is, managers can communicate directly with computers through interactive systems that use a CRT (TV-like screen) and a human language version of what is going into computers in program language. Even a small child without sophisticated training can now view a computer as a friend, not as a mysterious monster.

Compatibility is the second concept of critical importance to managers in developing a useful information system. The idea of compatibility has long been important in human relations (for example, in marriage). Computer specialists have adopted the idea and defined it as the ability of a program or component to be used with more than one kind of computer. From a manager's viewpoint, the concept of compatibility is even more comprehensive. Human compatibility is important; technical compatibility of computers is important, but management needs both human and technical compatibility. In other words, computer hardware in an information system must be compatible; the software selected must be compatible with the hardware; and finally, the computer hardware and software must be compatible with the thought processes of the managers. Computers in the future can best fit information systems when they are friendly to the users and compatible with other computers and managers.

**SUMMARY
OF KEY COMPUTER
TERMINOLOGY**

Managers can best understand the use of computers by learning at least one of the procedure-oriented languages (POLs). Moreover, they can secure better help from computer specialists if they understand some basic computer terminology. We can outline a limited number of the most important terms in this introductory chapter.

First, of course, we start with a clear definition of a computer: A **computer** may be defined as a data processor, control processing unit (CPU) that can perform substantial computations without intervention by a human operator during a run. A digital computer functions by interpreting discrete electronic impulses and is, by far, the most important type for general managers. An analog computer deals with measuring continuous waves and has specialized uses to engineers and production managers. The distinction has reappeared as important to managers, as more computers are interconnected via communication lines requiring modems. **Modems** (contraction of *mo*dulator-*de*modulator) are devices that modulate and demodulate signals transmitted over communication facilities, that is, they are used to convert digital signals into analog (voicelike) signals for transmission over telephone lines, and then to convert the analog signals to digital signals at the other end for business computer use.

A **computer program** is a sequence of instructions that directs the computer to perform a series of tasks to produce a desired output. The program is the means by which managers talk to the electronic brain and monitor the computer. A **data record** is an electronic collection on a single subject and serves as basic material for the computer. A **data file** is literally an electronic file of an organized collection of data records. These latter two terms are analogous to a group of file folders (data records) organized in a drawer of a typical filing cabinet (data file); the difference is computers require electronic filing instead of manual and physical filing.

The development of **microprocessors** (the computer on silicon chips) increased the speed of operations, decreased the size of computers, and eliminated the need for costly airconditioning previously required. The present state of the art consists of different sizes of computers: super, often called Mainframe, is large and exceedingly fast and has a large memory, which makes it ideal for central machines operated by computer departments of organizations. Midi and mini have intermediate size memories and operate at only 1 percent or less speed than the super does. A **micro** operates at less than half the speed of a mini and generally uses only one programming language, such as BASIC.

Supers have **time-sharing** capabilities in which each of several users can send and receive data via **remote terminals**—keyboards and a CRT (cathode ray tube) or televisionlike screen. Mini- and micro-computers can also access the super computer or, since they have computer capability, are referred to as *smart* or "intelligent" **terminals**. Supers also handle **batch processing**, which means that data are accumulated and processed as groups. Batch processing remains important when a large volume of reports is needed, and very high speeds reduce the cost of reports. **On-line operations** means that data are fed into the computer and stored as transactions occur, for example, grocery store sales and hotel and airline reservations.

The expanded use of remote terminals and smart terminals (mini- and micro-computers) is the basis for the trend toward decentralized or **distributed data processing**. The future will see more managerial work stations or executive terminals so that more executives will have interactive potential at their finger tips. Personal computers, in addition, will provide help for executives for work at home or while traveling.

FORMATION OF A COMPREHENSIVE INFORMATION INDUSTRY The entire industrial organizational structure of the United States is being transformed particularly with respect to information. This transformation is directly the result of advances in technology and the policy of deregulation. The largest corporations, which in the past have been leaders in a number of industries, are finding that they face new competition from large corporation leaders from other industries.

IBM remains dominant in computers, yet changes in its strategy by purchasing components from smaller, outside companies increase opportunities for a number of high-technology companies in Silicon Valley and other locations to be integrated with the large computer manufacturers. The consent decree for the breakup of AT&T, the largest American company, effective January 1, 1984, not only transformed the telephone industry but it released the resulting "Baby Bell" to compete in new industries including computers and other parts of the information industry. The U.S. Postal Service faces new competition from United Parcel Service, Federal Express, Purolator, Emery, and other delivery services and is directly affected by trends in electronic mail systems installed by large banks, brokers, and manufacturing and retailing companies.

Book and magazine publishers have visualized that their industry will move toward information retrieval using means outside of printing. Libraries have moved toward information retrieval outside the mere storing and distribution of books and periodicals.

Specialized companies in different industries have been affected by the increasing availability of communication satellites as well. In short, managing information of all firms not only faces the rapid changes in the computer industry but changes in the communications industry and others. These changes increase the alternatives available for installing management information systems. The good news is that managers have more opportunities to improve their systems; the bad news is that the complexity of making optimum decisions has increased.

ISSUES AND PROBLEMS OF COMPUTER SYSTEMS

Norbert Wiener, one of the pioneers in computer technology, early expressed concern about the ability of human beings to remain in control of electronic computers: "It is my thesis that machines can and do transcend some of the limitations of their designers, and that in doing so they may be both effective and dangerous."[3] Even if computers are governed by programs prepared by humans, Wiener argued, computer systems may take actions at such speeds that the human control may be too late to ward off disastrous consequences. He cited the analogy of a driver of a speeding automobile who is unable to correct the path of the machine before it hits a wall. Wiener's early observation is today the basis of some of the concerns about nuclear missiles, potential errors in electronic banking, and in a variety of issues involving the use of computers. We briefly discuss four leading issues concerning the computer's role in information systems.

Technical Problems

Four categories of technical problems continually needing attention are: (1) hardware related, (2) software related, (3) operations related, and (4) system related.

Hardware Problems Computer reliability may be a source of problems in the sense that a job may not be completed when it is desired because the computer malfunctioned. In this case, the job can be run properly later. Seldom do computers produce incorrect answers because of electronic or mechanical failure; instead, such failures normally result in no information at all being produced at the appointed time.

Computers are composed of many electronic, electrical, and mechanical components. Each component is subject to failure, in

[3] Norbert Wiener, *Science*, May 6, 1960.

much the same manner as parts of an automobile. Some computers fail less frequently than others, sometimes because of a superior engineering design, but more often because of the smaller number of different components required. A computer with millions of components will probably fail more frequently than one with, say, ten thousand components.

A very different sort of computer hardware problem relates to undercapacity of the computer itself. One cannot expect to go at a speed of 100 miles per hour in a car with only 30 horsepower; similarly, sufficient computer power must be available to process the expected workload.

Software Problems   Because software errors are not unusual, a staff of maintenance programmers is required in any large computing installation, to locate quickly and to correct errors when they become known. A careful and thorough testing requirement imposed by management can reduce software errors; however, no one knows how to eliminate them completely. It is in this area that highly experienced professional programmers earn their higher salaries by experiencing much lower software failure rates than beginning programmers.

Companies specializing in software, such as Microsoft and Lotus, relieve managers of many of the technical problems relating to software and are making software easier to use. Competition in the software industry has increased the options open to managers.

Operations Problems   The computer workload must be scheduled so that there is a sufficiently high probability that the needed processing can be done. Realistic times for job completion must be known, realistic amounts of time provided for reruns (where the first computer run was incorrect for some reason), and realistic estimates made of when accurate inputs will be available for processing. Without proper planning of computer operation, one cannot guarantee that all of the required workload will be processed when it is needed.

Systems Problems   A successful system must make the inputs to the computer available when needed, ensure the proper controls over accuracy and timing of the inputs and outputs, and ensure that the specifications for the software and operations are correct. Computers usually do what they are told, but the specifications which were originally provided may be incorrect or obsolete. One often hears, "The darned computer will not provide me with the information I need." While this assertion may well be true, these particular requirements may have never been included in the original specifications. Further, as time passes, new requirements occur which make existing systems obsolete and render them less useful. These types of needs must be respecified in a logical manner in order to initiate responsive system change.

Threats to Human Rights The possession of comprehensive data bases by the government and business organizations raises questions that the writers of the U.S. Constitution could not foresee. The human right to privacy and to the protection of a person in the home may be threatened by the trend toward the collection of all types of data about each individual. Technological progress has made available a powerful tool for management—so powerful, in fact, that society needs to improve its processes for controlling this vastly increasing supply of available information. Information necessary for one system may pose threats to individual rights if allowed to enter other systems for which it was not planned. In the last two decades, the issue received national attention when it was discovered that tax information collected by the Internal Revenue Service had been made available to other government agencies and threatened to serve as political blackmail. Rigid restraints have been imposed by legislatures and the Department of Health, Education and Welfare on the access to student grades in educational institutions by unauthorized people. Disclosure of the existence of large files of information held by the FBI and CIA raised serious questions about the potential misuse of information stored in large data bases.

Business firms have improved their knowledge for marketing and sales, so that mailing lists make it possible to pinpoint marketing opportunities. Word processing and Wide Area Telephone Systems (WATS) have increased the chances that each consumer may be subject to a deluge of "junk mail" and telephone calls by computers at any hour. The reduced cost of transmitting information has increased the social costs of receiving unwanted information mixed in with valuable information, so that the receiver needs a computerlike screening of information to avoid wasting time.

Systems analysts have been so effective in tying large information bases into a total system that they must now be particularly aware of the boundaries of their systems. If they are not, the counteracting threats may result in unnecessary constraints imposed by society in the name of human rights. Breakthroughs in assembling information pose new challenges to managers for ensuring that information systems are designed in such a way that they continue to provide valuable information without the potential of improper uses.

**Human Resistance
to Electronic Rationality**

The introduction of a computer-based management information system necessarily creates changes; a typical human reaction to change is resistance. At the clerical and worker level, the fear of being displaced by machines is based on both real and imaginary grounds. The routinized and boring jobs may be eliminated by computers, but history shows that new and challenging types of jobs emerge.

At the managerial levels, Chris Argyris has warned that there is a potential loss of status and influence by the manager when information can be obtained from the computer by the lowest-level worker.[4] The loss of power to regulate the flow of information by managers may be a threat to their status. Computers, thus, can trigger emotional problems and stress not only for the lowest-level worker in the organization but also for the top management.

**Security
of Information**

Increased use of computers in information systems has posed still another problem—the security of the information. Information is valuable. A dishonest person or even a young person who is experimenting with knowledge of the operation of the system has the potential of causing huge losses to the organization. Estimates of losses due to computer theft in the United States run in the billions each year. Another new term, *hackers*, has entered the expanding language of computers. The legal system needs to update its criminal law and the means of redressing wrongs.[5] Management, therefore, must provide tight controls on information systems. Technical means of control have been devised through the use of codes and electronic safeguards; however, studies show that management has been slow to spend the additional funds to make use of the technological advances. Again, technology has moved ahead of management's efforts and abilities to utilize the advancements.

The technical problems of developing comprehensive information systems are being answered rapidly. The development of management thought, which might make full use of the technical developments, has been slower. Of one thing we can be sure: Management will devote much time and creative thinking to making such systems operational.

[4] Chris Argyris, "Management Information Systems: The Challenge to Rationality and Emotionality," *Management Science*, February 1971.

[5] *Hackers* generally include bright, young computer buffs who experiment with their skills of accessing information systems of others. Hackers may perceive themselves as typical pranksters but society is recognizing that such pranks are serious crimes.

With this discussion of managing information concluding the part on managerial funtions, we are now ready to move to Part 3 and the practical applications of these functions in management. The next part will also provide illustrations of managerial functions in a variety of areas.

REFERENCES

AWAD, ELIAS, *Introduction to Computers in Business.* Englewood Cliffs, N.J.: Prentice-Hall, Inc., 1977

DIEBOLD, JOHN, *Managing Information—The Challenge and the Opportunity.* New York: American Management Association, 1985.

DOLL, D. R., *Data Communications: Facilities, Network and Systems Design.* New York: John Wiley and Sons, Inc., 1977.

HOLOIEN, MARTIN, *Computers and Their Societal Impact.* New York: John Wiley and Sons, Inc., 1977.

HUSSAIN, DONNA and K. M. HUSSAIN, *Information Processing Systems for Management.* Homewood, Ill., Richard D. Irwin, Inc., 1985.

KATZAN, HARRY, *Office Automation: a Manager's Guide.* New York: Amacom, 1982.

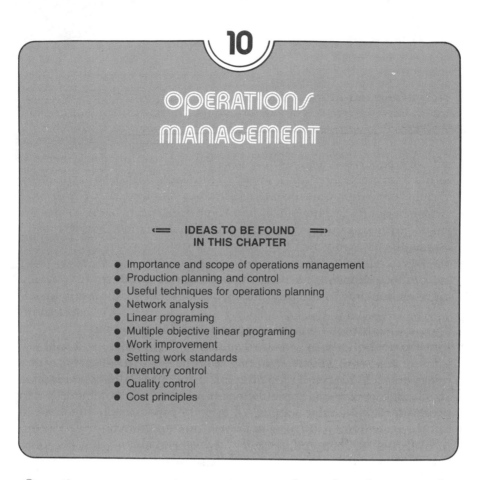

10

OPERATIONS MANAGEMENT

IDEAS TO BE FOUND IN THIS CHAPTER

- Importance and scope of operations management
- Production planning and control
- Useful techniques for operations planning
- Network analysis
- Linear programing
- Multiple objective linear programing
- Work improvement
- Setting work standards
- Inventory control
- Quality control
- Cost principles

Operations management concentrates on the technical aspects of a firm. In performing the managerial functions, the operations or production manager employs the tools of analysis provided by economists, accountants, mathematicians, behavioral scientists, and engineers. Early scientific managers expanded concepts originating in industrial engineering. The focus was on such topics as description and analysis of individual jobs, the technology of manufacturing, work flows, specifications of raw materials and the final product, location of plants, layout of work, methods for increasing productivity, standards, and planning and control of production. While these topics remain central to operations management, in the last two decades the new developments have been in systems thinking and quantitative methods of analysis.

AMERICAN INDUSTRIAL CRISIS AND OPERATIONS MANAGEMENT During the decade of the 1970s operations management received less attention. Rapid inflation enabled firms to increase their profits by raising prices of their products and services without worrying about retaining close control of their costs. Firms could agree to increases in wage costs and fringe benefits because these increases could be passed on to the consumer through higher prices. This inflation psychology resulted in American business operations becoming fat and less efficient. A rude awakening occurred when foreign manufacturers, especially Japanese auto and electronic producers, were able to take huge portions of the markets away from domestic companies by a literal flood of imports. By ignoring the techniques of cutting operating costs, American operations managers were caught with their costs too high!

In the early 1980s the American public began to ask questions about the decay of American industry and to view the quality of foreign products as superior to American products. Concurrently, criticism increased concerning the principles of American management. Some writers suggested that answers to these basic national problems could be found only by adopting Japanese management approaches. Many of these Japanese approaches were uniquely suited to the Japanese culture and environment and could not be transferred without changing American culture. On the other hand, many of the operations techniques used by the Japanese were actually developed by American writers. In all editions of this book, including the original in 1964, the importance of operations management has been emphasized. This edition retains the topics and techniques oriented to efficiency and cost reductions and summarizes the new developments of operations management which have been perfected in the last two decades.

The irony of the American developments in operations management during the twentieth century is that operations management was the focus of F. W. Taylor in the first decades. It was the area copied by the U.S.S.R. in the 1920s and by Western Europe and Japan in the 1920s and 1940s; it was the first area that introduced the powerful quantitative tools in the 1950s and 1960s; and its deterioration was the center of criticism of management in general in the 1970s. America had fallen behind in providing quality at low cost.

What were the reasons leading up to this American industrial crisis? Many have been cited, but two illustrate a basic flaw in the attitude of American managers and writers. First, in pioneering books on comparative management published in 1959 by two leading management writers, Frederick Harbison and Charles A. Myers, the following evaluation was made about management in Japan:

> Though respect for age and reliance on group decision making were admirable social customs in traditional Japanese culture, individual initiative and some atypical behavior are now recog-

nized as indispensable for healthy development of modern managerial organizations. Thus, foreign competition, union pressure, and concerted governmental measures may lead the Japanese to remove some of the incrustations of the traditional managerial order. But unless basic rather than trivial or technical changes in the broad philosophy of organizations building are forthcoming, Japan is destined to fall behind in the ranks of modern industrial nations.[1]

This surprisingly erroneous evaluation evolved from the attitude that American concepts were best for all nations; twenty-five years later many experts propose a similar but opposite, erroneous evaluation: Unless America adopts the Japanese ideas referred to in the excerpt above, it will fall behind. A more promising alternative is to return to the earlier American focus on operations management and its cost and quality control techniques that best fit the American culture and environment.

Second, in 1950, William Edwards Deming, an American, published a basic book on sampling and quality control[2] after initiating the first course in quality control at Stanford University early in World War II. This book never received wide attention in the United States because, as Deming observed, quality control had died out in the United States except for the production of quality control charts. But, Deming went to Japan where he obtained the attention of 45 top managers to whom he explained that quality control uses statistical methods but it also involves working with vendors "as if they were members of the family" and establishing consumer research to establish the customer "as the most important end of the production line." By 1985, Deming was recognized as the inspirational force behind the post war quality-control movement in industrial Japan. The Deming Award has been the top award in management in Japan for over ten years.

This second illustration clearly indicates that concepts developed by Deming, an American, were successful in Japan because top management listened to him while American top managers did not listen to one of their own and diverted their attention from operations management to financial and marketing management. In interviews in 1981 and 1984 Deming stated that he thought it would take 30 years for the United States to catch up with Japan. He reiterated his 14 points for improving management as shown in Table 10–1. In the

---

[1] Frederick Harbison and Charles A. Myers, *Management in the Industrial World: An International Analysis* (New York: McGraw-Hill Book Company, Inc., 1959), p. 265.

[2] W. Edwards Deming, *Some Theory of Sampling* (New York: John Wiley & Sons, Inc., 1950).

Table 10–1
Fourteen Points for Improving Management
Proposed by W. Edwards Deming

1. Achieve constancy of purpose.	7. Improve supervision.
2. Learn a new philosophy.	8. Drive out fear of failure.
3. Do not depend on mass inspections.	9. Improve communications
4. Reduce the number of vendors.	10. Eliminate fear of change.
5. Recognize two sources of faults:	11. Consider work standards carefully
Management and production systems	12. Teach statistical methods.
Production workers	13. Encourage new skills.
6. Improve on-the-job training.	14. Use statistical knowledge.

Source: "The Roots of Quality Control in Japan," *Pacific Basin Quarterly*, (Spring-Summer 1985). A publication of the Pacific Basin Center Foundation.

1980s many books imply that the answer to American problems will come from Japan although the real reason for the problems of the 1970s can be found in America's failure to concentrate on operations management as it had earlier.

By the mid-1980s American managers have found that a return to an emphasis on operations management is required as a competitive response to the increased attractiveness of foreign imports and as adjustments to a period of lower inflation (disinflation). In this chapter, we re-emphasize what is essential for a healthy business—continual effort to reduce the cost of producing a product or service.

A final introductory comment indicates the added importance of the techniques and processes of operations management. While many of the topics introduced by Taylor and the other scientific managers in the early twentieth century have been used in the operations of the steel mills and other "smoke stack" manufacturing industries, the ideas of "manufacturing" or production management can also be applied in all types of operations. Consequently, the title of this chapter replaces the term production with the term operations. In the present post-industrial society, the service industries have increased in importance in relation to the production of products. **Operations management** is aimed at the efficiency of changing the physical form of products (manufacturing) and the delivery of services where the output cannot be disassociated from the person receiving the services. Thus, almost any business has an operations function: manufacturing, converting or transforming, trucking, shipping, and well-being (e.g., education, health systems, military).

This chapter summarizes the responsibilities of operation managers and the applications of the seven managerial functions dis-

Table 10-2
Responsibilities and Techniques of Operations Managers

Design	Scheduling	Performance	Control
Product design	Long-run planning	Purchasing	Quality control
Job and process design	Detailed work activities	Forecasting re-	Inventory control
Capital equipment se-	Routing and scheduling	quirements	Cost control
lection	Schedules for stock	Maintenance	Resource alloca-
Setting standards	replenishment		tion
Training			
Plant location			
Layout			

cussed in Part 2. Table 10–2 summarizes these operations responsibilities and techniques.

The essence of the job of operations manager is in increasing productivity—processing of inputs in an optimum manner so as to add value to output, finished product, or service.

**PRODUCTION PLANNING
AND CONTROL** The operations manager is in charge of producing items or services that the marketing department can sell to customers. He or she must handle a vast amount of information from other departments, and must plan and control the internal operations. Production planning and control often is performed by a separate functional department and serves as the nervous system for the production department. Its chief functions are processing of information and planning work to be performed by operating departments.

The production control department supports the operating departments. Figure 10–1 summarizes the principal relationships between the production control department and other departments and indicates some of the important documents handled.

Production planning and control typically consists of five functions: routing, loading, scheduling, dispatching, and expediting. The first three are planning functions that take place before any production occurs; the last two are action functions that provide control.

1. **Routing** determines the operations to be performed, their sequence, and the path or flow of materials through a series of operations. The chief paper that describes what is to be done and how it will be done is called the *route sheet*, or operations sheet.
2. **Loading** is the function of assigning work to a machine or

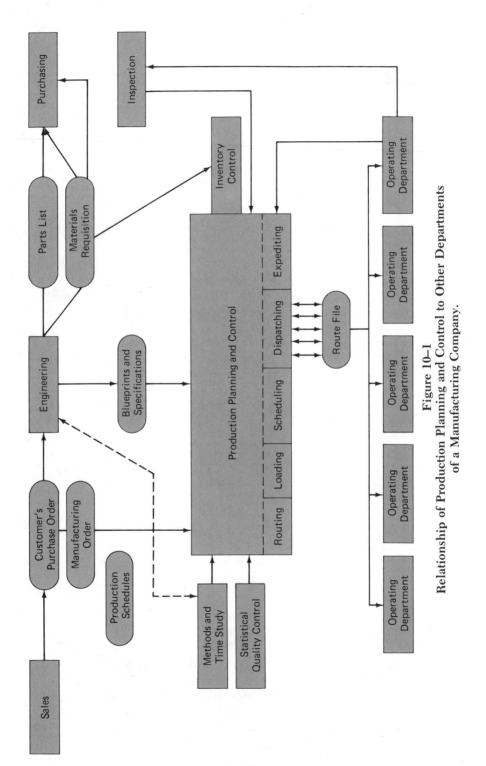

Figure 10–1
Relationship of Production Planning and Control to Other Departments
of a Manufacturing Company.

148

department in advance. The number of machines available and their operating characteristics, such as speeds and capabilities, are facts kept by the production control department so that it can develop an optimum plan for using plant facilities. The selection of the best machine, or the best substitute machine in case of break-down, is a part of the loading function.

3. **Scheduling** of production determines the time at which each operation is to take place. Master schedules show the dates on which delivery is promised to the customer. Detailed schedules are needed for each of the semifinished parts, so that all components will arrive at the proper place in time for the next operations. Assembly schedules depend on availability of all parts to be included in the finished product.

A useful tool of scheduling is a chart which portrays planned production and actual performance over a period of time for any or all of the factors that require planning and control. A **Gantt chart** is merely a bar chart with time on the horizontal axis and the factor to be scheduled on the vertical axis. Some are "progress charts" that show the various articles to be produced on the vertical scale and the planned time for production on the horizontal scale. Others are: "machine record" charts, which show the available machines and the time at which different jobs are planned; "order charts," which indicate the time to start different orders and the time of completion; and "man charts," which show the work planned for each person or group of people. In addition, network and critical path analysis have become powerful scheduling devices, and will be discussed in some detail in a later section.

4. **Dispatching** is the process of actually ordering work to be done. If the previously mentioned planning functions have been accomplished properly, the dispatching function may be merely a routine one of issuing authorizations to start operations. In some systems, dispatching is left to the head of the operating departments; in other systems, all orders are issued by the production control department. If the necessary information is available to the department head, greater flexibility might result from decentralizing the dispatching function, even if all the planning functions are central-ized.

5. **Expediting** is a follow-up activity that checks whether plans are actually being executed. Expediting can be accomplished by rou-tine reports and oral communications with operating departments. At times, specialists, known as expediters, may spend all their time insuring that key orders are being finished on schedule.

Table 10-3
Universal Production Questions and OM Techniques

Production Question	OM Technique
1. What products do we make?	Master production schedule (MPS)
2. What components go into them?	Bill of materials (BOM)
3. What is available now?	Inventory data
4. What do we need to buy or manufacture?	Materials requirement planning (MRP)

ACTIVITIES OF OPERATIONS MANAGEMENT

All manufacturers face universal questions they must answer. Table 10–3 shows both the questions and the operations management techniques to answer the questions.

All four of these techniques are really part of what is called a **materials requirement planning (MRP) system**. With the use of computers, operations people generate different "what if" scenarios. They can then see in advance if they have the correct numbers and types of machines, materials, and people. It may be that they cannot meet the customer order under the present set of conditions; they may have to request subcontracting to other firms, prepare the personnel department to hire additional people, or inform supervisors to put workers on overtime. They may not have enough materials in stock, and plans will be made to purchase the needed parts and components. One simple illustration of the MRP system follows.

Assume you manufacture a three-pac disposable razor. You would first develop a **master production schedule (MPS)**. This schedule represents a firm commitment to make so many razors during a seven-week period. Some MPS will contain both data for firm and tentative commitments.

The next step is to develop a statement of the components required for the final product, the **bill of materials (BOM)**.

An inventory check is made to find the status of handles, blades, retainer, and guards. The MRP process then takes the end-item production quantities from the MPS and uses the BOM file as well as inventory status data to determine component material needs and their planned order releases. This explosion process is logically simple but can involve hundreds or thousands of calculations for complex products.

The development of MRP demonstrates the gains from both the computer and information revolutions. For years manufacturing decisions had limited flexibility because of the constraints from inventories, machines, facilities, and people. Computers allow operations management to stimulate future options and thus generate flexibility in production decisions. Manufacturing is no longer at the mercy of its inventory, because information now extends the lead times necessary to meet demands.

Manufacturing resources planning II (MRP II) adds some new dimensions to materials requirement planning (MRP). MRP II developed from MRP, and since scheduling is fundamental to running a manufacturing business, the concept now brings all segments of the organization together. Scheduling focuses on *timing* and is fundamental to manufacturing (as we have seen above), to finance (cash flow is built around timing), and to marketing (customer delivery performance is based on timing).

MRP II is a company game plan. It requires participation from all members of the corporate team. There must be a common language. There must be a new set of values and objectives. Inventory records have to be correct, line accountability must be established, the bill of materials must become a control document valued by all (not just engineering), and the master production schedule must be realistic and not just a wish list or motivational tool. Everyone who supplies data into the information system must be sensitive to the integrity of the process. In one way, it is like a new philosophy of management.

USEFUL TECHNIQUES FOR OPERATIONS PLANNING

Network Analysis

Network analysis is a general-purpose schematic technique used to identify all the interconnecting links in a system. The technique is useful for describing the elements in a complex situation for the purpose of designing, planning, coordinating, controlling, and making decisions. The network approach has many applications; we shall discuss one which focuses on the critical path in scheduling.

Critical path analysis uses network analysis for scheduling production, construction projects, and research and development activities and in other situations that require estimates of time and performance. A sophisticated version of this technique (PERT—Program Evaluation and Review Technique) was first developed for use in defense projects, specifically in the development of the Polaris missile program, but it can be used in many scheduling situations.

The first step in network analysis is to separate each element, or link, and describe it in terms of other elements in the system. In order to present a network pictorially, one must distinguish the activities and events involved. An **activity** is a *time-consuming* effort necessary to complete a particular part of the total project; it is represented by an arrow (━━━━▶) that shows the direction of the sequential activities. An **event** is a specific *instant of time* that denotes the beginning and end of an activity; an event is represented by an ellipse or circle. An event cannot be accomplished until all activities preceding it have been completed. All activities begin and end with an event. The event is a "milestone," or signal, for dependent succeeding activities to begin. Events usually are assigned numbers sequentially for identification and analysis. In thinking through the process, one must repeatedly check three questions about the events and activities: (1) Which must be accomplished before a given event? (2) Which cannot be accomplished until an event is completed? and (3) Which can be accomplished concurrently?

After a network has been prepared and times for each activity have been noted, it is possible to determine the path that consists of those events and activities that require the maximum time (by adding the times for all activities along the path). This path is "critical," since it identifies the sequence of activities that will determine the minimum time in which the project can be completed. The **critical path** requires greater attention on the part of management for a number of reasons: (1) Any delay along this path will postpone the final completion date of the project. (2) Special study of each of the activities along the path may result in methods by which more resources or more concurrent activities or a change in the technology used may reduce the time required, which in turn would reduce the overall project time. (3) Advance planning and improvements along the critical path may cause another path to become critical. In short, the critical path approach directs management's attention to the "exceptional" and most significant facts, spots potential bottlenecks early, and avoids unnecessary pressure on the other paths that will not result in an earlier final completion date. Figure 10–2 illustrates a skeleton network and the critical path.

The **Program Evaluation and Review Technique (PERT)**, a special application of network analysis, has received the greatest amount of attention, because it has developed statistical refinements for estimating the time required for each activity and because it is of greatest help in new projects for which little past experience is available. In these cases, PERT has refined the network technique (usually with the help of electronic computers) and has provided danger signals for managment that require decisions for trade-offs in times required, resources allocated, or quality specifications.

In handling the times for an activity in a network, a single best estimate may not be reliable when compared with the time that the activities actually take. In order to arrive at a more reliable estimate, three time values are usually employed: the optimistic estimate (t_o),

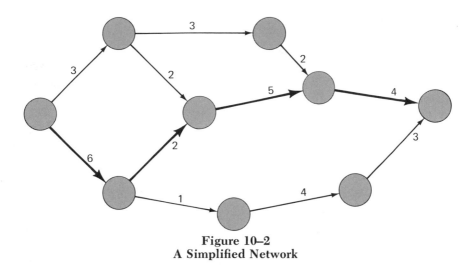

Figure 10–2
A Simplified Network

the most likely time (t_m), and the pessimistic estimate (t_p). The optimistic time is the shortest time possible if everything goes perfectly, with no complications; the chance of this optimum's actually occurring might be one in a hundred. The pessimistic time is the longest time conceivable; it includes time for unusual delays, and thus the chance of its happening might be only one in a hundred. The most likely time would be the best estimate of what normally would occur. If only one time were used, it would be the most likely time (t_m). The difference in the three time estimates gives a measure of the relative uncertainty involved in the activity. From these times, the expected time (t_e) can be computed by applying statistical techniques. The expected time (t_e) is the weighted arithmetic mean of the times. It may or may not be the same as the most likely estimate (t_m), since the differences between the optimistic and most likely and between the pessimistic and most likely would not necessarily be equal. The calculation of t_e is based on a statistical distribution of probabilities and can become quite complicated. However, it has been found that the formula

$$t_e = \frac{t_o + 4t_m + t_p}{6}$$

provides approximate results that are usable. The t_e provides the time in which there is a 50–50 chance of the project's being completed. The time required for each activity is shown on the arrow representing the activity; at times, it may be desirable to record t_o, t_m, and t_p, in which case the numbers are noted in that order along the arrow representing the activity.

A primary reason to estimate more than one time for an activity is to provide data by which management may determine the probabilities that each activity will be completed in a certain time. Moreover, most projects are assigned target dates, which may or may not be the same as the computed expected time (t_e) for the entire project. Slack is the difference between the target and the length of any path. Slack may be positive or negative, and it does not necessarily mean that there is time to spare. If the critical path has a time length that equals the target time, other paths will have positive slack. With these concepts, management has available information for making decisions for a variety of actions that will improve the chances of meeting the desired target.

Linear Programming

A fundamental technique for allocating available resources developed since World War II is called linear programming. **Linear programming** is a mathematical procedure for optimizing the use of resources, given an objective and resource limitations that are stated as linear functions. The actual calculations used in this technique are often complicated but can be handled by a general procedure called the simplex method. Although the details of this method are too involved to discuss here, it is possible to demonstrate the use of linear programming by a graphical illustration.

Suppose that a firm can produce either one or both of two products: toothpicks and matchsticks. At capacity, the available machines can produce either 15 million toothpicks per day or 10 million matchsticks per day, or any combination of both, subject to the limitation:

$$2T + 3M = 30,000,000$$

where T equals the number of toothpicks and M equals the number of matchsticks.

If we substitute zero for toothpicks, it can be seen that we could produce 10 million matchsticks. If the firm produced 9 million toothpicks, how many matchsticks could also be produced? Substituting 9,000,000 for T in the equation and solving for M (the equation would read: $2(9,000,000) + 3M = 30,000,000$) we get 4,000,000 matchsticks per day.

Suppose that as a further limitation the firm must (because of a labor contract) operate eight hours a day and hire exactly 100 workers

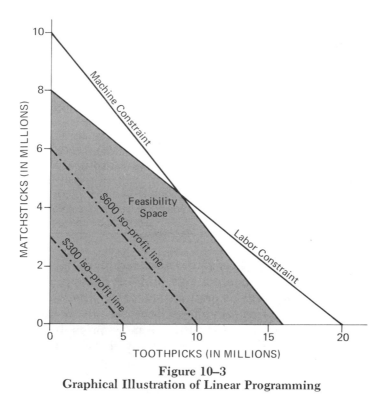

Figure 10–3
Graphical Illustration of Linear Programming

(800 manhours per day). These workers are needed to carry wood to the machines and to package the finished product. Assume that the workers can haul and pack 20 million toothpicks or 8 million matchsticks per day, or any combination of both. These assumptions could be stated as:

$$8T + 20M = 160,000,000$$

The above two equations could be shown graphically as a machine constraint and a labor constraint (see Figure 10–3). Assume that our objective is to maximize profit.

If matchsticks return a profit of $100 per million produced and toothpicks $60 per million produced, we could state an objective function as:

$$\$60 \frac{T}{1 \text{ million}} + \$100 \frac{M}{1 \text{ million}} = \text{Maximum}$$

In other words, we want to produce the optimum quantity of tooth-picks and matchsticks that will maximize our profit. Two illustrations of our objective function are plotted on Figure 10–3. Notice that an objective function can be drawn for any level of production, representing various combinations of toothpicks and matchsticks that yield equal profit (hence, each is called an isoprofit line).

Because our problem is to maximize profit, we will push the objective function as far from the origin as possible and still remain under or on the constraint lines, i.e., inside the feasibility space. (Notice that isoprofit lines represent larger profits as they move away from the origin.) The solution will always be found at some intersection. In this case, we can push the objective function out until we reach the point 5 million matchsticks and 7.5 million toothpicks. At that point our profit would be

$$\$60\,\frac{(7.5\ \text{million})}{1\ \text{million}} + \$100\,\frac{(5\ \text{million})}{1\ \text{million}} = \$950\ \text{per day.}$$

This simplified example serves only to indicate the class of problems that are solvable by means of linear programming. If we had additional constraints, we might find that some other combination of matchsticks and toothpicks would prove more profitable. If we had additional products and additional constraints, it would be impossible to show the relationships in a simple two-dimensional graph.

Multiple Criteria Problems in Linear Programming   A primary difficulty in modern decision analysis is the treatment of multiple objectives. The question becomes one of value trade-offs in the social structure of varying interests. A formal decision analysis capable of handling such situations is a new entrant in the field of management technology.

The organizational goals depend very much on the character and type of organization, the philosophy of management, and environmental conditions. Profit maximization, which is regarded as the sole objective of the business firm, is one of the most widely accepted goals of management, but is not always the only goal. The various formal solution techniques that have been needed for decision analysis are concerned primarily with making the right selection from a set of alternatives. However, in recent years, the nature of major decision problems has changed drastically and the adequacy of many solution techniques has been questioned.

Goal programming is a special extension of linear programming which is capable of handling a decision problem with multiple goals and multiple subgoals. Often goals set by management are achievable only at the expense of other goals. In goal programming, instead of trying to maximize or minimize the objective criterion directly, as in linear programming, the deviations between goals and what can be achieved within the given set of constraints are minimized. Thus the objective funtion becomes the minimization of these deviations, based on the relative importance of priority assigned to them. The true value of goal programming lies in its ability to solve problems involving multiple, conflicting goals according to the manager's priority structure, with a greater emphasis on "satisfying" rather than "maximizing."

Another extension of **linear programming** is in the solution of problems involving multiple objectives and is termed **multiple objective linear programming**. In this technique the ordering of the objectives is very crucial in obtaining the optimal solution. Forestry management, manpower allocation, water resource problems, and media selection problems in advertising are some of the areas in which the techniques mentioned above are being used.

Work Improvement

The goal of work improvement is the economizing of effort. The key to the attainment of this goal is an awareness of exactly what an operation involves, the details of what must be done, and an inquiring mind that searches for "the best way."

The inquiring mind needs certain questions to guide its thinking. Four such questions have proved useful in all work improvement: (1) Can some element of the work be *eliminated*? If there is any step that need not be done at all or any motion that is completely a wasted one, it should be eliminated. (2) Can some parts of the operation be *combined*? If two parts of an operation can be done jointly, combining them will improve it. (3) Can the *sequence be changed*? Anyone who has purchased disassembled furniture and has failed to follow the enclosed instructions will be especially conscious of failing to give proper consideration to sequence. (4) Can the operation be *simplified*? The simple way is usually the easiest, least expensive, and best way.

In using the four questions, it is mandatory to describe in detail exactly what is being done. One cannot improve an operation that one does not visualize and analyze.

Certain key ideas have helped guide thought about work improvement. Use *symmetrical* motions which have corresponding size, shape, and relative position when viewed from the center. The numeral "8" and the letter "S" are symmetrical when divided by a horizontal line through the center. *Opposite* motions contribute to the balancing of members of the body. *Ballistic motions* in which movement is "free"—uncontrolled—are best. *Continuous curved* motions require less effort. *Rhythm*, a term generally understood from its musical usage, is generally applicable in motion study. *Momentum* can help once an item is in motion. *Gravity* is a basic law of nature that is very beneficial to a worker if he finds out how to use it to his advantage instead of having to fight it. The *definite location* for tools, materials, persons, and work in process is particularly important in planning the workplace.

Considerable research indicates that the design of machines to fit the physical, intellectual, and psychological characteristics of people greatly affects the improvement of work. Results of this research can be summarized.

1. The human body is so constructed that its best position for work is an erect one. When a person is standing or walking, a perpendicular line best describes the relationship of the leg, back, neck and head. In carrying a load, it was found that the primitive yoke method proved superior because it distributed the load over a large area, making use of the strongest muscles. In lifting materials, the back should be kept straight and the legs bent because the back is relatively weak compared with the muscles in the thighs. Chairs that support the back in an erect position are universally considered to be superior.

2. The human body needs to change position. Equipment that permits the operator to either sit or stand reduces fatigue and increases productivity. A job that includes the use of different muscles, from time to time, will enable the worker to rest one set of muscles while continuing to work with another set.

3. Equipment should be adjustable to suit persons of different sizes. Because workers differ in height, weight, length of arms, and other physical characteristics, seats should be adjustable to the unique contours of the individual. The movable front seat of automobiles is an example of a use of this principle.

4. Controls and dials should be as simple and realistic as possible. For example, if an object is to be moved to the right, the control lever should move to the right. Dials with the fewest markings have proved to give the best results. Controls should be spaced to prevent mistaking one lever for another and should be grouped according to similar functions. A large number of individual controls increases the strain on the operator.

Setting Work Standards

The improvement of work should precede the setting of work standards. Obviously, if changes are made in the method of performing an operation, the time required for the performance will be changed.

Once the improved method is found, it should be standardized and all workers should be trained in using the improved method.

Managers use time standards to answer a number of important questions:

1. What is the time required for each operation in the *scheduling* of production?
2. How can production in one department, or at one machine, be *balanced* with other departments and machines in the plant?
3. How can the company develop a solid basis for a standard *cost accounting* system?
4. What amount of time will a job take for the purpose of estimating the *price* to place in a bid?
5. What basis is best for an *incentive* system?

The original method of setting time standards is F. W. Taylor's procedure of using a stopwatch to time a representative man actually working on a given job.

Because stopwatch time study has received considerable criticism, other methods of setting standards have been developed. Several of these (methods-time measurement, work factor, basic motion time study) make use of catalogues of motions, with a table of time values for each. The catalogues contain time data that have been developed through detailed research in laboratories. They are the basis for setting time standards without the use of a stopwatch.

Another technique of work measurement that has received increased attention is work sampling. It can be used for two purposes: (1) to determine the percent of time that workers are engaged in different activities (or not engaged in any productive effort), in order to find the proper allowances to be added to normal time, and (2) to set standards for irregular work and for indirect labor.

Work sampling depends upon random sampling theory. It involves the breaking down of the total working time of all workers who perform the operation into *instants* of time that are used as the basic unit for sampling. The exact instants of time for actual observations are determined by some random method. After the observer tallies the action occurring at a large number of different instants of time, the total number of instants at which each type of activity has been observed is divided by the total number of observations. The results are the percentages of instants at which each type of activity was observed. These percentages are the basic data provided by work sampling. They yield directly the information needed for determining allowances.

The setting of time standards is a difficult and important problem for management. Because time standards have many valuable applications, it is worth considerable effort to make them as sound as possible.

If a time standard is set hastily, management will have difficulty instilling confidence not only in that standard but also in the entire standards program. A "loose" standard is difficult to change once it has been adopted. A worker on a job having a "loose" standard becomes accustomed to the low requirements. If management tries to "tighten" the standard, the worker will charge that it is attempting to "speed up" and that there is no reason to try to meet or exceed the standard if management is going to take this as evidence that the standard needs raising. It is for this reason that a basic policy of management should be that once a time standard is set for an operation, it will not be changed unless the operation has been changed in some significant manner. With such a policy, management is faced with the problem of determining just what type of a change is significant. Typically, workers tend to make a number of small improvements in a job, none of which warrants a restudy. Accurate description of the job when it was timed, therefore, becomes especially important as a basis for determining just when a job has changed enough to need a new standard. Comparison of the description at the time of the previous study with the description of the current operation will provide a means of showing workers the reason for the new study.

INVENTORY CONTROL   The control of inventory is critical to the functions of production control. Often, the same department handles both inventory control and production control, because production directly affects the three main types of inventories: raw materials and parts, work in process, and finished goods. Raw materials must be ordered to arrive in time for production; the nature of the production process determines the size of work in process; the output of production must go either into finished goods inventory or directly to the customer.

Inventory control handles the following questions: (1) What is the optimum amount of inventory to carry? (2) What is the economic lot size for an order from a supplier or from a production department? and (3) What system of controlling inventory should be used?

1. The optimum size of inventory depends on the needs of the production department. Some parts, materials, and completed products have to be kept on hand in order to absorb discontinuities in production and to handle uncertainty. Some inventory must be held, if only for the purpose of having something to work on. At times, inventory may be kept as speculation on future price

changes. Finished stocks may be held to provide better service for customers.

2. The **economic lot size** depends upon two groups of costs: preparation costs and carrying costs. *Preparation costs* are primarily fixed costs relating to the starting of production or the writing of an order for a purchase and do not vary with the number of items in the lot; *carrying costs* vary directly with the number of items involved. Examples of typical preparation costs are the setup costs of machines, the clerical cost for writing an order, and the administrative costs of executive attention in placing a lot into production; examples of carrying costs are interest on capital, insurance, obsolescence, deterioration, handling, inventory taking, and so on.

Numerous formulas have been developed that weigh preparation costs, carrying costs, and rate of usage. One of the oldest and best known is:

$$Q = \sqrt{\frac{2RS}{I}}$$

in which Q = economic lot size
R = annual use of the items in units per year
S = setup cost each time a new lot is started
I = carrying cost per unit per year

Other formulas incorporate probability estimates for handling uncertainty—especially the uncertainty of the rate of usage and the uncertainty about the amount of time it will take to deliver the new order.

3. A number of systems of inventory control are available. A most popular one is the *periodic-order system*, in which cards indicate the pertinent information concerning usage rate, items on order, items reserved for specific usage, and balance on hand. In this system, four quantities serve as critical decision rules: maximum inventory (the most items ever to be stocked), minimum inventory (the safety reserve below which inventory should not fall), the reorder point (the level of inventory at which an order should be made so that receipt can be accomplished before the minimum level is reached), and the order size (the standard amount to be ordered). This system assumes that the picture of usage and ordering is that shown in Figure 10–4.

One of the developments in inventory control was developed in the materials on MRP. The computer-generated information system, driven by the master production schedule, links inventory control policies and practices with those of the production department.

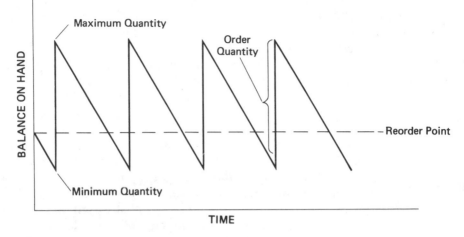

Figure 10–4
Routine Inventory Control in a Stable Situation

Developments in inventory control are not limited to the United States or the European countries; Japan has introduced operations techniques into the inventory control arena.

The Japanese have employed a concept uniquely suited to them. This concept is called **just-in-time system (JIT)**. The JIT idea is simple: Produce and deliver finished goods just in time to be sold, subassemblies just in time to be assembled into finished goods, fabricated parts just in time to go into subassemblies, and purchase materials just in time to be transformed into fabricated parts. Down-time for machines, waiting time for people, and any items in inventory are indications of waste, waste with a dollar figure attached to it. The ideal in a Japanese factory is zero inventory and stockless production. To them everything should be flowing and active; all elements in the production process should be integrated into the whole.

Inventory management under the JIT philosophy and practice would mean that production projects would be in small batches, inventories would be in small lots, and delivery would be frequent by the suppliers. Suppliers in Japan are more than independent parts of a total production system. They are partners in achieving the total corporate goal of a quality good at a competitive price. Suppliers frequently build factories or warehouses close to the production plants so that delivery times can be minimized. Suppliers are consulted if production problems arise in the main plant. Everyone is made to believe they are working for the same objective.

The emphasis upon small lots and simple procedures enables the Japanese to have workers operate in self-contained teams or groups. It also means that innovations like the kanban technique can work. The **kanban technique** is a simple manual card system that controls the manufacture of units. The card, attached to a container, signals the need to deliver more parts and an identical card signals the need to produce more parts. Such an inventory technique has limitations. It does not work well in process industries (brewers, bottlers, and canners). It is oriented toward discrete, not continuous, processes. The kanban technique also works best if it is integrated with a just-in-time procedure that places high priority on quality, the next topic under the operations function of control.

The subject of inventory management has received much attention in recent years. New techniques are helping to answer inventory questions. Because inventory is a very important problem, each manager should give considerable time to the development of a tailored system that will best answer his or her needs.

QUALITY CONTROL   Controlling the quality of products has greatly improved in the last fifty years as a result of refinements in systems that have become available for comparing the quality of products with standards set by engineers and designers. This improvement has been possible chiefly because of the application of statistical methods using probability theory. Using samples from work in process, the product can be checked against standards, so that the output contains a minimum number of rejects. The quality targets are set by engineers. Samples of products in production are tested at intervals to provide data on the current quality. These samples yield data that may vary from standard for two reasons: (1) the chance selection of the items in the sample or (2) the "real" cause of poor quality, such as wearing of a cutting tool. The problem in controlling quality using samples is in differentiating between these two factors, so that corrective action is taken only when it is probably needed.

Statisticians have provided tables for determining the size of samples, and the degrees of risk for inference from samples and other data using probability reasoning. The important skills needed by the nonstatistics-oriented manager are (1) a familiarity with the powerful tools provided by statisticians and (2) an ability to interpret the output of their work. Quality control charts offer a graphical means by which the manager can interpret this information supplied by the statisticians.

Quality circles is a Japanese technique receiving attention and credit for worker productivity and quality gains during the past ten years. Membership in these groups is voluntary, although the climate in the work place shows strong management support for such voluntary involvement. The QC members come from the same shop or work area, and the supervisor is usually, but not always, the leader of the circle.

Within the circle, however, the supervisor does not issue orders or make decisions. Circle members choose the problems and projects to work on, gather all the information, analyze it, and make decisions. Some management authorities state that the secret to Japanese success of QCs is the emphasis on worker participation in the process of improving the quality of the firm rather than an emphasis on the control of quality. QCs allow a revision in the authority system and tap the knowledge and experience of workers, those persons who in the last analysis actually determine product and service quality. Such an awareness of the importance of the worker and worker relations leads into the final operations management area, the operating function.

COST PRINCIPLES

Computation of profit is directly affected by the determination of what costs should be subtracted from total revenue. Because the conditions under which one decision is made may differ from the conditions under which another decision is made, it should be clear that costs should be tailored to a given decision. To an economist, the basic idea of **cost** is that it is a *sacrifice*. Measurement of cost involves an attempt to determine the amount of sacrifice that will be made in a particular decision. Because a decision is made in the present about consequences that will occur in the future, the manager's judgment may be important in estimating the total costs or sacrifices involved in the decision. This judgment can be improved by good analysis. Several cost principles are basic to this analysis.

Future Costs Are the Important Costs

Only those costs not yet incurred are important in a manager's decision. A manager makes decisions for future actions. The manager's viewpoint, like that of the managerial economist, requires concern with *future* rather than with *past* costs. It is true that the manager will know more about past costs, which concern actions already taken place, because they have been recorded; yet, historical costs (those usually provided by the financial accountant) have limited value for the manager. They are important because they help the manager learn to make better future decisions. Also, certain computations, such as income for tax reporting, must be based on past costs. However, the basic criteria for current decisions are the *expected benefits* to be realized as a result of the decision compared with *expected sacrifices* that will need to be made. If you had paid $1,000 for a useless item last year, it would be proper to forget the poor expenditure—it is a cost of a past decision. Any use (for example, scrapping) of the item in the future will involve only future sacrifices (certainly not the $1,000, which is a past sacrifice). On the other hand, if an item which cost $1,000 last year has become extremely valuable today, the use of this item will involve a greater sacrifice than its use last year involved. It should be clear, at this stage, that there are a number of cost classifications that are important under different conditions.

Opportunity Costs

Being interested in selecting the best alternative available, the manager must concentrate on the various opportunities that are open. A basic principle of economics is known as the **principle of opportunity** (*alternative*) **costs**, which is stated simply: The cost of any kind of action or decision consists of the opportunities that are sacrificed in taking that action. In deciding to use an hour of your time to file correspondence, you are sacrificing the chance of doing anything else with that hour. What is the cost of your filing correspondence for one hour? It depends. On what? If you otherwise would be waiting for someone and thus would have been idle, the cost is zero. If you are a doctor and could have performed an operation for which you would have been paid $200, the cost of filing would have been $200 (the sacrifice). If you could secure clerical help at the rate of $3.00 an hour so that you could perform the operation and have the correspondence filed, you would be able to allocate your time resources better (to the extent of $197, i.e., $200 less $3.00). Of course, it is often difficult to comprehend all the alternatives available and thus it is difficult to *know* all opportunity costs; yet the basic idea of opportunity cost is invaluable in helping to allocate resources properly.

Incremental Cost

We saw earlier that total costs, as shown on a breakeven chart, are useful to an analysis of operations. We indicated then that two other computations are possible: average cost per unit and changes in costs. The idea of average cost per unit is generally understood as dividing total cost by the number of units. Average cost is most useful when analyzing past costs; in fact, it can be misleading if used improperly in considering decisions for the future.

A most valuable concept in decision making is known as **incremental cost**—defined as the *additional* (change in) total cost that results from a particular decision. Incremental analysis involves a comparison of changes in revenue and the associated changes in costs. The idea is simple—you will want to do something if, and only if, you can expect to be better off than you were before. In a business firm, the manager would want to make sure that the additional total revenue would be greater than the additional total costs.

We have already employed the idea of incremental cost in Figure 4–2—by increasing volume, the extra revenue (change in total revenue) was greater than the extra cost (in this case, variable cost). We said that the difference was a contribution to fixed cost and profit—in other words, the incremental gain by deciding to increase volume. In many cases, therefore, the change in variable cost will give us incremental cost.

Incremental costs are valuable considerations in many other cases. For example, consider the problem of whether or not to accept a single order at a special price. The analysis would involve a comparison between the estimated profit based on accepting the order. In these estimates, we would have to consider the net effect on prices of other orders and all opportunity costs. Because opportunity costs are not recorded in accounting records, it is clear that we would have to tailor our costs to the particular decision. If we can offer a lower price on this one order without affecting prices on other orders and if we can cover all extra costs (including a possible loss of goodwill), it would be more profitable to accept the order even though all costs are not covered.

FUTURE OF THE ACADEMIC FIELD OF OPERATIONS MANAGEMENT

Since the birth of the field of management with Taylor and the other scientific managers, operations management has been the basic application of all management functions. Because of its general nature it was considered synomyous with management yet it lost status by its descriptive orientation in both engineering and business schools. But its revitalization came as it contributed new quantatative methods in the 1950s and 1960s, resulting in such promising new fields as management science and operations research. Concurrently, the other applied fields, marketing and financial management, received increased attention while the broad, but splintered, field of operations management was neglected. American industry in the 1970s suffered as both academics and practitioners reduced efforts to cut costs and improve quality. Great advances were made in many specialized fields, such as computer science, management science, systems, organization behavior, but less was done to improve operations by using the specialized fields. The industrial success of the Japanese caused a rude awakening with the result that operations management is one of the "in" topics of the 1980s and 1990s.

Operations management is the opening chapter in Part 3 because it always has served as the heart of the essentials of management. This chapter has summarized the subject as dealing with planning, organizing, and controlling operations. A significant portion of the chapter has introduced some of the basic techniques for decision making. It concluded with a short restatement of the cost principles from economics because the operations field aims at producing quality at low costs—the supply side of the economic picture. In the next chapter, we turn to marketing management which focuses on gross revenue, distribution of the product or service, and generally on the demand side of the economic picture.

REFERENCES

ADAM, EVERETT E., JR. and RONALD J. EBERT, *Production and Operations Management*. Englewood Cliffs, N.J.: Prentice-Hall, Inc., 1978.

BARNES, RALPH M., *Motion and Time Study* 6th ed. New York: John Wiley & Sons, Inc., 1968.

BARNDT, STEPHEN E. and DAVIS W. CARVEY, *Essentials of Operations Management*. Englewood Cliffs, N.J.: Prentice-Hall, Inc., 1982.

BUFFA, ELWOOD S., *Modern Production Management*, 5th ed. New York: John Wiley & Sons, Inc., 1977.

DILWORTH, JAMES B., *Production and Operations Management: Manufacturing and Nonmanufacturing*. New York: Random House, 1979.

LAUFER, ARTHUR C., *Operations Managment*, 2nd ed. Cincinnati, Ohio: Southwestern Publishing Co., 1979.

MAYER, RAYMOND R., *Production and Operations Management*, 3rd ed. New York: McGraw Hill Book Company, Inc., 1975.

MOORE, FRANKLIN G. and THOMAS E. HENDRICK, *Production/Operations Management*, 8th ed. Homewood, Ill.: Richard D. Irwin, Inc., 1980.

PLOSSL, G. W. and O. W. WIGHT, *Production and Inventory Control*. Englewood Cliffs, N.J.: Prentice-Hall, Inc., 1967.

REARON, HAROLD et al. *Fundamentals of Production/Operations Management*, 2nd ed. New York: West Publishing Co., 1983.

SCHONBERGER, RICHARD J., *Operations Management: Productivity and Quality*. Plano, Texas: Business Publications, 1985.

TIMMS, H. L., *Introduction to Operations Management*, Homewood, Ill.: Richard D. Irwin, Inc., 1967.

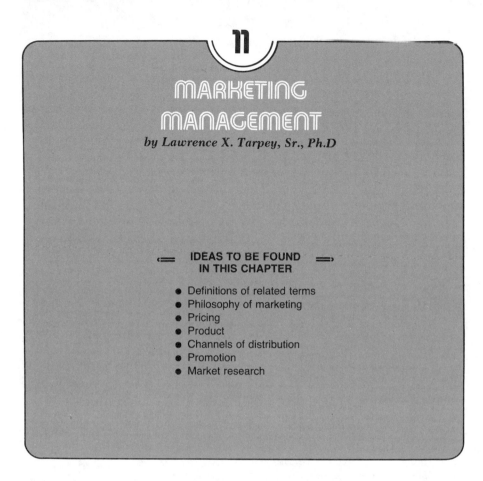

MARKETING MANAGEMENT

by Lawrence X. Tarpey, Sr., Ph.D

⟸ **IDEAS TO BE FOUND** ⟹
IN THIS CHAPTER

- Definitions of related terms
- Philosophy of marketing
- Pricing
- Product
- Channels of distribution
- Promotion
- Market research

While the last chapter illustrated applications of managing by operations in transforming goods and services, this chapter concentrates on marketing management. We shall clarify the terminology and related concepts and discuss the tasks of a marketing manager; specifically, the product, channels of distribution, promotion, and market research.

CLARIFICATION OF RELATED TERMS   The terms market, marketing, marketable, and marketing management are variations of a single unifying concept—exchange. Classical and neo-classical economics defined *market* as a place or situation where voluntary exchange took place between sellers and buyers to enhance the mutual benefits of all parties.[1] This meaning of the term is quite accurate today, but the marketing manager gives it a slightly different focus by emphasizing

---

[1] For an excellent explanation of this viewpoint, see Milton and Rose Friedman, *Free to Choose: A Personal Statement* (New York: Harcourt Brace Jovanovich, 1980).

the concept "transaction" which is an exchange of values between parties.

As a general rule, the economist is interested only in things that are *marketable*. A good or service is *marketable* if it is desired by someone and he or she is willing to give up something of value to obtain it. It must be relatively scarce and capable of yielding benefits of some sort to the buyer. *Value* implies worth and relates closely to the idea of usefulness or satisfaction. A key problem in marketing management is how to produce marketable products and how to further enhance the marketability of products already on the market.[2]

Marketing and marketing management are largely the consequence of rapid economic growth and large scale enterprise. Modern marketing was little more than a sales tool when agriculture and small business dominated the economy. In the micro context (i.e., emphasis on intra-firm activities) which is used in this chapter, **marketing** is the business function concerned with controlling the level and composition of demand facing the company or organization.[3] The paramount objective is creating and maintaining the demand for the firm's products as opposed to trying to force customers to buy goods because they have been produced and need to be sold. Finally, marketing recognizes the need to manage the demand for services, which are becoming a larger component of our GNP year after year.

Marketing management may be viewed as regulating the level, timing, and character of the demand for one or more products of the firm. Specifically, it is the planning, organizing, controlling, and implementing of marketing programs, policies, strategies, and tactics designed to create and satisfy the demand for the firm's product offerings or services as a means of generating an acceptable profit.[4] In essence, the marketing manager is the "demand manager" for the firm; the specialized expert for stimulating all activities relating to product planning and development, pricing, promotion, and distribution.[5]

All organizations must engage in marketing as a basic principle.

[2] Over 30 years ago Wroe Anderson *Marketing Behavior and Executive Action.* (Homewood, Ill.: Richard D. Irwin, Inc., 1957) saw that every phase of marketing can be understood as human behavior within an operating system. This "social system" involved customers looking for goods and suppliers looking for customers.

[3] Philip Kotler and S.J. Levy, "Demarketing, Yes, Demarketing," *Harvard Business Review* (November–December 1971), p. 75.

[4] Philip Kotler, "The Major Tasks of Marketing Management," *Journal of Marketing* vol. 37 (October 1973), pp. 42–499.

[5] Marketing experts are the new elites, experts based on science, technology, and specialized training in management. They constitute a core element of "technostructure" or business super powers. See J.K. Galbraith, *The New Industrial State* (Boston: Houghton Mifflin, 1967).

Non-profit organizations have a product (usually a service) which must be kept "marketable." So do universities, hospitals, libraries, museums, and so forth. In the public sector our elected officials are marketing managers, often under the guise of "lobbying" their colleagues to support some project, such as a new dam or product price supports, which the voters back home need.

PHILOSOPHY OF MARKETING Progressive business firms have adopted a "marketing concept philosophy" which guides marketing managers in fulfilling their responsibilities. Briefly defined, the **marketing concept** says that a company will prosper only as long as it gives consumers products that satisfy their needs and wants at prices they are willing to pay at a profit to the company. Thus, marketing begins and ends with consumer satisfaction.

The key elements of the marketing concept are:

1. *Customer orientation.* A thorough understanding of the consumer's needs and wants becomes the focal point of all marketing action, especially product planning and development.
2. *Integrated effort.* The firm's primary emphasis must be in integrating the marketing functions with those of R & D, production, finance, and so forth.
3. *Profitability.* The primary goal of the firm should be profits; sales volume should only be a proxy measure for satisfactory marketing performance in the short-run. Non-profit organizations should establish well defined and measurable goals for evaluating success of marketing efforts.
4. *Viability.* The company and its long-run survival and growth are paramount since the idea is to promote consumer loyalty.

Theodore Levitt delineated a philosophy by identifying what he referred to as *"marketing myopia."*[6] Essentially, it involves having a narrow, engineering concept of a product. For example, railroads conceived their product to be rail transport instead of the broader view that it was in the product-people movement service. Likewise, banks are not merely institutions for the lending or storage of money; they are full-service retailers who serve the financial needs of individuals, families, small businesses, financial and estate planners, meet off-hour cash needs by the 24-hour computerized teller, and so forth.

[6] Theodore Levitt, "Marketing Myopia," *Harvard Business Review* (July–August 1960).

PLANNING

Planning is the most important function of the marketing manager because it guides all subsequent actions or decisions. The strategic plan is developed at the corporate or highest level in the firm. It reflects the basic missions of the firm and specifies the long-run general marketing goals and/or objectives of the firm; its time frame is anywhere between one to five years. A strategic plan is likely to include such things as growth opportunities, profit goals, market shares, channel arrangements, product-line developments, and environmental issues. Figure 11–1 offers an outline of the elements in the marketing plan.

In the short run the marketing manager develops an operating plan generally called a **marketing program**. The marketing program, usually limited to a year, tells what is to be done, when it is to be done, and who is to be responsible for each activity or function. The marketing program, often referred to as the marketing mix, generally focuses on the following four areas: product, pricing, promotion, and channels of distribution. The vital elements of the program are policies, strategies, and tactics.

While policies may be defined differently from firm to firm, the essential element in a policy is "direction." Marketing policies involve a group of relative principles and consequent rules of actions which are designed to promote the successful achievement of marketing objectives. A marketing program will have established policies in each element of the marketing mix. For example, a common pricing policy states that "extraordinary" price discounts must comply with antitrust laws and be cleared by the legal department. However, it must be understood that each marketing activity will be governed by a set of interrelated policies. In the case of products, there will be policy statements relating to such matters as service (pre-sale and post-sale), warranty, inventory of parts, returns, physical distribution, deletions, and so forth. It should be noted that policies are flexible and may be altered during a current year if warranted by competition or changes in current business conditions.

MARKETING MIX AND STRATEGIES

The **marketing mix** is the blend of the four controllable variables that make up the nucleus of the marketing program—product, pricing, promotion, and channels. In addition, each business must have an operating plan for dealing with environmental factors which are non-controllable. Non-controllable factors include technology, competition, laws, social structure, cultural norms, economic conditions, and political considerations.

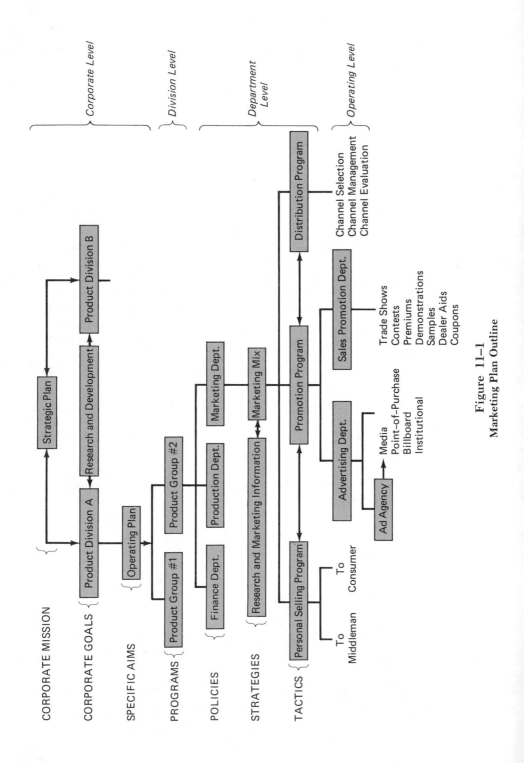

Figure 11-1
Marketing Plan Outline

Strategies and tactics are the two elements of the marketing program that reflect the various techniques used to enhance the effectiveness of the marketing mix. A **strategy** is a set of broad, directional, action decisions required to achieve a predetermined objective. Firms have general strategies, such as "growth strategies," which reflect the thinking of corporate management and impact on the entire business. However, developing strategies for each of the elements of the marketing mix is an important part of putting together the marketing program. For example, product strategies may encompass specific categories such as new product development, width and breadth of the product line, product deletion, planned obsolescence, and inventory.

A **tactic** specifies details, methods, or techniques to implement the strategy.[7] For example, over the years McDonald's has attempted to stay ahead of competition by the use of several product strategies to broaden its market. It enlarged its product line to include breakfast and added chicken (McNuggets) to its menus. All its new product strategies are market tested and backed up with strong promotional campaigns. A long term promotional strategy of McDonald's has been the clown character, Ronald McDonald, who promotes McDonald's goodwill image by visits to the franchises and sick children in hospitals.

McDonald's has used tactics common to many retailers by giving customers coupons and running contests for big prizes. K mart stores, for example, offers "unadvertised specials" on different days, a tactic designed to encourage shoppers to drop-in and browse. In the auto industry part of the pricing strategy is giving the consumer the option of leasing a new car; a pricing tactic is giving potential buyers indirect price cuts by offering them long-term financing at rates below the banks or those of competing auto dealers.

PRICING Probably the marketing manager's most important task is pricing because pricing is the economic consideration for which management must balance the product's costs with the requirements of the marketplace. It requires the decision maker to make judgments concerning consumer income, business conditions, competitive reaction, corporate goals, and costs of production and distribution.

---

[7] The best metaphor for explaining the difference between tactics and strategies is in sports. Prior to a football game, the coach will have worked out a "game plan" which contains general features, such as confine running plays to end-sweeps because the opponents are too strong up the middle. A tactic is part of the coach's repertoire utilized for specific situations which might develop during the course of the game, such as a fake punt.

Prices represent values. By setting prices management is really translating into quantitative terms (i.e., dollars and cents) not only the costs of products produced at a point in time, but also some measure of profits, such as return on capital investment. For consumers, value is a personal thing; it is what one is willing to give up or trade off in order to acquire the product. Marketing managers have to be able to do three things to be effective price setters: (1) estimate the product's value to particular market segments and produce a product in line with this estimate, (2) convince the consuming public that the product price is fair and the best value for the dollar, and (3) develop pricing policies and strategies that will generate sufficient revenues in the long-run to satisfy investors and assure survival.

Pricing Policies

In making pricing decisions, the marketing manager must take into account the following factors: (1) the nature and extent of consumer demand; (2) the short- and long-run costs of manufacturing and selling the product; (3) the competitive reactions; (4) the antitrust laws; (5) the promotional strategy (6) the channels of distribution; (7) profit goals; and, (8) life cycle of the product.

Price policies are those management guidelines that control the day-to-day pricing decisions as a means of meeting the objectives of the firm. These policies are actually strategies. For example, price discrimination is a common policy employed to exploit differing price elasticities of demand in specific market segments. Some foreign manufacturers will "dump" their surplus inventories in our markets at prices far below their total costs. Another price policy is to sell new products at relatively high prices (called skimming the market) recognizing that some market segments have different price elasticities of demand that will vary over the life cycle of the product. A penetration price policy targets that market segment which is very responsive to low prices.

The firm's policies help determine how the prices are established, but most companies have formulas for determining the actual dollar-and-cent figures to place on products. In economic theory the forces of demand and supply set the price; in practice, however, prices are determined by the company's management. This is referred to as administered pricing.

Pricing Formulas

Many pricing formulas can be reduced to two basic approaches: (1) the cost approach and (2) the market or demand approach. The cost approach is easy to understand. Three commonly accepted price formulas are: (1) Prices are set equal to allocated total costs, plus a

Table 11-1
Key Factors Affecting the Pricing Decision

1. Market Structure—the number and size of competing firms and ease of entry
2. Market Conditions—general enconomc conditions
3. Competitive Behavior—collusion, price behavior, price matching
4. Product—its perishability; durability; stage of life cycle; type—producer or consumer good; cost of production and distribution; distinctive substitutes
5. Customers—their urgency of needs; ability to pay; location; potential number; purchase behaviors; use of product—intermediate or ultimate; perception of seller or brands; susceptibility to promotion
6. Goals or Objectives of Seller—desire for market share; target rate of return on capital; beating or matching competition; recapturing full costs; exploiting excess capacity; maximizing sales rather than profits; exploiting monololy power; market leadership

certain standard percentage markup. This is a *full-cost formula* where price reflects the average total cost of each unit plus a margin of profit. (2) Prices are set equal to a certain percentage of product cost at each level of production and distribution. This method, the *markup formula*, is basic in the wholesale and retail trade. (3) Prices are set equal to variable direct costs plus some amount added to cover allocated overhead and profit contribution. This is known as the *profit margin formula* and uses only variable costs as a starting point. (See Table 11-1.)

The Cost Approach   Using the cost approach one must find answers to two key questions: (1) What should be used as the cost base? (2) What factors should be considered in planning the margin? If, for example, a company prices its products based only on the variable costs of each unit produced, it is using *incremental cost pricing*. This method is viable only in the short-run because overhead costs and return on capital investment must be covered in the long-run.

A cost-plus approach to pricing has certain inherent risks. Today's price often outlasts the conditions that determine today's costs. Forecasting future costs of key production factors such as wages, raw materials, purchased components, and capital are required for most pricing decisions. Here replacement costs are more vital than historical costs. Finally, a cost-plus pricing formula should adequately reflect the competitive situation and the unit sales volume at various price levels. Average unit costs depend on sales volume but in certain markets sales volume depends on the price charged. Thus the marketing manager is faced with a modest dilemma. From a marketing management viewpoint the practical solution is to adjust costs to fit a predetermined price ("customary price") which takes into account generic demand, competition, and advertising elasticity in each target market. It should be recognized that the prices for manufactured goods are "administered" prices which require a lot of planning around data supplied by accounting and marketing research.

The Demand Approach   Since marketing is primarily a "demand management" activity, understanding how to price goods in relation to market forces is critical. For the economist, demand is an expression of willingness to buy. Economists often portray demand as a schedule of prices and quantities that will be bought at each price. Marketing enlarges upon this concept of demand. In the broadest sense of the term some authorities equate the demand with consumer behavior; however, given the known relationship between price and sales volume, the marketing manager must devise policies and strategies that allow price to be integrated with the other marketing mix elements (promotion, product, place).

The marketing manager must make a distinction between two key demand concepts—market demand and company demand. Market demand is also known as industry or generic demand. Generic demand is the total amount of purchase potential for a type of product, such as beer or gasoline. Company demand is known as selective demand. Tylenol is marketed as a non-prescription pain-killer but chain drug stores sell the identical product, acetaminophen, under the store brand at a much lower price.

Pricing a product that has close substitutes pressures the marketing manager to de-emphasize price competition and place more emphasis on promotion to create product differentiation. With industrial goods, however, price is much more critical. Purchasing agents are experts in doing value analysis as a means of obtaining the best product for the least cost. They have good knowledge of the offerings of all vendors, and the prices their competitors are paying for the same good. For consumer goods most managers use a mixed marketing strategy which will reflect the nature of the product, market structure, available channels of distribution, consumer needs, and so forth. Curtis Mathes employs a marketing strategy for television sets emphasizing its higher price and four-year warranty as a means of reaching that market segment where a higher price is equated with higher quality; its distribution strategy is to market exclusively through company owned stores which permits price control.

Pricing is affected by market structure. Technically market structure includes: physical attributes of the product; uses of the product; cross-elasticity of demand; the number and location of competitors; cost structures, and so forth. If the seller has a monopoly, he then has wide amounts of pricing discretion. In the case of perfect competition the situation is just the opposite.

Concluding Generalizations Pricing is often viewed as the most
About Pricing complex problem facing the mar-
ket manager. Prices are always un-
der pressure—from costs, competition, the law, or the consumer.
Authority to change prices is not usually delegated to the sales force
but remains a top-management responsibility because of the direct
connection between prices and profits. Generally, a vice-president
will decide when and how much to charge, but sometimes a marketing committee is given this authority. In any case, the changes are
made only after much deliberation. An important part of marketing
management is to review the price structure constantly to see that it is
in line with costs, competition, product life cycle, and the other
policies and objectives of the company.

PRODUCT

"A company's product is what it
has to sell." Under the marketing
concept philosophy, a product is viewed as a reservoir of satisfactions
that accrue to its owner either from possession or use. These satisfactions are often more than functional and fulfill other needs such as
aesthetic gratification, convenience, social status, psychological well-
being, and so forth.

Prior to the adoption of the marketing concept philosophy the
technological or engineering dimensions of a product were the primary focus. Today, however, products are designed and marketed
with a strong emphasis on the unique attributes and benefits (relative
to price) which the physical product represents. Primary attention is
placed on consumers' needs and wants at the planning and development stage. For example, Revlon does not just sell cosmetics; it also
sells the promise of beauty and glamour. IBM sells more than
technologically advanced office products; it also sells communication
technologies plus reliability. In air travel, budget airlines, such as
Peoples Express, are marketing transportation at lowest cost per-air-
mile while competitors are selling transportation plus convenience
and personal comfort—at a higher price.

A product is the company's main link with the consuming public.
In the marketing mix under the marketing concept philosophy,
product is the critical element. A poorly conceived product, no matter
how well it is promoted, priced, or distributed, will fail in the
long-run. The task of developing products and product-lines and
positioning them in the marketplace to maximize consumer satisfaction is called **merchandising**.

Merchandising The essence of product policy is
forecasting all the dimensions of
the environment along with consumer desires to determine the types

of products the various market segments desire and then integrating these forecasts with an analysis of the firm's existing and non-existing marketing strengths, skills, resources.

A policy of **product differentiation** involves modifying particular product attributes with the goal of tapping a new market segment or enlarging demand in a current segment. Another rationale for this policy is to make a product more unique and less of a substitute for competing products as in the case of breakfast cereal manufacturers who promote such attributes as "more fiber and less sugar"—ideas in vogue for the prevention of diseases as well as good nutrition.

Market segmentation recognizes the fact that markets are not homogeneous. It makes more marketing sense to talk about sub-markets. Automobile manufacturers use this policy by producing sub-compacts, compacts, and mid-size, luxury models. Another example is in the food industry where the manufacturers of condiments, canned vegetables, and coffee produce institutional size packages. Here again the result is to broaden or deepen the product line.

Planned obsolescence is another product policy where the goal is to introduce products, usually with superficial or minor variations, in order to get current owners to purchase the new model. The college textbook industry focuses on revisions every two or three years to reduce the impact of the used-book market. Laundry detergent manufacturers introduce "new and improved" versions periodically.

Product positioning strategy refers to the manner in which the product is targeted at specific consumer segments either through the intrinsic attributes of the product or through the image created for the product through promotion. The key product variables, e.g., style, durability, versatility, and package, are paramount in matching product with a particular market segment. Gilette's "Right Guard" was originally positioned as a deodorant for men but later was repositioned as a deodorant for the family. "Trading up" is a strategy used to enhance the product's image to appeal to a more affluent and quality conscious market segment. Sears and J C Penney have done this by adding more expensive clothing lines carrying the name of a well-known designer or celebrity.

Finally, a strategy related to all of them is **benefit segmentation**. This involves identifying a particular market segment which is highly sensitive to the presence of one or more key product attributes. For example, some travelers will stay only at motels or hotels which have indoor swimming pools and/or saunas.

Product design, packaging, and materials are three of the more important aspects of product strategy. Product design begins with marketing research. Emphasis should be on consumer needs; production requirements should not dominate. Packaging in this era of self-selection is critical for the product because aside from protecting the product it (1) gives information, (2) promotes, (3) often reduces selling costs, and (4) facilitates the use of the product. For example, Campbell Soup produces a single-serving size can and many of the cans used to package products such as soups or chili have pull-off lids to eliminate the need for can openers.

A **brand** is a name, term, symbol, or design that identifies the products of a manufacturer and distinguishes them from those of competitors. However, from a consumer behavior point of view, a brand serves as a "cue" which triggers in the buyer's mind (memory) the relationship between a particular brand and the satisfaction associated with its prior consumption. Some manufacturers will produce merchandise and allow chain stores or discount houses to place their private brand on the product. Often a manufacturer will make use of the "family brand" concept and sell many products under that brand to utilize the investment in quality associated with the brand name, such as (the Craftsman line of tools sold by Sears). A brand manager usually heads up the product team.

Today, new-product management is an important part of a firm's competitive strategy. When a company selects and develops a product, it is choosing the kind of business it is going to be; therefore, a new-product program is a top-management responsibility. Within industry a number of organizational arrangements have recently evolved.

1. A product manager sometimes is charged with the responsibility of keeping the product up-to-date.
2. A new-product manager (also called the product planner or product development manager) may have the task of maintaining a steady stream of new products for the various product managers.
3. A product planning committee, composed of top executives, represents the functional areas of business.
4. A new product department.

Managing product lines is a never-ending process since all products have a life cycle: (1) introductory stage, (2) growth stage, (3) maturity stage, (4) saturation stage, and (5) decline. Perhaps the best example of this is in personal computers where technology shortens the product's life cycle to months rather than years.

Finally a product must include all of the social and psychological aspects associated with marketability. To illustrate, customers judge the food in some restaurants to be of high quality simply because the higher priced restaurant promotes itself as being better by the use of expensive decor, linen table cloths, valet parking, and so forth. The marketing manager must match the product-offering with the consumer's expectations. Other things being equal, many consumers still equate price with quality even though price differences do not always represent differences in quality.

CHANNELS OF DISTRIBUTION

Developing and managing the channels of distribution are a major line responsibility of the marketing manager. Developing a channel strategy emphasizes the spatial and temporal dimensions of marketing. A **channel of distribution** is the route that the product follows in its passage from the producer to the consumer. Critical factors affecting this route are: (1) nature of the good (industrial, perishability, bulk), (2) nature and location of the markets, (3) price of the product, (4) availability of middlemen, transportation and storage facilities, (5) sales effort required by middlemen, and (6) resources of the manufacturer. Thus a bar of soap may be sold by a manufacturer to a broker to a wholesaler to a retailer whereas industrial goods, such as equipment or raw materials, are often sold directly to the user.

Channel management involves two basic problems: the selection of the proper channel for the product and maintaining the channel. Three policy alternatives may be considered in the selection of the channel:

(1) The policy of *general* or *intensive distribution*, whereby the firm seeks to obtain the widest possible distribution for its product by allowing it to be sold everywhere by anyone willing to stock it.

(2) The policy of *selective distribution*, where the manufacturer chooses only those outlets that are best able to serve that company's needs.

(3) The policy of using *exclusive dealerships*, which allows only one distributor to stock and sell the product in a given market.

A company may use more than one channel, particularly if its market is diversified. Light bulb manufacturers, for example, sell direct to industrial markets but also sell to regular consumers through brokers and wholesalers. The use of middlemen can be justified only on the basis of increased efficiency, lower costs, reliability, and cooperation.

The second problem of channel management is maintaining the channel so that no blockages develop that can adversely affect the company's competitive and profit position. If a firm is selling part of its product by means of its own sales force, the channel maintenance problem is one of maintaining fair and consistent policies. When other types of middlemen are employed (such as agents and wholesalers), the marketing manager has to do three things: (1) See to it that the terms of the contract are followed by all parties. (2) Maintain good relations with the middlemen and encourage them to cooperate fully. and (3) Represent his company to the middlemen by seeing that sufficient cooperation and assistance are provided.

As a general rule, middlemen operating under a selective or exclusive distribution policy are expected to expend more effort in marketing the product. Two basic strategies are used to facilitate cooperation: (1) a *push strategy* where the producer makes heavy use of all of its promotional funds and selling efforts among channel members to secure cooperation and loyalty, and (2) the *pull strategy* where the producer emphasizes advertising and sales promotion to the ultimate consumer to pull the product through the channel. Most sellers employ a combination of both strategies.

Franchising represents a special type of channel which has grown in importance over the last 20 years. The franchising concept is derived from an older channel arrangement known as wholesaler sponsored voluntary chains, mainly in the grocery field, e.g., IGA and Ace Hardware. The current idea is that the franchisor (manufacturer or wholesaler) gives the franchisee the legal right to sell the franchisor's good or services in a restricted market; the franchisor provides the franchisee with equipment, the product or services, marketing management know-how and often some financial assistance. The franchisee agrees to market the product or service according to the conditions specified by the franchisor.

In essence there are three general types of franchise arrangement: (1) the manufacturer sponsored franchise as in the case of auto dealers; (2) the manufacturer or wholesaler sponsored franchise as in the case of Coca-Cola; (3) the service firm sponsored franchise system which is probably most familiar as in the case of Hertz, McDonald's, Holiday Inns, Kelly Girls. A key to the rapid growth of the franchise channel arrangement is that it enables the small independent business to compete effectively with the large corporate chain stores by providing them with buying power, management skills, and strong promotional effort.

PROMOTION

Promotion is communication to the potential consumer and refers to the nonprice selling activities of the firm. Three important types are advertising, personal selling, and sales promotion. **Advertising** is any paid form of nonpersonal presentation of merchandise to a group by an identified sponsor. **Personal selling** is the process of assisting and persuading a prospect to buy a commodity in a face-to-face situation. **Sales promotion** includes such devices as trading stamps, dealer aids, incentive travel, premiums, contests, and so on. In practice, sales promotion activities are used primarily to supplement advertising or personal selling. The general goal of the promotion element in the marketing mix is to increase sales, but the strategic objective is to enhance the effectiveness of the other marketing mix components.

Advertising and personal selling are different means to the same end—increasing sales. Usually they are employed together. Advertising appeals to the mass mind, whereas personal salesmanship is directed to the individual. Advertising assists salespeople and makes their efforts more productive by giving preliminary information about the product to prospects or developing goodwill toward the sponsor.

The successful marketing manager is always aware of the fact that the promotional activities are a cost to the firm. Therefore, selling expenditures have to be justified in terms of increased sales and profits. Using incremental reasoning, the added expense of any promotional outlays should equal or exceed the additional profits generated. This is not always possible because some types of promotional outlays are common to more than one product while others are intended to be long-term as in the case of institutional advertising or trade shows. For example, paying athletes large sums of money to use your products is necessary because competitors do it, but the sales benefits are taken on faith.

The advertising manager is usually in charge of a firm's advertising program, and has the responsibility to plan the entire advertising program, to draw up a budget, and to justify the request for funds—often with expert help from an advertising agency. The advertising agency is a service institution composed of specialists that assist clients in planning, preparing, and placing advertising. Agencies are paid by the various media (usually a 15 percent commission). Some firms have their own internal advertising department.

The promotional manager has two key responsibilities: (1) to develop a promotional mix for each product, and (2) to formulate the promotion budget. The mix depends on many factors, such as funds available, nature of the product, stage of product's life cycle, market structure, channel of distribution, and location and size of the markets. Budgeting must start with the objectives or goals to be achieved. Some of the approaches used are: (1) spend all you can afford; (2) spend a fixed percent of past or expected sales; (3) imitate competition; (4) spend so much per unit of product. Logically, the objective-task approach is the most sensible; this means the advertiser starts out by establishing a hierarchical list of goals or objectives to be met during the budget period.

Personal selling is usually the responsibility of the sales manager, who hires, fires, trains, and supervises the sales force. Most personal selling is directed to the middleman; some to the ultimate consumer. Some selling is creative in nature because it involves the process of arousing demand and persuading the buyer, whereas some is simply routine because the customer has already decided to buy. In general, the salesman helps the buyer solve his problems and is a good ambassador. For example, in marketing high tech products the salesman can be a valuable source of information about product innovations and technological research being done in the industry.

The sales manager must organize the sales force for maximum effectiveness. Bases for organization include: (1) the geographic area; (2) the type of product; (3) the kind of customer (consumer or industrial); (4) the channel of distribution (middlemen versus direct buyers); or (5) the nature of the selling task (new business or servicing old accounts).

In one sense promotion is the firm's attempt to communicate with the market which includes the channel members as well as ultimate consumers. However, communication is only a means to an end—short-run and long-run sales. The bottom line is purchase behavior and product loyalty. Nevertheless, in terms of a specific promotional campaign, the immediate objectives are product information, persuasion, and image reinforcement. Some advertising is used to provide price information, but in general, the idea is to use promotion to minimize price competition. Finally, every marketing manager knows that good advertising cannot sell an inferior product and that, in the long-run, the best advertisement for a product is a satisfied customer. Following the logic of the marketing concept philosophy the goal is repeat sales.

MARKET RESEARCH   **Market research** can be defined as the systematic gathering, recording, and analyzing of data about problems relating to the distribution and sale of goods. The market-research department is a staff function that services the entire organization, because the need for market-research information is pervasive. The justification for market research is that it helps to keep the executive informed and thus serves as a basis for making decisions. The qualified market researcher is a highly qualified expert in designing studies, collecting and analyzing data, and storing and processing it for future use.

Progressive companies are establishing **marketing information systems (MIS)** to coordinate the several information flows affecting marketing. A MIS may be defined as "a structured, interacting complex of persons, machines, and procedures designed to generate an orderly flow of pertinent information collected both from intra and extra firm sources for use as the basis for decision making in specific responsibility areas of marketing management." The MIS concept recognizes that too much information may be as bad as too little information in this age of electronic technology for collecting and processing data. The goal is to make certain the marketing managers have access to marketing intelligence so that they are able to perform the key tasks of planning and control. Here the bottom line is marketing intelligence.

Market-research departments usually are headed by a director who reports to the top marketing executive. Research personnel are specialists (for example, statisticians, psychologists, economists) in using the technical tools of their work. If a company cannot afford to maintain a full-time marketing-research department, the responsibility for research will be assigned to one of the marketing executives and an outside agency will be relied upon to provide the actual technical research. These external agencies are varied as to mode of operation, but in general there are eight basic types:

1. Consulting firms that work for the company as independent contractors.
2. Syndicated data services (for example, A. C. Nielson, Daniel Starch) that assemble certain types of data and sell them on a subscription basis.
3. Specialized service organizations that perform limited functions such as computer programming, field interviews, data storage, and statistical analysis.
4. Trade associations supported by contributions from firms in the industry that serve an entire industry.
5. Media that have full-time research staffs to perform certain kinds of marketing studies on a continuing basis and perform specialized services only upon request.
6. Advertising agencies that perform marketing-research studies for clients on a fee-plus-expense basis.
7. Universities with bureaus of business research that contract to do studies for businesspeople or industries.
8. Government agencies (for example, the Small Business Administration, the Agricultural Market Service) that sponsor or perform research for an industry or for a certain kind of business.

Below are listed some typical market-research projects and applications:

1. *Product studies*, which include developing and testing new products, measuring product preference, and testing package design.
2. *Consumer studies*, which identify potential consumers, measure characteristics (income, habits, attitudes, etc.), motivation research, brand loyalty, consumer polls and panels.

3. *Market analysis*, which tries to measure current sales potential and sales trends forecast, short-run and long-run sales; analysis of business conditions and trends.

4. *Sales analysis*, which appraises sales policies, measures distributor and dealer performance, evaluates sales territories, sales compensation studies, store audits, establishment of sales quotas and territories.

5. *Advertising studies*, which attempt to measure the effectiveness of evaluating advertising campaigns, determine advertising appeals, and measure media audiences.

6. *Distribution cost analysis*, which seeks to measure the actual cost of distributing a product by marking channel cost studies, transportation costs including handling and insurance, and storage costs.

Marketing managers must know enough about research techniques to be able to evaluate reports and to communicate with the market-research personnel. A working knowledge of statistics and accounting is vital in the interpretation of market-research information. The typical marketing-research report will contain a summary of the key findings and will have several technical appendixes at its end. For example, almost all market surveys are based on some type of probability sample, and sales forecasting relies heavily on trend analysis and statistical correlation. The marketing executive is not expected to be an expert in every field, but he has to know enough about methodology to ask intelligent questions of the researcher. Likewise, it is vital for the manager of marketing research to have an understanding of the firm's marketing plans, programs, and procedures.

CONCLUDING GENERALIZATIONS   The following summary generalizations will enable the reader to appreciate more fully some of the complex issues and questions involved in the study of marketing.

First, the scope of marketing is being broadened to include the marketing needs of business and nonbusiness organizations. Second, as our economy becomes more "high-tech" the marketing of services will become more important—American society in the 1990s might be labeled a "service society." Third, the development of social marketing, which refers to the application of marketing principles and techniques by social causes and programs relating to issues such as health care, ecology, highway safety, child abuse, and so forth. Fourth, despite government pressures, marketing managers have become more sensitive to the ethical effects of their actions on society. Fifth, marketing is becoming more scientific by using scientific decision-

king tools including statistics and mathematics, utilizing the behavior sciences, and developing computerized management information systems. Sixth, since marketing students are being trained for
business leadership, they need to have a well thought out philosophy
of enterprise. Seventh, marketing is slowly developing sizable models
relating to consumer behavior. Finally, over the past several decades,
marketing has become more of a hard-core academic discipline which
is being taught by professors with doctoral degrees and substantial
training in the social and management sciences, but who have had
"hands-on" experience in the world of business.

REFERENCES

BRITT, STEWART H., *Marketing Manager's Handbook*. Chicago, Ill.: Dartnell
Corp., 1983.

CUNDIFF, ED, ET AL, *Fundamentals of Modern Marketing*, 4th ed. Englewood Cliffs, N.J.: Prentice-Hall, Inc., 1985.

DORFF, RALPH, *Marketing for the Small Manufacturer*. Englewood Cliffs,
N.J.: Prentice-Hall, Inc., 1983.

FENWICK, SAM AND JOHN QUELCH, *Consumer Behavior for Marketing
Managers*. Boston: Allyn-Bacon, Inc., 1984.

HARTLEY, ROBERT F., *Marketing Mistakes*, 2nd ed. Columbus, Ohio: Grid
Publishing Co., 1981.

JAIN, SUBHASH C., *International Marketing Management*. Boston: Kent
Publishing Co., 1984.

KOTLER, PHILLIP, *Marketing Management: Analysis, Planning, and Control*,
5th ed. Englewood Cliffs, N.J.: Prentice-Hall, Inc., 1984.

LOVELOCK, CHRISTOPHER H. AND CHARLES B. WEINBERG, *Marketing for
Public and Non-Profit Managers*. New York: John Wiley & Sons, Inc.,
1984.

MACSTRAVIC, ROBIN S., *Marketing by Objectives for Hospitals*. Rockville,
Md.: Aspen Systems Corp., 1980.

MCCARTHY, JEROME E., *Basic Marketing: A Managerial Approach*, 8th ed.
Homewood, Ill.: Richard D. Irwin Inc., 1984.

NASH, EDWARD L., *The Direct Marketing Handbook*. New York: McGraw-
Hill Book Company, Inc., 1984.

STANTON, WILLIAM J., *Fundamentals of Marketing*, 7th ed. New York:
McGraw-Hill Book Company, Inc., 1984.

WIND, YORAM, J., *Product Policy: Concepts, Methods and Strategies*. Boston:
Addison-Wesley Publishing Company, 1981.

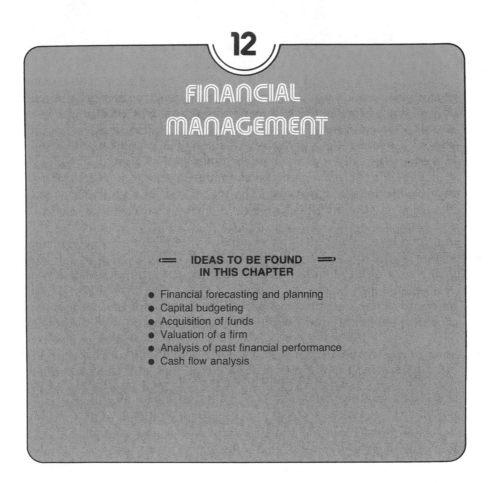

12

FINANCIAL MANAGEMENT

⟸ **IDEAS TO BE FOUND** ⟹
IN THIS CHAPTER

- Financial forecasting and planning
- Capital budgeting
- Acquisition of funds
- Valuation of a firm
- Analysis of past financial performance
- Cash flow analysis

The operations function concentrates on transforming the product or providing the service for sale to customers. Marketing management, as we saw in the last chapter, focuses on distribution of the product or service to customers to provide revenue to the firm. Both of these functions require investment in order to produce a flow of funds. Financial planning and control involve this flow of funds from customers back into operations and marketing in search of profits. This chapter deals with this third major function of a business enterprise.

ROLE OF FINANCIAL MANAGEMENT Financial management is the operational activity of a business that is responsible for obtaining and effectively utilizing the funds necessary for efficient operations. The objective of financial management is to see that adequate cash is on hand to meet required current and capital expenditures and otherwise to assist in maximizing profits.

A financial manager usually is located at a high level in an organization, and is one of those who advise the president and board of directors, under whose authority policies are formulated and final decisions are made. Typically, the chief financial officer carries the title of vice-president, serves as chairman of the finance committee, and reports directly to the president and board of directors.

Recent developments have changed the environment in which the financial manager functions. The rise of large-scale business units, increased product and market diversification, acceleration of corporate mergers, increased governmental regulation, and innovations in information-processing techniques have significantly broadened the responsibility and usefulness of financial control. Hence, the demands for careful planning and control, incident to the realization of profit goals, have made the financial officer a key executive. Three functions of the financial manager are financial forecasting and planning, acquisition of funds, and assistance in valuation decisions.

FINANCIAL FORECASTING AND PLANNING

The financial planning function involves long-range plans for plant expansion, replacement of machinery and equipment, and a miscellany of expenditures, causing large cash drains. The financial manager assists in the analysis of cash flows over the planning period.

Financial forecasting and planning involve: (1) financial analysis ascertaining the capabilities and needs of the concern; (2) prediction of the needs for funds over the short-run operating period, including cash flow, cash budgets, and sources of current capital; (3) prediction of the need for funds over a long-run period including investment fund flow, capital budgets, alternative capital expenditure proposals, cost of capital, and conditions of the capital market.

Financial analysis consists of a comparison of a company's current status with industry standards. It points out the firm's operating weaknesses, its potential capacity, and the volume and types of financing needed to enable the company to accomplish the objectives of the management. The raw material for this analysis consists of the historical accounting records of the company and appropriate industry standards. Financial ratios serve as guideposts for management by helping to spotlight the areas that call for financial attention. A check list for comparing the performance of a company with norms for the industry is presented in Table 12-1. Data for several consecutive accounting periods will strengthen the usefulness of these comparisons. The norms used in the table are for illustrative purposes only; in practice they should be obtained from sources that collect information on the specific industry concerned.

Table 12–1
Check List for Financial Ratio Analysis

Name of Ratio	Formula	Industry Norm (assumed merely as illustration)
I. *Liquidity Ratios* (measuring the ability of the firm to meet its maturing obligations)		
Current ratio	$\dfrac{\text{Current assets}}{\text{Current liabilities}}$	2.6
Acid-test ratio	$\dfrac{\text{Cash and equivalent}}{\text{Current liability}}$	1.0
II. *Leverage Ratios* (measuring the contributions of financing by owners compared with financing provided by creditors)		
Debt to equity	$\dfrac{\text{Total debt}}{\text{Equity}}$	56%
Coverage of fixed charges	$\dfrac{\text{Net profit before fixed charges}}{\text{Fixed charges}}$	6 times
Current liability to equity	$\dfrac{\text{Current liability}}{\text{Equity}}$	32%
III. *Activities Ratios* (measuring the effectiveness of the employment of resources)		
Inventory turnover	$\dfrac{\text{Sales}}{\text{Inventory}}$	7 times
Net working capital turnover	$\dfrac{\text{Sales}}{\text{Net working capital}}$	5 times
Fixed-assets turnover	$\dfrac{\text{Sales}}{\text{Fixed assets}}$	6 times
Average collection period	$\dfrac{\text{Receivables}}{\text{Average sales per day}}$	20 days
Equity capital turnover	$\dfrac{\text{Sales}}{\text{Equity}}$	3 times
IV. *Profitability Ratios* (including degree of success in achieving desired profit levels)		
Gross operating margin	$\dfrac{\text{Gross operating profit}}{\text{Sales}}$	30%
Net operating margin	$\dfrac{\text{Net operating profit}}{\text{Sales}}$	6.5%
Sales margin	$\dfrac{\text{Net profit after taxes}}{\text{Sales}}$	3.2%
Productivity of assets	$\dfrac{\text{Gross income less taxes}}{\text{Total assets}}$	10%
Return on capital	$\dfrac{\text{Net profit after taxes}}{\text{Equity}}$	7.5%

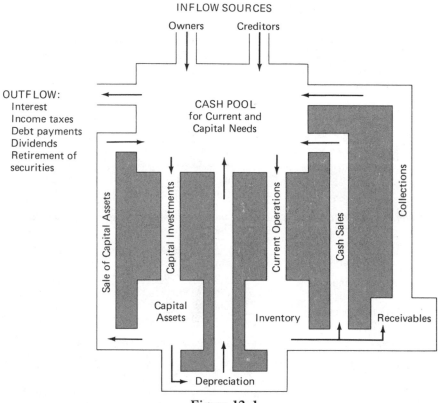

Figure 12–1
Flow of Cash Through a Business

Prediction of the short-term needs for funds is interrelated with long-term requirements. A combined short- and long-run cash flow analysis, the framework for which is illustrated in Figure 12–1, may be helpful in judging future cash needs. Cash and capital budgets may further facilitate decision making with respect to the sources and expenditure of funds.

The **cash budget** is basically a tool by which the analyst attempts to predict the various additions and withdrawals from the cash reservoir over a normal operating period. It aims to discover the extent of funds needed to meet current operating expenses. The cash budget is a part of the master budget.

Other aids for the prediction of short-term needs include pro forma income and balance sheet statements, pro forma statements of working capital and source and use of funds, and breakeven charts. These devices facilitate the comparison of actual results with expected results, pointing up the strong and weak points of the periodic performance.

Long-term differs from short-term planning primarily in the purpose to be achieved. Accountants distinguish between the two terms by separating cash uses into capital expenditures and current expenditures. Generally, a **current expenditure** is one from which principal benefits are realized within a year, and a **capital expenditure** is one from which benefits are realized over a period longer than a year.

Long-term financial planning starts with the preparation of a capital budget. **Capital budgeting** is an attempt to appraise the long-range monetary benefits of alternative capital expenditures. The first step in this process is for each department head to determine the various capital expenditures believed to be desirable. Each department head faces three problems: (1) the determination of available alternatives, (2) the classification of proposals according to purpose, and (3) the final selection.

Several approaches may be useful in the evaluation of investment opportunities. The job in all approaches is to find the difference between the net benefits that accrue from each alternative and the financial burden incurred to secure the benefits. The following three methods are used:

1. *Payback Period.* An estimate is made of how long it will take for the investment to pay for itself, called the payback period. Then the period is compared with some standard period. If the asset would pay for itself in less time than the standard period, the investment would be made. The payback formula is simple:

$$P = \frac{C}{R}$$

where P represents the payback period, C the cost of the investment, and R the expected net annual return from the investment.

2. *Present Value.* A more precise method of evaluating capital expenditures is to calculate the present value of the net cash benefits discounted at the company's cost of capital rate (the weighted average annual cost computed as a percentage of present total capitalization). If the amount computed is greater than the new investment, monetary gain should result from the outlay. To illustrate: Assume that the cost of capital is 10 percent after taxes and that the benefits after taxes from a $10,000 investment are $4,500 per year for three years. Using present-value tables, the present value of this stream of income discounted at 10 percent is $11,192 or a net realizable gain of $1,192. The basic formula is

$$P = \frac{R_1}{(1 + i)} + \frac{R_2}{(1 + i)^2} \cdots \frac{R_n}{(1 + i)^n}$$

in which P = present value of the investment; R_1, R_2 ... R_n = expected dollar returns in each year; i = the appropriate interest rate.
3. *Discounted Rate of Return.* The object in a third method of evaluation is to find the rate of return that will discount those returns to equal the cost of the proposed investment when applied to the future-dollar returns. Using the same assumptions as in the present-value illustration, the rate that will equate the stream of $4,500 per year for three years with the required investment of $10,000 is computed. A series of trial calculations will reveal that a net cash inflow of $4,500 for three years is equivalent to a rate of return of approximately 16.6 precent. If this exceeds the present cost of capital, the investment should be profitable as compared with overall past performance.

ACQUISITION OF FUNDS The acquisition of funds involves a consideration of the available sources and the time period for which they are needed. A first step for these considerations is the determination of the types of funds to be used and the mix best suited to the situation.

Broadly speaking, there are two basic types of funds: **debt** (fixed claims by outsiders) and **equity** (ownership). Four factors influence the choice between the two types:

1. Maturity of the obligating agreement.
2. Priority of claim on income.
3. Priority of claim on assets.
4. Voice in management.

Some considerations that influence the types of funds to use are:

1. *Suitability.* The types of funds must harmonize with the kinds of assets being financed.
2. *Volume and stability of income.* The more substantial and reliable the flow of income, the more feasible is the adoption of financial leverage (debt financing).
3. *Control.* The types of funds used reflect the residual owners' desire to maintain control of the company.
4. *Flexibility.* The ability to adjust the source and nature of the funds in response to changes in needs for funds.

5. Characteristics of *the economy,* including the level of business activity, money, capital markets, and tax developments.
6. Characteristics of *the industry,* including seasonal variations, nature of competition, regulation, and growth potentials.
7. Characteristics of *the organization,* including legal form, size, status in the industry, credit status, and management attitudes and policies.
8. *Economic and social responsibilities.*

Acquisition of funds is affected by whether the funds are anticipated for short-term, intermediate, or long-term use. One general rule is to match the maturity of the obligation with the income-producing life of the asset being financed. A second rule is that regular working capital should be derived from long-term sources, whereas fluctuating working capital normally requires short-term debt financing.

A major portion of the funds employed by a successful business is generated by the business itself in the form of depreciation allowances and retained earnings. Outside sources include the sale of equity shares, long-term debt securities for investment purposes, and the use of various credit facilities for short-term and intermediate-term financing. Trade creditors, finance companies, insurance companies, commercial paper houses, factoring companies, government agencies, and commercial banks are some possible outside sources. Circumstances prevailing at the time of the need will dictate the final choice.

For most businesses, commercial banks are relied upon heavily for current funds. Firms generally maintain a close working relationship with one or more commercial banks to provide depositories for the company's monies, meet payrolls, distribute interest and dividend payments, and handle other money matters; the financial manager turns to commercial banks for aid when short-term credit is needed.

In the early stages of a company's life, banks normally demand extensive information before extending credit, including personal information about the borrower, information about the business, historical accounting data, and facts about the need and use of the loan. After credit is granted, it is expected that the bank will be furnished a record of the borrower's subsequent business performance.

Successful acquisition of long-term (capital) funds depends upon the competence of the financial manager in knowing who the principal buyers are, the best contacts with the capital market, and the factors that underlie a good capital structure. The manager must keep informed of recent trends in the market for corporate securities (such as the increasing importance of pension and retirement funds) and of the impact of institutional buyers on the market. He should know the important classes of buyers such as life insurance companies, commercial and mutual savings banks, investment companies, and individual investors.

Various methods may be employed in contacting potential buyers of securities. The most important are: (1) contractual underwriting arrangements with investment bankers; (2) offers to existing shareholders on a preemptive (prior-privilege) basis; (3) direct placement with an institutional buyer or trust fund administrator; and (4) competitive bid by all prospective purchasers. The final selection of the method of contacting buyers depends on the relative cost, conditions prevailing in the capital market, effects of the issue on capital structure, effects on stockholder relations, and the amount of government regulation involved.

In building the capital structure of a company, the following policies may be helpful:

1. Don't use bonds unless the estimated earnings will give a *factor of safety* of at least 100 percent. (Ratio of what is left after interest payments to the amount of the interest.)
2. Keep the capital structure as *simple* and *conservative* as is feasible.
3. Keep the contracts between the security holder and the corporation as flexible as possible.
4. Safeguard the control of the company.
5. Keep the annual cost to a minimum.
6. Keep the best security (most appealing; minimum risk) for emergency financing.

Of critial importance in investment analysis is the determination of the *cost of capital*. Since capital may be raised by selling shares of equity and by long-term debt (leverage), a firm's cost of capital must involve a weighted average from both sources. It is important for two main reasons: first it provides a basis for evaluation of investment opportunities; second, it emphasizes how the degree of leverage is useful in the development of a balanced capital structure. The *cost of capital*, therefore, is a weighted, after-tax average computed on the combined capital structure mix. The future cash payments that must be made on the entire mix of capital sources constitute the cost of capital. Estimating the average cost of capital involves three steps:

1. Determine the optimum capital structure.
2. Determine the after-tax cost of each type of fund used or sought.

3. Weight the cost of each type of fund by its proportion in the optimal capital structure.

Although the idea of cost of capital is clear, there is considerable controversy concerning the average cost of capital when the degree of financial leverage (debt) increases. The Miller-Modigliani view suggests that the average cost of capital decreases as debt increases, because the interest on debt is tax deductible. The traditional view stated that the average cost of capital increases because the cost of debt and equity increases. Recent research in financial management has been devoted to simulations of models of different capital structures. The general manager, therefore, is well advised to check assumptions carefully and consult recent literature before employing a figure for cost of capital.

VALUATION METHODS OF A FIRM

The financial manager from time to time must participate in decisions relative to the purchase of major assets and to consolidations and mergers. During the negotiations for acquiring parts or all of other companies, he has the job of arriving at the dollar value of going concerns. The job is made more difficult inasmuch as value must be based not only on present or past value but on careful forecasts of future income-producing ability under conditions of uncertainty. Some of the conventional methods of valuation are:

1. *Original asset cost less depreciation* is based on the theory that an asset is worth what was paid for it, less the value lost through useful wear and tear. Objections are raised to this method because prior cost is no measure of present worth.

2. *Asset replacement cost less depreciation* avoids the question of changing price levels, but is objected to because of the lack of agreement on what replacement means (for example, identical replacement or present worth of replacement).

3. *Total book value of claims on assets* is another way of saying that the value of the claim is represented by the value of the asset to which the claim applies.

4. *Market value of outstanding securities* constitutes a composite expression of value incorporating all the factors that influence investment decisions. Wide fluctuations in security prices, however, do not facilitate a sound estimate of established values.

5. *Capitalization of earnings* is based on the proposition that, in the final analysis, an asset is worth what it will produce in the

form of a stream of income over a period of years, discounted at a "fair" rate of return. For example, the assets of a given company may be capable of producing "normal" annual earnings of $217,333. A capitalization rate of, say, 12½ percent is judged reasonable for a business of this character, considering the degree of risks inherent in the venture. Thus, through the simplest capitalization formula, $.12\frac{1}{2}V = \$217,333$, the value of the business would be $1,738,665. At a capitalization rate of 15 percent the estimated value would be $1,448,890, and at 10 percent the value would be $2,173,330. Of course, the valuation decision would be no more reliable than the accuracy of the estimated future earnings, and the acceptability of the capitalization rate. Furthermore, better but more complicated formulas are available in more rigorous studies of financial management.

The financial manager sits on the horns of a dilemma, being charged with the responsibility of having money ready to *spend* for current and investment purposes and at the same time having to get and *keep* sufficient money on hand to enable the business to achieve its profit objective. A workable balance between cash inflow and cash outflow must be constantly maintained. This calls for continuous planning, controlling, and maintaining relationships with the source of current and capital funds. A sound business rests on a sound financial foundation, the construction of which is the foremost responsibility of the financial manager.

ANALYSIS OF PAST PERFORMANCE

Financial statements contain valuable information that managers can use to analyze past performance. In order to use such information, they must recognize the limitations of such data and apply techniques to overcome these weaknesses. At the same time, out of the great mass of financial information that is available, managers must sift out that which is relevant.

Financial Statement Analysis

Management can analyze financial data by (1) comparisons of two or more periods and (2) comparison within one period. The former includes the analysis of successive balance sheets and income statements to determine trends in individual items. The latter involves the analysis of current financial statements to determine the state of the firm with respect to its solvency, stability, and profitability. Good financial statement analysis uses both approaches. Individual items can be compared over a period of time, with increases and decreases expressed as percentage changes.

The financial ratios illustrated in Table 12–1 have long been useful for analyzing past financial performance. Both the greatest advantage and the greatest disadvantage of ratios come from the ease of computing ratios. With some knowledge of accounting the computation of any financial ratio is simply a matter of relating two absolute sums as a fraction—simple division—a major advantage. The disadvantage is that the computation is so simple that many managers carry this simplicity over into interpretation. Certain values of each of the ratios have been illustrated in Table 12–1, but often these are assumed to be "good" values.

For example, most readers have picked up the idea that a 2:1 value is a good ratio because $2 of current assets seem "good" for covering $1 of current liabilities—but this is merely a first approximation. If the current assets consist of little cash, questionable accounts receivables, and inventories not readily marketable, a 2:1 ratio may not be high enough. Furthermore, different types of businesses require different ratios. A water company which receives payments monthly and has few liabilities that demand monthly payment may be in excellent condition with a low current ratio whereas a furniture store which requires large inventories and routinely allows several months for payment of accounts receivables may be in a tight financial condition if its current ratio is 3:1.

Recently, more differences of opinion have been voiced about the debt/equity ratio. **Leverage** or **trading on the equity** seeks to increase the rate of return to owners of equity who borrow funds at interest rates lower than the rate required for equity. This technique is even more attractive because interest payments are deductible for tax purposes. Interpretations differ regarding debt-equity ratios (leverage or trading on the equity) purely because opinions differ as to the degree of risk that is statisfactory. A conservative realizes that the debt must be paid and that bankruptcy can occur only to firms with debts while the high roller seeks to use borrowed funds whose interest is tax deductible even if the risks are high.

Cash Flow Analysis   Another very useful technique is **source and application of funds analysis.** This technique involves the determination of where funds have come from and how they were used, that is, a focus on cash flow. Although the term "funds" has a variety of meanings, in this analysis it means working capital; that is, current assets minus current liabilities. Most of the information needed for the analysis can be obtained from a comparison of two

Table 12–2
Example of a Source and Application of Funds Statement

Sources of Funds	
Proceeds from sale of stock	$10,000
Proceeds from sale of fixed assets	5,000
Net income from operations	4,000
Depreciation expense	1,000
Decrease in working capital	3,000
Total sources of funds	$23,000
Applications (Uses) of Funds	
Retirement of long-term debt	$16,000
Purchase of fixed assets	4,000
Payment of dividends	3,000
Total uses of funds	$23,000

balance sheets plus some supplemental information added to reflect the flow of funds.

From management's point of view, the value of the analysis of source and use of funds is that it gives valuable insight on the efficiency of management in allocating funds. Table 12–2 illustrates a hypothetical example of the analysis.

From Table 12–2 it appears that the largest source of funds was the sale of capital stock; net income for the period provided a relatively small part. The decrease in working capital indicates that internal sources of funds were necessary to meet the requirements of long-term liabilities, dividend payment, and replacement of fixed assets. The entire analysis is straightforward, with the exception of depreciation, which does not require the outflow of cash. It is subtracted from revenue along with other expenses in the income statement, but, unlike other expenses, depreciation does not involve outlay of funds. Therefore, to obtain the correct amount by which funds are augmented by the firm's operations, it is necessary to add the depreciation as a source.

Source and application of funds statements accompany annual reports. They aid materially in the evaluation of management's ability to generate funds through normal business operations and to allocate the funds to various needs. As a management tool, the statement is valuable as a basis for forecasting future sources and uses of funds; however, such analysis will normally be a part of the formal budgeting process. The primary purpose of the analysis is to evaluate past performance and to raise issues regarding management's efficiency in managing its cash flow.

NEW DEVELOPMENTS IN FINANCIAL MANAGEMENT

Financial management in the 1990s will be different than in past decades. First, the institutional structure has undergone probably its greatest change during the last decade. Second, changes in interest rates, the reduction in governmental regulations, and the development of new ideas (popularly called creative financing) have raised interesting issues for financial managers. In the 1980s a group of corporate raiders have developed techniques for raiding even the largest corporations through tremendous debt financing. These raiders contend that the value of the common stock of many of these corporations is much less than the value of their individual assets and thus the shareholders have not been effectively represented by the operating management. This threat of takeovers and actual mergers results in shifting the attention of top managments from improving operations and marketing to techniques for protecting themselves through defensive financial measures. A complete new group of picturesque words has evolved to identify these measures, for example, golden parachutes and white knights.

These new developments are forcing top management to give special attention to financial management at a time when foreign threats are being made in operations management, especially in quality and in productivity. As a result, financial management as a scholastic endeavor cannot be separated as easily from general management and its operational and marketing functions.

REFERENCES

BRIGHAM, EUGENE, F., *Fundamentals of Financial Management* 3rd ed. New York: The Dryden Press, 1983.

COHEN, NEIL and LOIS GRAFF, *Financial Analysis with Lotus 1-2-3*. Bowie, Md.: Brady Communications, 1984.

FRANKS, JULIAN R., JOHN E. BROYLES, and WILLARD T. CARLETON, *Corporate Finance*. Boston: Kent Publishing Co., 1985.

GITMAN, LAWRENCE J., *Principles of Managerial Finance*, 4th ed. New York: Harper & Row, Publishers, Inc., 1985.

JOHNSON, ROBERT W. and RONALD W. MELICHER, *Financial Management*, 4th ed. Boston: Allyn and Bacon, Inc., 1982.

KEOWN, A. J., DAVID SCOTT, JOHN D. MARTIN, and J. WILLIAM PETTY, *Basic Financial Management*. Englewood Cliffs, N. J.: Prentice-Hall, Inc., 1985.

OSTERYOUNG, JEROME S. and DANIEL E. MCCARTY, *Analytical Techniques for Financial Management.* Columbus, Ohio: Grid Publishing, Inc., 1980.

VISCIONE, JERRY A., *Financial Analysis.* Boston: Houghton Mifflin Co., 1977.

WALKER, ERNEST W., *Essentials of Financial Management.* Englewood Cliffs, N.J.: Prentice-Hall, Inc., 1965.

WESTON, J. FRED and EUGENE F. BRIGHAM, *Essentials of Managerial Finance.* Chicago: The Dryden Press, 1985.

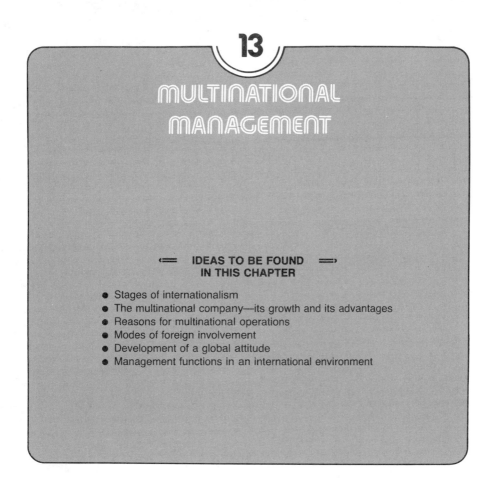

13

MULTINATIONAL MANAGEMENT

During the last three decades, management has developed rapidly in the international sphere. Business firms have expanded across national boundaries. Emerging nations have invited management specialists to advise them in economic development. International organizations, such as the International Labor Organization and the United Nations, have promoted interchange of ideas about managerial approaches. Cultural exchanges among university professors have broadened the horizons for research in management. These developments are the result of (1) the improvements in transportation and communications, (2) the growth of regional economic cooperation, e.g., the European Community (EC), (3) the relative attractiveness of foreign markets for mass produced goods, and (4) an increased intellectual awareness of a need for international understanding. As a result, the subject of management has expanded and has faced new basic questions. Is international management different from domestic management? If there are differences, how can these differences best be studied? Originally, international business was chiefly a matter of **international trade;** that is, raw materials were imported by the developed countries from the less developed ones and finished products were exported through various marketing channels to other countries. The essential subjects for attention at this stage were those covered in international economics, such as the law of comparative advantage, foreign exchange mechanisms, and marketing channels. While these subjects are still very important, they are normally covered by other disciplines and do not necessarily involve specific problems in the managerial process.

STAGES OF INTERNATIONALISM Despite the long and interesting history of international trade, until recently little attention has been paid to management aspects. Some early companies such as the East India Company and the Hudson Bay Company operated as political subdivisions of colonial powers long before management became a separate discipline.

A second stage of international development involved international finance and investment. Those countries with available capital sought to invest funds outside the home countries. These investments were treated strictly from the financial viewpoint and involved the flow of funds through banks, investment firms, and governments. The management of the operations was chiefly within national boundaries, with the flow of goods treated solely as imports and exports.

Beginning in the twentieth century, however, some large firms entered a third stage, in which the management of overseas operations was controlled by subsidiaries which handled all international business. These subsidiaries were treated as appendages of the parent company and served chiefly as export agencies. The countries outside the home nation view these business operations as efforts by foreigners to gain profits from their economies while providing only minimal employment for local people and without contributing to the local economies. The headquarters of these subsidiaries were usually located in the home country, with only warehouses, service offices, and sales agencies located in other countries. Management functions were handled as they were in the domestic company.

A fourth stage in the development of international companies (immediately after World War II) was seen in the appointment of vice-presidents of international operations as members of the domestic companies. The vice-president of a firm acted as contact and liaison with the various subsidiaries involved in international manufacture and trade. This was the first time that management began to recognize the unique problems of international operations.

A fifth stage saw the evolution of a global company in which the overseas operations were integrated into a single organizational structure. This stage developed during the 1960s and resulted in the forming of divisions in foreign countries to handle not only sales but also production, personnel, and finance. It was at this stage that international management emerged as a separate field of study, concentrating on management problems of a multinational nature. The emergence of this fifth stage was directly related to the formation of regional trade groupings of countries, such as common markets and free trade areas, which created markets large enough to warrant separate production and distribution organizations. Thus the managerial problems of the multinational company became a separate area of study.

In addition to the different types of organization for foreign operations, two special cases of international business firms deserve mention. One type is the company organized in a particular country for legal, tax, or political reasons. This type of firm chooses as its headquarters a small country which offers special advantages to firms seeking locations for legal headquarters. The differences among these firms are usually based on tax or legal rather than managerial grounds. Another kind of international firm is evolving from the growth of several distinct companies in different countries which maintain a loose coalition but do not necessarily have common overall policies. The managements of these companies tend to operate as domestic firms with no centralized policies or organizational structure.

THE MULTINATIONAL COMPANY

A recent development in world business is the **multinational** or global company (**MNC**)—a corporation which maintains world headquarters in one country but performs production, marketing, finance, and personnel functions within many nations. Although some of these companies were started early in the twentieth century, their importance as major factors in the international business world became evident only after World War II. Chief reasons for their development are: (1) the corporate form of organization with its infinite life and legal recognition as a separate entity; (2) the vastly improved systems of communication and transportation which facilitate global strategies; (3) the concentration of capital funds in advanced countries; (4) the rapid growth of markets in many countries, together with the maturing of markets in the home country; and (5) the creation of larger regional markets through common market and free trade agreements.

The chief advantages of the multinational firm are: (1) the access to organized capital markets and the resulting size of their investment potential; (2) the means by which management personnel can be recruited, formally trained, and developed; (3) the advanced stage of their accounting techniques, which provide controls and comparisons not available in many countries which operate on a less scientific basis; (4) the greater possibility of applying the law of comparative advantage and thus shifting procurement and production to low-cost areas; and (5) the power over governments wielded by their size and their impact on the entire economies of individual, small countries.

New problems and policy issues emerged with the growth of multinational operations. Since some of these problems are unique to this new form of organization, we shall discuss these in some detail.

First, a multinational company, by its very definition, finds itself a citizen of more than one nation and, therefore, must reconcile its loyalty to more than one sovereign power. It must at times cope with basic conflicts among foreign policies of several countries to which it has obligations. Embargoes by one country against another may create obstacles; one country may prohibit the sale of goods to a second country in which the company operates; to honor the laws of one country may force disastrous unemployment in the second. Every country attempts to enforce some of its laws extraterritorially; the U.S. antitrust laws restrict the American company's action in other countries; tax treaties or the lack of them cause double taxation or havens for avoiding taxation. Political activity may be difficult to avoid in many governmental situations; a multinational manager tends to become involved in the activities of local governments, and these activities may be opposed to the political position in the company's parent country.

A second policy issue unique to the multinational firm is the attempt to maintain coordinated policies consistent with its global strategy; at the same time, it must operate in different societies with different customs, languages, religions, and legal systems. Policies which may be desirable for one country may create international incidents with other countries. Different wage levels and labor practices may be required for each country in which the company operates. Variations in laws and tax systems prevent the establishment of consistent policies for all countries.

The employment of local nationals in management of a local plant is a third policy question that causes many headaches. Whereas the multinational company must attempt to identify with the society in which it operates and thus has many reasons to lean toward the use of local nationals, it may find that the quality of management is difficult to maintain or that a good local manager, with his different cultural background, may not fit in with the overall management policies of the multinational corporation.

There has been a trend toward decentralization in multinational operations as a result of national conditions which differ to such a great extent as to make it impossible to maintain centralized policies and decision making. This fourth issue at times creates a centrifugal force which pulls against a unified strategy. Once a manager has been delegated large powers of operations in a given country, it is difficult to replace him, even if his performance does not reach the standards of the company as a whole. Variations resulting from decentralization make transfer of management personnel more difficult. Furthermore, well trained managers in the parent firm may not view a transfer to an undeveloped country as the best means of promotion to top levels of management. Although American and British managers are accustomed to moving among countries, some nationalists—e.g., the French—often view a managerial position in another country as undesirable.

The foreign countries in which operations are conducted are referred to as **host countries.** The nation in which the corporation has been chartered and in which its headquarters is located is referred to as the **home country.**

Multinational companies can be relatively small and operate in only a few countries. Many are very large and operate in more than 100 countries. Large American companies earn over 50 percent of their profits from foreign operations. Coca-Cola, Exxon, Goodyear Tire, Pfizer, Inc., IBM, and Ford Motor are only a few of the American companies with major international interests. In addition to American multinationals, we all have become aware of foreign multinational companies operating in the United States, such as the Japanese companies (Bridgestone, Toyota, and Sony), the German companies (Volkswagen and Bausch and Lomb), the French companies (Michelin and Renault), the British companies (British Petroleum and Baskin-Robbins), the Dutch companies (Philips and Heineken), and the Swiss companies (Ciba-Geigy and Nestlés). With this trend of increase in the number and size of multinational companies, some observers have estimated that, within the next decade, over 50 percent of the combined gross national products (GNPs) of all countries will be generated by multinational companies.

REASONS FOR MULTINATIONAL OPERATIONS

The growth and expansion of multinational companies have been the result of increasing direct investments into foreign operations. **Direct foreign investment** involves the transfer of funds from the home country to foreign (host) countries in order to build warehouses, sales offices, and manufacturing plants or to acquire existing facilities in foreign countries. Later, the MNC may expand through the reinvestment of earnings in host countries, or it may use the financial markets within host countries for the sales of equity securities or bonds.

The central idea of direct foreign investment is that a multinational company maintains managerial control over foreign operations. (In the United States, any company with 10 percent or more equity in a foreign company is considered to have de facto managerial control.) If a company wants to invest funds in foreign countries merely as an investment but it does not plan to manage these foreign operations, it is said to have **portfolio investment.**

The reasons for a company to become multinational are numerous and varied. However, we can summarize four reasons that underlie the tendency to expand operations across national boundaries.

1. A company that requires a stable supply of basic raw materials for its operations must seek these raw materials wherever they may be found. Even in a large and well-endowed country like the United States, companies find that certain essential raw materials are not found within their country's boundaries or that these raw materials are available in insufficient supply (for example, oil) at reasonable cost. Thus, historically, one basic reason for expanding internationally is to *seek and gain control of raw materials at a satisfactory cost.*

In the nineteenth century, American companies such as Standard Oil, Kennecott Copper, and U.S. Steel were able to satisfy their needs for raw materials within the United States. Furthermore, if small amounts of materials were needed from abroad, they could merely import supplies. But when a major percentage of the raw materials was required from foreign sources, those companies found it desirable to **integrate backward,** that is, they expanded backward toward the source of supply in order to gain managerial control of their raw materials to support their manufacturing and refining operations.

Examples of companies seeking control of raw materials are the large, integrated oil companies; metal processing companies in the tin, copper, aluminum, steel, nuclear, chrome, asbestos, and chemical industries; forest and agricultural processing companies in rubber, lumber, food, and chemical industries; and producers of precious metals and stones such as gold, silver, platinum, and diamonds.

2. A second basic reason for becoming multinational is *to develop new markets* and to satisfy the demand of foreign consumers for products produced by the company. Companies with successful

domestic products recognize that many of these products could reach vast new markets in other countries. These companies discover that further continued growth depends on moving into other countries, especially if their domestic market has become relatively saturated or mature. Of course, these companies might initially export products from their domestic operations without expanding their managerial control outside their own nation. Yet, they tend to recognize that they need greater control of their marketing efforts and **integrate forward,** that is, they expand their operations and managerial control from manufacturing toward sales to the ultimate consumer.

Many present-day companies have developed multinationally in order to secure greater managerial control over the marketing of their products. Automobile companies, such as Ford and General Motors, integrated forward through sales divisions in many foreign countries. Pharmaceutical companies today are often multinational. General Electric, Philips (Dutch), and other electrical manufacturers have become global companies. Unilever, Nestlés, Corn Products, and other food and soap companies have also integrated forward. International airlines, shipping companies, and hotel chains such as Hilton and Holiday Inn have become multinational in order to serve the international traveler. In many other industries, the search for new markets has caused companies to grow internationally.

3. A third reason for becoming international is to reduce the production and transportation costs of parts and assemblies. In labor-intensive industries, the cost of labor may widely vary among nations as a result of the varying supplies of different types of labor and the local demands for that labor. A number of countries such as Hong Kong, Korea, Taiwan, India, and many Latin American and African countries have a significant labor-cost advantage, especially in assembly-type industries.

An increasing number of manufacturing companies have used a strategy called **horizontal integration** of international operations, that is, the establishment of plants at the same stage of production in different countries. These strategies reduce risks through geographical diversification and enable the company to shift production from a plant in one country to a plant in another country when cost changes or labor problems develop. The resultant increased power held by these companies raises issues among governments.

4. A fourth reason for a company to become multinational is simply *to keep up or to get ahead of its competitors*. In oligopolistic industries with a few large competitors, each company's management keeps an eye on its competitor's strategy. If one company in

an industry attempts to seize foreign opportunities, competitors will also move to prevent the first one from becoming entrenched in the new markets. For example, for years General Electric aggressively sought international business. In the 1970s Westinghouse moved to become multinational for fear that GE would gain a commanding lead in the growing market. Recently, in order to acquire new technologies developed in other countries, European, American, and Japanese MNCs moved into global operations to remain competitive. In such high-technology industries as computer chips, the rate of change is so rapid that every company must search for international opportunities to avoid losing competitive advantages through a new discovery by a foreign competitor.

MODES OF FOREIGN INVOLVEMENT The modes of foreign operations differ in terms of both the amount a firm commits to foreign operations and the percentage of resources located at home or in host countries. Among the many modes available to the company from which it can choose, the following six are the principal ones:

1. *Export of products from home country.* If a company wishes to minimize risks and costs of **exporting,** marketing, and manufacturing abroad, it might secure an export broker or other specialist who would handle all foreign negotiations and procedures. The company can, therefore, avoid the complexity involved in managing multinational operations and can thus simply trade internationally. Usually, this mode of operation is preferable to a company that has little experience in international operations. Exporting as an initial stage can then be followed by one of the other modes.

2. *Licensing.* Under an international licensing agreement, a firm (the licensor) grants rights to a foreign firm (the licensee). The rights may be exclusive or nonexclusive and may refer to patents, trademarks, copyrights, or special know-how. Under **licensing,** the licensor agrees to furnish technical information and assistance; the licensee agrees to exercise its rights aggressively and to compensate the licensor for services rendered. For example, a publishing company may grant rights to its copyrighted books to foreign publishers; a drug company may license foreign companies to sell its patented products in other countries.

3. *Franchising.* **Franchising** is essentially a way of doing business in which the franchisor gives an independent franchisee use of trademarks, patents, or other valuable intangible assets: the franchisee conducts the business within an agreed area under the limitations of the agreement. Sometimes the franchisor provides

supplies, managerial assistance, and other resources not generally available to the franchisee. Foreign hotel chains such as Holiday Inn and Hilton, rental car agencies, including Hertz and Avis, and fast-food outlets like McDonald's and Kentucky Fried Chicken, widely use franchises as a means of securing local acceptance in foreign markets and a mode for rapid expansion.

4. *Joint ventures.* The **joint venture** involves sharing ownership with others and is usually formed for the achievement of a limited purpose. Joint ventures have increased in use because many countries give preference to local businesses. A multinational company with foreign ownership and control can often interest a locally owned and operated business to join with it and thereby provide local identification. Many joint ventures are on a fifty-fifty basis; some involve 51 percent ownership by the multinational giving it managerial control; others have 51 percent ownership by the local company in countries requiring local control. The greatest advantage of joint ventures is in their flexibility and adaptability. The Japanese early recognized the advantages of joint ventures as a means of implementing their expansion into foreign markets.

5. *Management contracts.* In the last decade, **management contracts** have become a popular form of MNC involvement since it is merely a service contract requiring no capital investment. In communist countries, which, by definition, restrict private company operations and in some developing countries such as Saudi Arabia, where management skills and other operating services are limited, the management contract may be the only means by which the MNC can participate. The MNC can receive compensation for its management skills without any direct foreign investment. Occidental Petroleum, Pullman Company, and others experienced in dealing with controlled economies have extensively used management contracts.

6. *Foreign subsidiary.* The **foreign subsidiary,** often 100 percent owned by the MNC, makes initial direct investments in other countries and operates foreign plants as part of its global network of manufacturing and marketing. This mode is preferred by those MNCs desiring maximum managerial control and willing to assume greater risks of foreign operations. The selection of the subsidiary as a mode of foreign involvement requires rigorous analysis of many variables, since it commits the company to the greatest exposure to risks of foreign operations and management.

With these six modes available, the choice of the best one to use for a company in a particular situation is crucial. Among the many variables that need to be considered, the following ones are the most important in selecting the best mode.

1. *Risks.* The degree of risk associated with each mode is of major importance. In a joint venture, the risks of investment can be shared; in licensing and franchising, the risks of investment are assumed by the licensee or franchisee, thus relieving the foreign company of owning property in the country; in management contracts and exporting, capital is not required outside the home country, and thus the risks are considerably less than when a foreign subsidiary is used. For companies without foreign experience, the less risky modes are initially more attractive. After gaining valuable experience, other modes with greater risks can be used.

2. *Legal restrictions.* The MNC must operate within the legal restrictions of both the home and host countries. The home country may restrict actions through extensions of its antitrust laws, foreign exchange controls, and tax structure. The host country may restrict the amounts of profits that can be repatriated and may prohibit private ownership in sensitive industries such as extractive ore, banking, and those critical to economic development. The host country can restrict foreign exchange and use its tax structure to regulate operations of foreign companies. Finally, host countries may have different legal systems from the home country. An MNC with a home office in a country having a common law system may have complex legal problems in operating in countries using a civil law system or a Moslem legal system.

3. *Competition and markets.* The selection of the mode of foreign operations depends upon the modes used by competitors and by the intensity of competition in the prospective market. The size of the market and sales potential together with the intensity of competition from local companies and other multinationals are important, for example, in choosing to build a plant in the host country or merely to export from the home country.

4. *Foreign expertise and experience.* Companies with extensive experience in foreign operations can better afford to make the commitment of investing in a foreign subsidiary, while a company with limited expertise in foreign operations would choose to export, license its product, or use a franchise agreement.

5. *Degree of managerial control.* Probably of greatest importance to the decision of mode selection is the degree of managerial control desired. A 100-percent ownership in a foreign subsidiary offers maximum control. Exporting and licensing offer limited managerial control.

NEED FOR A CHANGE
IN ATTITUDE TOWARD
OTHER NATIONS

The management of an MNC must adapt to different host environments with the help of international institutions; yet it should develop a compatible, unified global approach that handles the interactions among the varied environments.

Howard V. Perlmutter[1] has observed three types of managerial attitudes that may be adopted by managers in adjusting to the global environments: ethnocentric, polycentric, and geocentric.

An **ethnocentric attitude** is oriented to the home environment. Managers who are inexperienced in international operations often have an ethnocentric viewpoint; that is, they are imbued with the beliefs and customs that have worked well at home and assume that they are suitable to all countries. This attitude ignores the impact of the diverse environments on managerial practices. Comments illustrating this attitude are "Americans have the best managerial approach," "My job is to teach the American way to others and to bring foreigners around to our way of thinking," "Japanese and Latin Americans are sure peculiar—why don't they do things the way we do?" and "I'm right and foreigners are wrong." A person may unconsciously take an ethnocentric view unless he or she is alerted to cultural factors of the relevant nations in which he or she participates.

The second attitude is **polycentric,** that is, an understanding that each country has unique cultural characteristics that require an international manager to attempt to do things the way they are done in the host country. In short, "When in Rome, do as the Romans do." With extended first-hand experience outside the home country, a manager may evolve a polycentric viewpoint. The problem is that every move to a different country requires that the manager "learn the ropes" in a new environment. The manager might "go native" and lose contact with the home culture and its management fundamentals. A polycentric manager may react against earlier cultural experiences and cause increased difficulties with superiors at headquarters. Many problems between foreign subsidiaries and home-country headquarters are conflicts between ethnocentric superiors and polycentric host-country managers. In such conflicts, headquarters may treat foreign-resident managers as though they were in "Siberia." In such cases, managers located outside the home country may be overlooked when their promotions are considered. Polycentric managers may have trouble fitting into the global thinking desirable in multinational companies.

[1] Howard V. Perlmutter, "Social Architectural Problems of the Multinational Firm," *Quarterly Journal of AIESEC International*, vol. 3. no. 3 (August 1967).

The experienced top manager in trying to resolve the conflicts of the two attitudes attempts to develop a third viewpoint—a **geocentric attitude.** This global view recognizes the strengths in one's home environment (ethnocentrism) and the strengths of other nations' cultures (polycentrism). The managers at headquarters need to integrate these strengths in order to develop a unified, world perception. The geocentric or global view accepts the differences in cultures as conditions of reality. Cultures may not be superior to one another but they are just different. A geocentric view maximizes the advantages of these differences. The result may be that adaptations will strengthen a company's managerial approach, facilitating the transfer of ideas and practices tested in one environment and potentially useful in others.

The modern world has become increasingly interdependent. International institutions have emerged to facilitate the interchange of goods, technology, and management. The ethnocentric, polycentric, and geocentric attitudes have basic impacts on this interchange.

MAJOR PROBLEMS FACED BY INTERNATIONAL MANAGERS

Diverse environments create many problems for the international manager not faced by the domestic manager. A geocentric attitude helps keep the problems in perspective. In this book we can only list some of these problems.

1. Different languages create problems of translation and communications. Interpreters may be needed for oral communications; translators may be required for written communications. The best method for handling this problem is undoubtedly for managers to be multilingual or, at least, to learn the languages that enable them to communicate in the language of the home country and the languages of the host countries.

2. Different currencies are used by the many sovereign nations. The values of these different currencies introduce risks of changes in **foreign exchange rates,** that is, the value of one currency stated in the units of another currency. Companies with profitable operations may have financial difficulties solely from losses due to currency fluctuations. Companies with otherwise efficient operations have faced bankruptcy simply as a result of losses in the foreign exchange market.

3. Laws and regulations differ among governments and political systems. Common law, which is used in the United States, differs from civil law (the Napoleonic code, which is predominant in Europe), and religious law (such as Moslem law, which is used in the Middle East).

4. Differences in accounting systems introduce problems of reporting and comparing operations in different countries.

5. Systems for measurement of weight and distances pose adjustment problems. For example, items sold in countries using the metric system (liters and meters) require conversion from quarts and yards.

6. Custom duties (tariffs) and health, safety, and business practices imposed by different sovereign governments make international operations more difficult in spite of advances made by General Agreement on Tariff and Trade (GATT) and other international institutions.

7. Diplomatic and political pressures call for policy decisions concerning the degree of company involvement. The fact that an MNC is viewed as an outsider may make life more complicated.

These problems faced by international managers result from the differences among the national environments in which multinational companies operate. Some of these differences have become less and some have become greater in the last few decades. The multinational company in its attempt to maintain a unified strategy must bridge these differences and transfer resources and managerial techniques in order to gain optimum performance.

THE SEVEN MANAGEMENT FUNCTIONS APPLIED IN INTERNATIONAL OPERATIONS

The seven functions—decision making, planning, organizing, staffing, leading, communicating, and controlling—are applicable in all managerial situations. Nevertheless, we have observed that performance of these functions must be adapted to diverse environments

Decision Making

Although the MNC requires the same decision-making process, new variables, such as politics and culture, make the process more complex. Furthermore, in some nations, such as Japan, the decision-making process involves modification of the general pattern discussed in Chapter 4.

Planning

The planning function is particularly critical to successful multinational operations. The selection of specific countries for operations should be the result of careful scanning of the opportunities and constraints in each of the number of countries available for expansion. Long-range planning and forecasting of the degree of receptivity expected by each host country are initial steps in planning multinational operations. Since the MNC will enter a new country as an outsider, it should develop a plan and strategy to increase its receptivity. It can then select the form of involvement and the type of entry strategy to be used. Some of the factors to be considered in an MNC's planning include the following:

1. An assessment of the needs and national plans of the host country will enable the MNC to provide evidence of how its entry will help each country achieve its own goals. Most developing and many industrial countries have five-year plans that provide a basis for this assessment. The MNCs can select niches, for profitable operations that fit the interests of the host countries and increase receptivity by increasing employment of labor, supplying needed capital and technology, or strengthening the host's balance of payments through increasing exports or through import substitution.

2. A forecast of the risks associated with operations within host countries should seek to uncover possible future problems and attempt to solve these problems prior to entry. The degree of commitment of company resources depends on an understanding of the history of the host country and its treatment of other MNCs. Political stability, degree of labor unrest, convertibility and stability of the host's currency in foreign exchange, understandings for repatriation of profits to the home country, and records of nationalization and expropriation of private property are some of the potential problems that should be investigated.

3. Plans should include the development of strategies to reduce the fears of host countries of being controlled by outsiders. Employment of nationals as managers, decentralization of authority to local managers, use of raw materials and parts produced within the host country, participation in local community improvements, and the maintenance of low profit tend to provide a cooperative climate for successful operations.

4. Realistic appraisal of incentives offered by host countries for attracting foreign investment should be made prior to making commitments. Host countries often provide strong incentives for entry through tax exemptions, import concessions, immigration agreements, and supportive legislation. In planning, the MNC should recognize that initial incentives may not be permanent and that the government attitude toward the MNC might change. Receptivity may decline once the MNC becomes committed to operations within the country.

Planning is always an important managerial function, but in

international operations, the function is most important and often very complex. Plans by home-country personnel must take into account the plans of the host country and those of each subsidiary.

Organizing   Typically, a company on first entering the international arena establishes an "international department" supplementing its domestic structure of departments. An advantage of this method of organizing is that the scarce number of managers with international expertise can be grouped together, thus economizing on training of all personnel in international matters. Yet, the international department fails to internationalize the thinking of the entire organization.

With increased experience in international operations and the training of more international managers, the MNC may use one of the three usual types of departmentation: geographical, functional, or by products. Since the varied environments differ in the regions of the world, the geographical basis is predominant with the world organization divided into regional divisions and subsidiaries. The functional type is least used because of its tendency toward centralization of authority and its less adaptability to environmental forces. Although the geographical type of structure has been found to be suitable to single-product companies, large multiproduct MNCs, such as General Electric and IBM, have found that the product type provides a global orientation for all products and increases the internationalization of all managers with the companies.

More recently multiproduct MNCs have experimented with a fourth type of organization: **grid, or matrix, organization.** The product type of organization has each product division represented by a manager in each country. The geographical type of organization tends to focus on the adaptability to the different environments but with less expertise concerning each product. Therefore, in an effort to gain the advantages of both geographical and product organization, some companies use a grid organization, in which departmentalization is both geographical and by products. A regional manager becomes an expert for a region, and a product manager specializes in particular products. The grid type of organization has proven useful in spite of the organizational problems of coordinating regional and product managers in each of the countries.

The development of the organizing function in international companies has contributed new ideas for organizing domestic firms. Organizational experimentation has increased in the international area, and an increasing body of literature has developed on special forms for international companies. This literature has enriched the development of the organizing functions in all types of companies.

The management of human resources in an international company is considerably more complex than in a domestic company. The company must develop personnel policies relative to the number of managers who will be sent from the home country (expatriates) and the number of nationals who will be trained to manage within their own countries. If a domestic manager is to be sent to a foreign assignment, he or she will need special training on the environmental factors important to the new assignment. If a national is to be assigned managerial responsibilities in his or her own country, special management training programs must be developed to provide the necessary understanding of the company's philosophy and managerial practices.

Staffing

Staffing of an international company is faced with special problems, whether home-country personnel or nationals are to be used. The home-country expatriate will tend to better understand the managerial approach of headquarters in the home country and thus, when placed in a foreign assignment, he or she will "speak the same language" as the superiors in headquarters. However, the expatriate will face difficulties in managing nationals in the host country and in being accepted in the local environment. The local national selected to manage operations in the foreign country will be more skilled in handling the unique environmental problems, but he or she may have problems in understanding the global plans of the home headquarters and in communicating with headquarters.

Recruitment and training of managers require special attention on the international level. Furthermore, the differences in the cost of living, travel costs, and salary scales are important. The salary costs, travel expenses, and overseas differential required to maintain an expatriate in a foreign country are particularly high.

Leadership

Probably the most diverse set of problems in managing an international firm is in the variety of leadership styles that may be required to fit the diverse environments. As we saw in Chapter 7 on the function of leadership, leading occurs when one person induces others to work toward common goals. In international operations, the personal characteristic of the leader must be consistent with the needs and expectations of the people in the foreign country. If the employees in a country expect a leader to assume an authoritative attitude, a leader who has developed a subordinate-centered style with a wide area of freedom for subordinates may find that the style found to be effective in the home country might not be as effective in the host country. In some countries, charismatic leaders are most effective; in other countries, the class or position of the leader is prerequisite for others to follow; in others, a leader who encourages followers to participate in decisions fits best. The style of leadership suitable to a particular situation inherently depends upon the cultural characteristics of the country in which operations are conducted.

Communicating   International managers, of course, find that communications require knowledge of the language used in the country. If the country uses a different language, the manager must either (1) learn the language or (2) communicate through interpreters. Certainly, a manager who is fluent in the language has tremendous advantages. Even if a manager has not yet achieved fluency, the attempt to speak the language of the host country is most important psychologically. Usually, the mere evidence of trying to speak the national language will be perceived as evidence of goodwill toward subordinates.

Communicating, however, involves more than the spoken or written language. Nonverbal gestures and body postures, especially important in crosscultural discussions, have hidden meanings. Often this **silent language** gives unintended meanings; that is, actions speak louder than words. Edward Hall, a cultural anthropologist, has for years identified examples of the importance of what he calls *silent language* in high context cultures.

In the United States with a low context culture, a manager tends to place less emphasis on these nonverbal characteristics than do cultures in Latin America, Asia, and other locations in which American managers may face unintended consequences. In the United States, we are taught not to stare in the eyes of others, whereas in the Middle East individuals closely watch the pupils of the eyes of those with whom they are talking, seeking evidence from pupil changes to indicate the attitude of the other person. Americans are accustomed to a conversational distance of five feet, whereas in many parts of Asia and Latin America, the conversational distance is about two feet. It is not surprising that when Latin Americans seek to adjust the distance to two feet, the Americans back away to five feet. Although the Americans may feel that they are being friendly, the Latin Americans perceive them as distant and difficult to get to know.

Sadat was accustomed to the Egyptian culture of considerable touching and thus placed his hand on the knee of the individual with whom he was having a friendly conversation. In India a person who is agreeing with another habitually moves the head in such a way that an American might interpret the head movement as shaking the head in disagreement. At times bodily movements are perceived as contradicting the message given in words. Many other examples of differences in silent language may cause trouble to an American engaging in international communications. The essential aspect for American managers is to become aware of these subtle elements in international negotiations.

The technology of the means of communicating varies in sophistication and type. Even in countries with well-developed telephone systems, the use of the telephone requires study. Dial tones may be confusing, and the operations of pay stations vary. Typewriters differ, and word processors are in different stages of use. The degree of formality of business letters and reports differs. The need for written agreements and distribution of memos is subject to different cultural interpretations.

Networks for communications differ. For example, the simple matter of dealing with superiors and subordinates may be affected by a customary procedure not used in other countries.

Communication is a function of management that requires special attention in international operations. The differences among countries are so great that we can only offer general classifications and a few examples of the impact of culture on communications.

Controlling

The importance of the control function is just as great in international operations as it is in domestic operations. In all operations, standards are required, measurements of performance must be made, and corrective action must be taken after comparing the standards with performance. The international differences in controlling relate to (1) the differences in the units of measurement among different countries, (2) the differences in the means of collecting information on performance, and (3) the differences in the methods of taking corrective action.

Standards of performance must be in terms understood by those being controlled. Some countries use the metric system; others use units tailored to their history and environment. Countries use different currencies. The multinational company must be able to convert the standards understood within different countries to a common method of stating standards at the global headquarters. For example, accounting data in a local currency must be converted to a common currency, usually the currency of the home office. Production quotas may be stated in liters in one country and in quarts and gallons in another. The standard used at the global level must be adaptable and convertible to those used in each country.

The measurement of an individual's performance must have

clear significance to each individual. Problems of measuring output are great even when the measuring units are the same, but the problems increase when these measurements have different meanings to different individuals.

Corrective action must be accommodated in any control system. In an international company, a paramount issue is whether to centralize control at headquarters or to decentralize the control to plants in different countries. The time frame for corrections is usually longer in many countries outside the United States with its concentration on the "bottom line" in monthly, quarterly, and annual reports.

CONCLUSIONS

Technological and social changes have forced managers to consider the international dimension. Even domestic firms are directly affected today by developments in other nations. As expansion continues on a global basis the subject of multinational management will become increasingly important.

REFERENCES

BALL, DONALD A. and WENDELL H. McCULLOCH, *International Business*, 2nd ed. Dallas: Business Publications, Inc., 1985.

BARNET, R. J. and RONALD E. MULLER, *Global Reach*. New York: Simon and Schuster, 1974.

DANIELS, J. D., E. W. OGRAM and L. H. RADEBAUGH, *International Business: Environments and Operations*, 3rd ed. Reading, Mass.: Addison-Wesley Publishing Co., Inc., 1982.

EITEMAN, DAVID R. and ARTHUR I. STONEHILL, *Multinational Business Finance*, 3rd ed. Reading, Mass.: Addison-Wesley Publishing Co., Inc., 1982.

KORTH, CHRISTOPHER M., *International Business: Environment and Management*, 2nd ed. Englewood Cliffs, N.J.: Prentice-Hall Inc., 1985.

MASON, R. HAL, ROBERT R. MILLER, and DALE R. WEIGEL, *International Business*, 2nd ed. New York: John Wiley & Sons, Inc., 1981.

ROBOCK, S. H., K. SIMMONDS and JACK ZWICK, *International Business and Multinational Enterprises*, revised ed. Homewood, Ill.: Richard D. Irwin, Inc., 1983.

RUGMAN, ALAN M., DONALD J. LECRAW, and LAURENCE D. BOOTH, *International Business*. New York: McGraw-Hill Book Company, Inc., 1985.

RUTENBERG, DAVID P., *Multinational Management*. Boston: Little, Brown and Co., 1982.

SERVAN-SCHRIEBER, J. J., *The American Challenge*. New York: Atheneum Publishers, 1967.

VERNON, RAYMOND and L. T. WELLS, *Manager in the International Economy* 3rd ed. Englewood Cliffs, N.J.; Prentice-Hall, Inc., 1976.

WEBBER, ROSS A., *Culture and Management*. Homewood, Ill.: Richard D. Irwin, Inc., 1969.

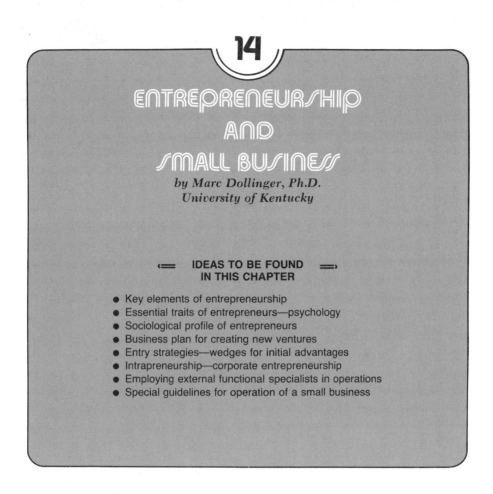

14

ENTREPRENEURSHIP AND SMALL BUSINESS

by Marc Dollinger, Ph.D.
University of Kentucky

⟸ **IDEAS TO BE FOUND** ⟹
IN THIS CHAPTER

- Key elements of entrepreneurship
- Essential traits of entrepreneurs—psychology
- Sociological profile of entrepreneurs
- Business plan for creating new ventures
- Entry strategies—wedges for initial advantages
- Intrapreneurship—corporate entrepreneurship
- Employing external functional specialists in operations
- Special guidelines for operation of a small business

Our knowledge of entrepreneurship, like our knowledge of management, comes to us from many different disciplines. Anthropology, sociology, psychology, and economics have all contributed to our understanding of the entrepreneurial phenomenon. However, because of the diversity of approaches to the study of entrepreneurship, there is difficulty in defining just what entrepreneurship is and identifying just who is an entrepreneur.

Even Webster's dictionaries disagree among themselves. Webster's *New American Dictionary* defines an **entrepreneur** as "one who undertakes an enterprise" or "an employer of workmen." Webster's *Third International Dictionary* offers a more complete definition: "an organizer of an economic venture, especially one who organizes, owns, manages, and assumes the risk of a business." The difference between the definitions is one of scope and emphasis. The first definition is very broad and can include organizing a Little League team or hiring a contractor to fix the roof. The second definition is more useful because it narrows the focus of entrepreneurship to its important qualities: economic activity, ownership, venturing, and risk.

Some writers on entrepreneurship, such as economist Joseph Schumpeter, have stressed "innovation" as being the key factor in entrepreneurship. **Innovation,** the creation of new products, markets, services, sources of supply, or forms of industrial organization, is viewed as the dynamic force that moves the capitalist system. Entrepreneurs take capital from less productive sectors of the economy and invest it in new, growing, more profitable industries. This "creative destruction" of capital makes the entrepreneur the linchpin of a strong free enterprise economy.

Another key element of entrepreneurship is risk-taking. John Stuart Mill, a nineteenth-century British economist, saw risk-bearing as the distinguishing factor between entrepreneurs and managers. Entrepreneurs stand to lose or gain for their own purse as a result of their own efforts. Managers are merely office holders and they bear none of the risks or liability of loss. Today, however, with employee stock ownership plans, managerial stock option incentives, and large pension fund investments, managers and employees are often important risk-bearers in their organizations.

Sociologist Max Weber offered a significant insight into our understanding of the entrepreneur. To Weber, the entrepreneur was the ultimate source of power and authority in an economic organization. In his analysis of bureaucracy, Weber saw no role for personal power in managerial positions. Only the entrepreneur possesses this. The distinction then between entrepreneur and manager rests on this presumption. However, recent commentators have noted that managers do act entrepreneurial in certain situations. We will look at these cases later in the chapter. But first, we will examine what makes an entrepreneur from a psychological and sociological perspective. Then, the discussion will cover how entrepreneurs create new ventures and what entry wedges they employ as competitive strategy. Since many ventures become small businesses, we will offer a managerial perspective of small business operations. The chapter ends with a look at corporate venturing and the role of innovation in larger firms.

THE PSYCHOLOGY OF THE ENTREPRENEUR

Psychologists have investigated the personality characteristics of entrepreneurs in an attempt to understand why some people become entrepreneurs and others don't. This is known as the trait approach. Among the traits thought to be related to entrepreneurship are: flexibility, extroversion, independence and aggressiveness. In this section, we examine three traits which investigators have shown to be entrepreneurial: the need for achievement, the internal locus of control, and a tolerance of ambiguity.

The **need for achievement**, or **n-ach**, is one of the traits studied by David McClelland in his book *The Achieving Society*. McClelland developed the theory that individuals, indeed whole societies, that possess n-ach will have higher levels of economic well-being than those that do not. McClelland's work indicated that there are five major components to the n-ach trait: responsibility for problem solving, setting goals, reaching goals through one's own effort, the need for and use of feedback, and a preference for moderate levels of risk-taking.

The individual with high levels of n-ach is a potential entrepreneur. The person views the economic undertaking as a problem to be solved and enjoys solving problems. Solving the entrepreneurial problem requires setting goals with hard but achievable expectations. The potential entrepreneur also believes that these goals can be achieved by his own efforts—that he possesses the skills, abilities and resources. Along the way, the entrepreneur is open and responsive to feedback. This feedback may come from other individuals, organizations, the environment, or even the entrepreneur himself. The entrepreneur uses positive feedback for encouragement and negative feedback for correction. Lastly, the achievement of the goals and the possibility for failure are perceived as moderate risks. The n-ach individual neither plays it safe nor takes unnecessary chances.

A trait related to n-ach is locus of control beliefs. People who do not believe that their efforts in a business venture will be related to its success or failure are unlikely to become entrepreneurs. These people are known as "externals" since they believe that outcomes are determined by forces external to their own behavior. "Internals," on the other hand, believe that they have the ability to influence the outcome of an event. These people are potential entrepreneurs.

A third important trait is tolerance of ambiguity. Ambiguous situations are defined as novel, complex, or unsolvable. These conditions parallel entrepreneurial activity and, therefore, becoming an entrepreneur requires the ability to tolerate these factors. Entrepreneurs view ambiguity as an opportunity to solve a problem, achieve a goal, or impose their own will on the situation. People who are intolerant of ambiguous situations are threatened and uncomfortable in this context.

While the trait approach is useful for understanding the psychological makeup of potential entrepreneurs, it doesn't offer a model of

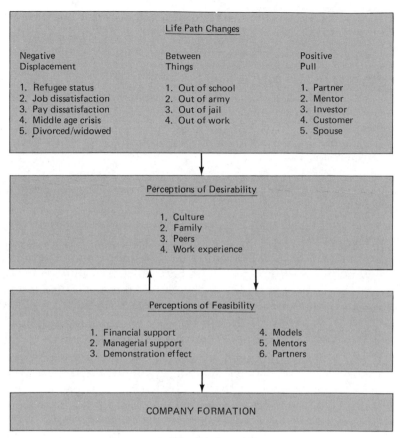

Fig. 14–1.

the person who actually goes into business for himself or herself. For this we turn to a sociological explanation.

THE SOCIOLOGICAL APPROACH

While personality characteristics may provide evidence of entrepreneurial tendencies, the actual activity of starting an enterprise is a process. The entrepreneurial event formation process has been described by Albert Shapero and is illustrated in Figure 14–1.

The process begins with a life plan change. The potential entrepreneur may have just experienced a displacement, be between things, or have a positive force encouraging entrepreneurial activity. For example, the negative displacement of being a refugee helps explain overseas Chinese entrepreneurship and Jewish entrepreneurship world-wide.

Table 14–1
Differences between Entrepreneurs, Executives,
and Small Business Owners
(All figures in percent)

	Entrepreneurs	Fortune Executives	Small Business Owners
Age (percent under 45)	63	9	40
White Anglo-Saxon protestant	48	65	68
Began business while in school	32	19	16
Finished 4 years of college	76	94	47
Worked for 4 or more companies	42	21	30
Has never been fired or dismissed	31	9	10

However, perceptions of desirability must also be positive if the process is to continue. Some cultures have a disdain for entrepreneurship and, generally speaking, find alternatives to venture creation. Although there are always exceptions, most Irish immigrants found assimilation in the United States through civil service, as policemen and teachers. In addition, family tradition sometimes makes commercial activity seem undesirable. Many families have traditions of professional work (medicine or law), the family firm, or strong labor and union ties. These tend to decrease the desirability of entrepreneurship.

Perceptions of feasibility must also be present. Entrepreneurial activity must appear do-able. This means there must be models of successful venturing and resources available for venturing. Only when all the conditions of the entrepreneurial event process are met can new company formation be predicted.

Are there any other differences between the characteristics of entrepreneurs and non-entrepreneurs? A recent survey by the Gallup Organization conducted for *The Wall Street Journal* provides us with insight and information.[1] The groups surveyed consisted of 258 small business executives (company sales less than $50 million), 153 entrepreneurs (chief executives of *Inc. Magazine's* 500 fastest growing firms), and 207 CEOs and other executives from *Fortune Magazine's* list of the 500 largest American corporations. Table 14–1 shows some of the statistical results.

The survey tends to confirm some of the psychological and sociological theories . Entrepreneurs are younger on an average than executives and less likely to be a white Anglo-Saxon protestant. These

[1] Ellen Graham, "The Entrepreneurial Mystique, Special Report on Small Business," *The Wall Street Journal*, p. 4C, May 20, 1985.

two findings, coupled with the findings on changing jobs, indicates that entrepreneurs are more likely to be displaced, unsettled, or between things. The need for achievement is evident in that entrepreneurs tend to begin their business activity while still in school, and most (76 percent) finish college. Overall, from both theoretical and empirical perspectives, entrepreneurs are a different breed of executive.

NEW VENTURE CREATION

It is the goal of almost every entrepreneur to start a new business someday. For the entrepreneur this challenge can lead to personal development and satisfaction as well as wealth, power, and status. Furthermore, in democratic capitalism the primary role of the entrepreneur is new venture creation. A healthy, thriving capitalist system needs new ventures for jobs, productive capacity, innovation, and creativity. It is a fact that while larger, older firms in steel, autos, and chemicals are slowing down and becoming smaller, new ventures in computers, services, robotics, and genetic engineering are creating jobs and growing.

The nucleus of the entrepreneur's attempt to create a new venture is the **business plan**. This is the document that describes the who, what, where, when, and how of the venture. The plan and the planning process serve a number of important functions. Primarily, the process of developing the business plan informs the entrepreneur of all the potential threats, opportunities, problems, and strengths facing his venture. It is an educational process. The entrepreneur, who may be a specialist in an area, must learn how to be a generalist and understand all of the factors which affect his creation. Even if events don't occur as the entrepreneur has envisioned, his responses are likely to be more effective if he has gone through the planning process and prepared himself for contingencies.

There are a number of other functions of the business plan. Few new creations arrive with munificent financing. One of the major barriers for the entrepreneur is raising the money for the venture. The business plan serves as the document that will help the entrepreneur finance the business. All potential sources of capital will want to familiarize themselves with the business plan before investing: friends, relatives, business associates, banks, small business investment companies, and venture capitalists. A highly stylized form of the business plan is the initial public offering prospectus which is required by the Securities and Exchange Commission when stock in a venture is sold to the public at large.

The elements of a business plan will vary from venture to

Table 14–2
Elements of a Comprehensive Business Plan

A. Entrepreneur's philosophy and goals	E. Form of Business
B. Venture's mission statement	1. Legal form
C. Strategy of the firm	2. Tax strategy
1. Entry wedges	F. Schedules
2. Generic strategy	1. Checklists of milestones
3. Strategic posture	2. Timetables
D. Feasibility of the venture	G. Key Executives
1. Market analysis and competition	1. Resumes
2. Location analysis	2. Compensation plans
3. Operations policies	
4. Personnel policies	
5. Financial projections and requirements	

venture but certain types of information are always (or should be) included. Table 14–2 provides an outline of a comprehensive business plan.

The elements outlined in Table 14–2 indicate the comprehensiveness needed for the business plan and the generalist qualities required of the entrepreneur who authors the plan. While much of the outline is self-explanatory, a few items dealing directly with the entrepreneurial nature of the venture plan need elaboration. These are the mission statement, the firm's strategies, and the feasibility study.

The mission statement describes the new venture's products and services, the markets to be served, and the technology which will be employed to (a) make the product and (b) deliver the product. This key element of the plan answers the question: "What business are we in?" This is not as trivial nor as simple as it may seem. The entrepreneur has a great deal of discretion in terms of product, market scope, and technological configuration. Consider an entrepreneur about to open a computer store. Questions that need to be answered include:

Will the store be retail, wholesale, mail-order shipping?

Computer hardware? Software? Both?

Established brand names? New innovative products?

Hobbyists? Home computers? Business applications?

The mission that promises to do everything for everyone will have as difficult a time succeeding as one where the market is defined so narrowly that there aren't enough customers to be profitable. In addition, a mission statement should include the nature of the entrepreneur's competitive advantage. It answers the question: "Why

Table 14–3
Entry Wedges

Wedge	Description
1. New Product	Invention or commercialization of previously unavailable product, service, or product type.
2. Parallel Competition	Entry into already established industry or market based on a minor variation of what is offered and/or how it is provided.
3. Franchise Entry	This employs a proven product or service without variation, but in a new geographical area under license.
4. Partial Momentum	Exploiting the momentum of established enterprises, e.g., by filling a suply shortage or tapping under-utilized resources.
5. Customer Sponsorship	Entering at the behest of the customer, e.g., with contract in hand or as a second source.
6. Parent Company Sponsorship	Creation of a new firm assisted by a larger firm with existing resources, e.g., joint venture, license agreement, or spin-off.
7. Government Sponsorship	Creation of a new firm at the behest of the government or to meet the government market, e.g., due to a favored purchasing agreement or a rule change (set aside).

Source: Karl M. Vesper. *New Venture Strategies*, (Englewood Cliffs, N.J.: Prentice-Hall Inc, 1980), pp. 176–204.

should anyone do business with us?" Again, this is not trivial and if no answer can be found, the potential entrepreneur may wish to re-evaluate his options.

The strategies of the firm describe how the mission will be accomplished. It answers the questions of how the business will be entered, how a sustainable, competitive strategy will be maintained, and what tactics will be employed to implement the strategy. This section details the strategic management of the new venture. While a complete analysis of strategic management is beyond our scope here, of special importance to the entrepreneur are the entry wedges used to overcome market entry barriers.

Entry wedges are the firm's initial advantages. Karl Vesper has developed a typology which includes three major competitive wedges—new products/services, parallel competition, franchising—and a number of partial wedges. Table 14–3 describes these strategies and Table 14–4 shows how they interrelate.[2]

[2] Karl M. Vesper, *New Venture Strategies* (Englewood Cliffs, N.J.: Prentice-Hall, Inc.,1980), pp. 176–233.

Table 14–4
Cross-referencing of Entry Wedges

| | Main Entry Wedges | | |
Other Entry Wedges	New Product or Service	Parallel Competition	Franchising
Exploiting Partial Momentum			
1. Geographical transfer			X
2. Supply shortage		X	
3. Tapping unutilized resources		X	
Customer Sponsorship			
4. Customer contract		X	
5. Becoming a second source		X	
Parent Company Sponsorship			
6. Joint ventures	X		
7. Licensing			X
8. Market relinquishment		X	
Governmental Sponsorship			
9. Favored purchasing		X	
10. Rule changes		X	

Source: Adapted from Karl M. Vesper, *New Venture Strategies* (Englewood Cliffs, N.J.: Prentice-Hall, Inc., 1980), p. 206.

SMALL BUSINESS OPERATIONS

Often, the fruit of entrepreneurial activity is the founding of a small business. After the entrepreneur has determined what business to be in and has developed a strategic plan of entry, he or she must focus on the operational aspects of running a small business enterprise. This requires a different set of skills and attitudes. Where once the entrepreneur could be a specialist in some area and be concerned with the big picture, now the details of running the firm are important and the entrepreneur must be a generalist, doing a little of everything.

Running the firm requires attention to the various functional activities of an enterprise: accounting and legal, personnel, finance, marketing and merchandising, manufacturing and engineering (operations), maintenance, and security. In larger firms, of course, each of these functions is executed by a departmental team of managers and employees. In the smaller firm, often the entrepreneur has only a manager or two to help him coordinate the entire operation.

We will briefly examine the major areas of responsibility for the entrepreneur in operating a small business. Within each functional area, the entrepreneur must be aware of how the activities affect the firm and how the functional areas work together. Most importantly, the entrepreneur needs to keep the firm's strategy clearly in focus and insure that lower—level operational decisions help to implement and achieve the overall strategy.

Accounting and Legal   The most important accounting decision the entrepreneur must make is which legal form of business to organize the firm. This choice will affect how accounting records are kept and how the firm will be taxed. The choices the entrepreneur has are: sole proprietorship, partnership, corporation, and subchapter S corporation.

The sole proprietorship is the simplest form of legal structure. It establishes the entrepreneur as owner and the profits of the business are passed through to the proprietor as ordinary income. The advantages of the sole proprietorship are:

It gives the entrepreneur total control.

It is easy to start and terminate.

All profits go to the owner.

There are the fewest government regulations and reporting requirements.

The disadvantages are:

The entrepreneur's personal assets are at risk if the small business has financial obligations that it cannot meet.

The ability to expand is limited due to financial and managerial limits.

The owner has no other interests looking out for the business.

The business terminates when the owner dies.

The partnership form of organization may be appropriate when there are two or more founders to the firm. Usually, a partnership agreement is executed among the principals, outlining the contributions, responsibilities, duties, and rights of the partners. The advantages of a partnership include:

Greater freedom for each partner while other partners "mind the store."

Greater possibilities to raise capital or receive a bank loan because of a larger capital base.

Each partner has special skills to contribute.

Partnership income is taxed as ordinary personal income.

Some disadvantages are:

All partners are subject to all the liabilities of the firm and each partner may incur business liabilities upon the other partners.

The partnership is terminated at the death of a partner.

The entrepreneur and each partner may disagree on how to run the business.

Many entrepreneurs choose the corporate form of legal structure for their firms. A corporation is a legal entity, like a person, endowed by law with rights, duties, and a legal life of its own. Corporations are taxed at different rates than individuals and, depending on the entrepreneur's other sources of income, rates may be higher or lower than the individual rates.

Advantages of the corporate form include:

Limited liability of the entrepreneur up to the amount invested in the corporation.

The corporation has a perpetual life and survives the entrepreneur, thus making possible family ownership and succession.

Corporations can raise capital by selling equity (stock) to increase financial flexibility.

The primary disadvantages of a corporation are:

Potential loss of managerial control if the entrepreneur sells stock to outside shareholders.

Increased reporting and regulatory requirements by all levels of government.

The last possibility for the entrepreneur is the subchapter S corporation. This type of organization is a corporation and has the advantages of one, but it is taxed as a partnership or sole proprietorship. It offers the benefits of limited liability and potentially lower tax rates. Shareholders can also offset subchapter S income (or losses) with losses (or income) from other sources.

The decision of which legal form to take should be made by the entrepreneur with counsel from an attorney and a tax accountant.

Personnel

If the small business is relatively large (maybe 75 employees or more), it may be big enough to have a personnel department and a personnel manager. Until the firm reaches sufficient size, the entrepreneur is the decision maker. The personnel responsibilities include staffing, the determination of salaries, wages, fringe benefits, training, job description, and performance appraisal. These activities together are known as human resource management (HRM). The proper execution of the personnel function in the small business is similar to that in larger firms and that information is covered elsewhere in this book. But there are some differences.

One major difference is the role of the entrepreneur. Entrepreneurs occasionally have trouble delegating responsibility and authority for getting the job done. Their tendency to do it all themselves, which was of paramount importance in starting the business, interferes with the normal delegation process once the business is operating. As a result, the supervisory style of the entrepreneur may be authoritarian and his assumptions Theory X. Many small businesses remain small because the owner can't let go and allow others to help make the business grow. Successful entrepreneurs learn they must enable and encourage others to do their jobs without interference.

The second major problem faced by smaller firms is the lack of career paths. Employees of smaller firms often find that because of the size of the firm, there are few opportunities for advancement and promotion. If a small firm grows, this problem may take care of itself. If the firm is stuck at a slow rate of growth, people without opportunities may seek employment elsewhere. This is unfortunate for the small business because recruiting, training, and developing good workers is an expensive and time consuming function. While it would be nice to say there is a solution, there really isn't. The consequences of high turnover in small firms can be mitigated, however, through job enrichment and job enlargement programs.

Finance

The entrepreneur must be the firm's chief financial officer (CFO) during the initial capital formation phase and often remains the CFO for the firm. In the simplest terms, the CFO is responsible for managing the balance between the sources and uses of funds. The objective of this balancing act is to provide the firm with enough capital to meet its needs and minimize the firm's cost of capital. These responsibilities include securing equity for the firm, arranging for short- and long-term debt financing, analyzing the financial statements, and making capital budgeting decisions.

Financial analysis of the small business is similar to that summarized in Chapter 12. However, the single most damaging factor in small business failure is undercapitalization. This means that the firm is always short of capital and is unable to obtain enough to meet its financial obligations and expand. Early bankruptcy is often caused by under-capitalization because the entrepreneur underestimates how much money it will take to bring the firm up to break even. Later bankruptcy may be caused by a firm's expanding too quickly, and trying to grow without proper financing. In either case, inadequate attention to the finance function can spell doom for a small business.

Marketing

Marketing consists of the purchase, merchandising, pricing, distribution, and selling of goods and services. It is *not* just sales. Sometimes the activities of marketing are characterized by the four "p's": product, price, place, and promotion. The entrepreneur, who may have exceptional skills as a promoter, needs to manage the active marketing function if the small business is to profit and grow. The discussion in Chapter 11 is particularly important to small business managers.

Operations

The management of operations is crucial. While all the previous managerial functions help the small firm operate efficiently and effectively, they are at the periphery of either production or service. The others are staff functions and their goal is to support operations. Operations is the line function—it makes the product or delivers the service. Operations is the technical core, the heart of the firm.

Unlike the staff functions of small business management, operations management and the management of the line require a particular orientation. The managemant of the operations of a small business depends almost completely on what kind of business it is. Accounting, marketing, finance, and personnel activities are each a bit different depending on the type of firm, but each has a universal set of techniques which can be applied to any type of small business. While Chapter 10 on operations management and production summarizes the universals, it doesn't teach how to manage or produce anything in particular. Only personal knowledge, experience, and on-the-job training can provide that. The small business owner/operator brings this knowledge to the firm if it is to be successful. Table 14–5 summarizes the most important topics to be considered when forming a new enterprise.

OUTSIDE ASSISTANCE

In many cases, "smallest" firms (under 10 employees) to "just-small" firms (between 100–250 employees) need expertise that lies outside the knowledge of the entrepreneur and his immediate com-

Table 14–5
Checklist of Small Business Operations

I. Accounting and Legal
_____ Form of organization (proprietorship, partnership, corporation)
_____ Tax treatment (Subchapter S)

II. Personnel
_____ Staffing
_____ Compensation
_____ Training and development
_____ Performance appraisal

III. Finance
_____ Sources of capital (debit and equity)
_____ Uses of capital (capital budgeting)
_____ Financial statements (balance sheet, income statement, cash flow statement)

IV. Marketing
_____ Product
_____ Price
_____ Place (location and channels)
_____ Promotion (advertising, publicity, point-of-purchase promotion, personal selling)

V. Operations
_____ Hands-on experience
_____ Close to the customer

pany. In the previous section, we encountered the problem of choosing a legal form of organization, and it was recommended that the entrepreneur seek the advice and counsel of an accountant and an attorney. These professionals can be thought of as external functional managers. An **external functional manager** is a person who doesn't belong to the small business organization but is hired (or volunteers) to offer counseling, consulting, or technical expertise.

In addition to accountants and lawyers, there are others who serve as external functional managers. Many of these professionals operate under the banner of consultant. Thus, there are personnel consultants, financial consultants, marketing and market-research consultants, and consulting engineers.

All of these areas have professional orientations and the consultants should be members of their respective professional organizations before they are employed. Professional certification is often a requirement before a consultant in a particular field can practice. Entrepreneurs are advised to check certification and references carefully before hiring a consultant. Furthermore, all paid consulting engagements should begin with a written proposal of the work to be done, a timetable, and a schedule of fees.

The use of hired external functional managers to augment the entrepreneur's technical sophistication is an expensive proposition.

There are other alternatives. Three of these are: establishing a board of directors, using government sponsored counseling, and networking with other entrepreneurs and small business owner-operators.

Large firms have boards of directors composed of people who have fiduciary and oversight responsibility for the management of the corporation. Many times managers are directors, but almost all corporations have outside directors, too. These outside directors are hired (large firms pay high directors' fees) from the pool of captains of industry, political figures and ex-office holders, and respected public servants.

Small businesses can also have boards of directors. For nominal fees, the small business owner-operator can create a board of knowledgeable experts who can help advise and manage the firm. Prospective candidates for a small business board would include: accountants, lawyers, bankers, Chamber of Commerce staff members, local political figures, college professors, and other business people in similar or related businesses. A motivated, skilled, and enthusiastic board can provide the small business with insights, technical expertise, and perspectives that are hidden to the entrepreneur. It also generates valuable goodwill among important local community leaders.

There are also a number of government-sponsored programs designed to offer management counseling and assistance to small businesses. The federal government has three such programs originating from the Small Business Administration: the Small Business Development Center (SBDC), the Small Business Institute (SBI), and the Service Corps of Retired Executives (SCORE). The SBDC can offer the services of management consultants on a short-term basis as well as offering seminars and market-research information. The SBI program uses teams of senior-level business students to work on a semester long project in cooperation with the entrepreneur. SCORE is a voluntary organization composed of retired executives who can offer advice and the benefit of their years of experience to help the small business owner-operator solve problems.

Networking is a term used to refer to making business contacts, finding common problem areas, and offering support to people within the network. For the entrepreneur, networking can be a source of technical and managerial assistance, as well as emotional support. Networks can be built from Chamber of Commerce committees, church groups, philanthropic organizations, and local political activity. By meeting people from different parts of the business environment and cultivating these people as advisors and confidants, the entrepreneur can create a team of external advisors for his small business.

CORPORATE ENTREPRENEURSHIP

So far we have discussed entrepreneurship and entrepreneurs in the context of new venture creation. Recently, however, the importance of entrepreneurship has been recognized within the corporate environment. Corporate entrepreneurship can be defined as the development of new products, services, and innovative technology within a large, mature organization. Sometimes this is referred to as **intrapreneurship** indicating that the activity takes place within an existing business.

In the corporate environment, entrepreneurship is not an all-or-nothing phenomenon. Parts of the corporation may be mature, stable, and oriented toward professional administrative management; however, other parts of the firm, new product development groups, venture teams, applied research task forces, may be quite entrepreneurial. These parts of the firm possess the entrepreneurial mindset and try to recreate for the corporation the environment that stimulates innovation and creativity. The entrepreneur's thought patterns define the entrepreneurial process by asking the following questions[3]:

1. *Where is the opportunity?* Entrepreneurial teams are sensitive to changes in market conditions and buyer preferences. They monitor improvements in product manufacturing technology and product quality characteristics. These teams are empowered by the corporation to take political action to mobilize the firm.

2. *How can we take advantage?* The action-oriented venture group must be able to act quickly to gain an advantage once opportunities are identified. These groups are risk-takers. Corporations must be willing to tolerate and accept failure since many, if not most, products never prove to be commercially successful. But the payoffs can be large, too. Members of venture groups understand that their jobs are not on the line with every risk they take.

3. *What resources do we need?* Entrepreneurial teams make imaginative use of limited resources. They *borrow* people, equipment, material, and money from other parts of the corporation where these resources exist. Project development for venture groups is a multistage process. Commitment of major resources may be appropriate only as progress to commercialization is made.

4. *How do we control our resources?* When entrepreneurial groups receive their *borrowed* and formal appropriations from the firm, the emphasis is on the results that can be obtained. This allows the new venture team more flexibility in how to use their resources. Since the team has limited resources and may exist on a temporary basis,

---

[3] Howard H. Stevenson and David E. Gumpert, "The Heart of Entrepreneurship," *Harvard Business Review* (March–April 1985), pp. 85–94.

entrepreneurs avoid owning equipment or hiring people. This is valuable because the teams can have greater resource specialization (they can get exactly what they need) and avoid the risk of obsolescence.

5. *What structure is best?* Entrepreneurs within a large corporation prefer a flat organizational structure with multiple lateral networks. These lateral networks are groups of colleagues who can help the entrepreneurs get things done. They facilitate coordination and provide a buffer between the administration's need for stability, hierarchy and orders, and the entrepreneur's challenge to hierarchy and desire for independence.

CONCLUSIONS   Bernard A. Goldhirsch, publisher of *Inc.* and *High Technology Magazines*, has said that an "entrepreneurial revolution is taking place."

> It has come into being because society has come to recognize the value, importance, and productivity of the entrepreneurial business unit. The awesome capabilities of small to mid-sized companies to adapt to changes, to bring new products to market, to generate jobs and to create wealth has been recognized.[4]

Goldhirsch gives a number of reasons for this revolution. The rise of two-family incomes in the under-50 age bracket has created accumulated capital which enables one of the partners to go out and take a risk. The shift to a service economy poses low capital requirements for small but emerging growth industries. Furthermore, college graduates are redefining the relationship between work, risk, and fulfillment. He notes that college graduates are thinking in terms of risk and the entrepreneur alternative looks more and more promising.

REFERENCES

COHEN, WILLIAM S., *The Entrepreneur and Small Business Problem Solver.* New York: Ronald Press, 1983.

Directory of Small Business Investment Companies, 1981. U.S. Small Business Administration, P.O. Box 15434, Ft. Worth Texas 76119.

DRUCKER, PETER F., *Innovation and Entrepreneurship.* New York: Harper and Row, Publishers, Inc., 1985.

[4] Bernard A. Goldhirsch, speaking to the Advertising Club of Pittsburgh, Penn., in "Notable and Quotable," *The Wall Street Journal*, June 17, 1985.

GUMPERT, DAVID E. and JEFFREY A. TIMMONS, *The Encyclopedia of Small Business Resources*, Harper and Row Publishers, Inc.: New York, 1982.

Inc. Magazine, 38 Commercial Wharf, Boston Mass. 02110, published by Inc. Publishing Corp. 1642 Westwood Blvd. Los Angelos, Cal. 90024.

JONES, SEYMOUR, and M. BRUCE COHEN, *The Emerging Business*. New York: Ronald Press, 1983.

Journal of Small Business Management, Bureau of Business Research, West Virginia University, P.O. Box 6025, Morgantown, West Va. 26506.

KENT, CALVIN A., DONALD L. SEXTON, KARL H. VESPER, *Encyclopedia of Entrepreneurship*. Englewood Clffs, N.J.: Prentice-Hall, 1982.

MCCLELLAND, DAVID C., *The Achieving Society*, Princeton: D. Van Nostrand, 1961.

TIMMONS, J. A., L. E. SMOLLEN, A. L. DINGEE, *New Venture Creation: A Guide to Small Business Development*, 2nd ed., Homewood, Ill.: Richard D. Irwin, Inc., 1985.

Venture Magazine, 35 West 45th Street, New York, N.Y. 10036.

VESPER, KARL H., *New Venture Strategies*. Englewood Cliffs, N.J.: Prentice-Hall, Inc., 1980.

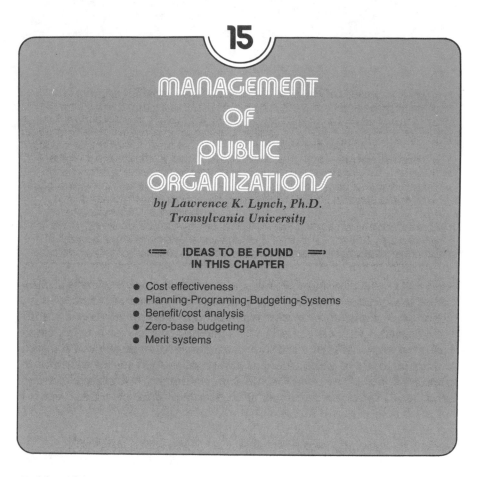

15

MANAGEMENT OF PUBLIC ORGANIZATIONS

by Lawrence K. Lynch, Ph.D.
Transylvania University

⟸ **IDEAS TO BE FOUND** ⟹
IN THIS CHAPTER

- Cost effectiveness
- Planning-Programing-Budgeting-Systems
- Benefit/cost analysis
- Zero-base budgeting
- Merit systems

Public administration—management of public organizations—emphasizes goals which differ significantly from the goals emphasized by business organizations. The functions and disciplines of management described in earlier chapters apply to both private and public organizations, but have some unique orientations in the public sector because of problems created by this difference in goal emphasis.

Recall that business firms primarily seek to earn profits, although they have other goals such as growth, stability, and public service. Public organizations have public service as their primary goal, with efficiency (and perhaps growth) as secondary goals. Public organizations include federal, state, and local government agencies, school systems, public colleges and universities, and "independent" quasi-governmental agencies such as the Postal Service, the Tennessee Valley Authority, and the Federal Reserve System.

The work of early management scholars, especially Henri Fayol, was adopted by public administrators in the 1930s, largely through the work of Luther Gulick, who coined the acronym POSDCORB to describe the critical functions performed by administrators (planning, organizing, staffing, directing, coordinating, reporting, and budgeting). More recent developments in public sector management include the introduction of "cost effectiveness" analysis in the Department of Defense by Robert McNamara under President Kennedy, the adoption Planning-Programing-Budgeting-Systems (PPBS) by the federal government in the Johnson Administration, and the requirement for Management by Objectives imposed on federal agencies by the Nixon Administration. The influence of each of those planning tools which will be discussed further below, has peaked and declined, but each has left its mark on the way public administrators think. The newest decision-making technique is zero-base budgeting, which was introduced by the Carter Administration.

GOALS AND MEASUREMENT

Business firms have one tremendous advantage over public organizations: it is easy to *measure* profits. Public organizations, for which the major goals must be articulated in phrases such as "reduce crime," "improve public health," "protect the country from nuclear attack," and "issue Social Security checks to all qualified people," have a much harder time in measuring goal attainment.

The fundamental goal of any public organization is a legislatively prescribed impact on society, or on some subpopulation of society. Some quantitative measures of impacts have been developed (such as number of crimes in different categories, numbers and percentages of people with various diseases, retaliatory nuclear response in terms of estimated "megadeaths," or family income levels), but all suffer from imprecision of measurement due to sampling and reporting problems. Moreover, society changes over time for a number of reasons, and the impact of change due to a particular government program is often difficult to identify. As one example, suppose the number of violent crimes in a particular city declines from 3500 in 1976 to 3000 in 1977. What portion of the decline is due to the efforts of police? to a new psychological counseling program? to improving economic conditions? to the weather?

Because societal impacts of public programs are difficult to measure, these impacts, or "external goals," are often transformed into easier-to-measure internal goals. These internal goals may be classed as output goals or input goals. **Output goals** relate to the products of some governmental unit; examples are "pieces of first-class mail delivered," "number of Social Security checks written," "number of clients visited," or "number of reports produced." **Input goals** include numbers of manhours spent on a particular program, equipment purchased, or funds expended. Educators, for example, often use expenditures per pupil as a measure of the quality of education.

Measurement of internal goals is a poor substitute for measurement of an agency's impact on society. As we shall see, however, even accurate measurement of external goals does not solve the problem of allocating government resources among agencies or programs.

POLICY MAKING

Strategic planning, or deciding on broad courses of action, is termed **policy making**, and is, in theory, performed by the legislative branch of government. In practice, however, senior public administrators from the executive branch also make policy: in the first place, they draft legislation and press for its enactment; and secondly, they fill in gaps in legislation through **administrative regulations**. While such regulations are supposed merely to implement the intent of the legislation, they often create new policy, and take the agency in directions never anticipated by the legislators.

The judicial branch of government also makes policy—through court decisions which strike down legislation, require modification of legislation, or even imply the need for new legislation. For example, the famous U.S. Supreme Court *Brown* vs. *Board of Education* decision, in which racial segregation in public schools was found unconstitutional, has led to major civil rights legislation at both the national and state levels. Just as U.S. Supreme Court decisions make policy at the national level, state highcourt decisions make policy for states.

The importance of policy making in the executive branch has recently led to the development of *policy analysis* as a high-level administrative activity. A **policy analyst** looks for conflicts among different policies and applies various analytical tools to determine the impact and value to society of alternative policies. Policy impacts are often assessed through the use of sophisticated economic and social forecasting tools.

One such tool is the **econometric model**, a highly complex system of hundreds of equations used to predict economic conditions for each of several policy alternatives and several sets of assumptions about the behavior of businesspeople and consumers. The assumptions are called *exogenous variables*; the variables produced by the model are called *endogenous variables*. For example, the effects of a tax cut policy versus a public works program on employment and Gross National Product might be forecast. Or the demands created by a national health insurance program for additional health personnel might be predicted, along with the additional needs for federal and state spending on education. These simulations provide data from which a policy decision may be made.

The **Delphi Technique** is a behavioral tool in which a panel of experts is asked for a prediction of the implications or effects of some policy, frequently termed a *scenario*. Sometimes each expert develops several scenarios, based upon different assumptions about society's behavior. The experts are kept separate from one another to eliminate group social pressures. After each expert has given a scenario, or scenarios, the results are compiled and sent to the other participants, who are asked to revise or maintain their predictions in the light of the others' opinions. The process is repeated several times until a consensus is reached. The consensus may reflect agreement on a single policy or agreement on a set of policy alternatives. An example of the use of Delphi was that by the National Institute of Drug Abuse when it commissioned a study to develop a range of policy options for drug-abuse control.[1]

Another influence on policy making comes from lobbyists, paid representatives of business, labor, and, more recently, consumer and public interest groups, who attempt to influence the content of both legislation and administrative regulations. A recent and continuing example of lobbying at the federal level has been in connection with automobile air pollution standards. Environmental lobbyists have argued for more stringent standards to be applied at earlier dates, while the auto industry has pressed for relaxed standards and delays in implementation. The severe economic recession of 1974–75 and conflicts between energy policies and environmental targets led to some victories for the automobile industry in delaying the imposition of standards from the late 1970s into the 1980s.

Planning is hierarchical in government as well as in business. The narrowest goals and policies established at one level of government become the broad goals for the next lowest level—which in turn develops its narrower goals and operational plans.

PLANNING AND DECISION MAKING   The disciplines of managerial economics and accounting, quantitative methods, and computer technology are now widely used in government as well as business. Because of the difficulty in quantify-

---

[1] I.A. Jillson, "The National Drug-Abuse Policy Delphi: Progress Report and Findings to Date," in H. A. Linstone and M. Turoff, eds., *The Delphi Method: Techniques and Applications* (Reading, Mass.: Addison-Wesley Publishing Company, 1975).

ing public sector goals, certain specialized technologies—which make use of the disciplines—have been developed for government.

Cost effectiveness analysis, imposed by Defense Secretary Robert McNamara on the Department of Defense in the early 1960s, attempts to compare alternative approaches to goal attainment by measuring the impact per dollar spent on each alternative. In order to make such comparisons, common measures of goals must first be developed. For example, suppose you are considering the alternatives of intercontinental ballistic missiles or long-range bombers for a nuclear "second strike" capability. The common measure for each of the two alternatives might be numbers of enemy deaths, and the estimated deaths for each alternative would be divided by the cost of the alternative to determine which was most cost effective. Obviously, if you measured enemy deaths for one alternative and number of factories destroyed for the other, you couldn't directly compare their cost effectiveness. Actual military planning uses many measures of effectiveness, and actual alternatives are based upon complex mathematical models which simulate the effects of various combinations of weapons, delivery systems, and personnel; but the essence of cost-effectiveness analysis is to determine which alternative provides a given level of goal attainment at the least cost.

Management by objectives (MBO) was used as a planning and control tool by the Nixon Administration, and has been implemented in many state government agencies. MBO emphasizes the control function: Administrators are held accountable for achieving the goals they themselves established. Suppose you are the Director of a state Occupational Safety and Health Program; you might establish the following goals for your program and yourself for a one-year period:

1. Perform 500 factory inspections (an increase of 10 percent over the previous year) with no additional staff.
2. Hold six informational workshops for businesspeople in each of six principal cities of the state.
3. Reduce the accident rate in each industry to specified levels.
4. Read at least 20 technical articles related to occupational safety and health (a self-improvement objective).

The abbreviated list of objectives contains two output objectives, one impact objective, and one input objective. All of the objectives are measurable, however, and you as the Director could be held accountable for achieving them. Note that there is no quality dimension to objectives 1 and 2—the inspections could be cursory, the workshops dull. If the achievement of objectives 1 and 2 were at the expense of quality, however, it is doubtful that the third objective could be accomplished.

Planning-Programing-Budgeting-Systems (PPBS) are extensions and refinements of cost-effectiveness analysis, in which each governmental activity is evaluated according to what it accomplishes for a given expenditure. In PPBS, governmental functions are classified into a hierarchy of programs, subprograms, activities, and subactivities, which may or may not correspond to the organization of government. For example, C. West Churchman describes A. H. Schainblatt's case of a state government alcoholism program, in which 13 different state agencies participate.[2] Goals are defined for each level of the hierarchy, and goal attainment per dollar spent is the measure of activity and program value. One subprogram in an alcoholism program might be rehabilitation, and the agencies which participate and their activities might include:

1. The courts, which either jail or fine those arrested for alcohol-related offenses (such as drunken driving).
2. A state social agency, which provides counseling to those arrested, as well as to those who seek aid.
3. A state hospital, where people may go or be sent for "drying out."

A PPBS system would attempt to determine the combinations of those agencies and activities which would provide the maximum number of rehabilitated cases at the lowest cost.

Although PPBS is useful in evaluating alternative approaches to attaining the same goals within a single program, it is less useful for comparing programs themselves. How can you compare the impact per dollar spent on higher education with the impact of spending on criminal justice, for example, when their goals are measured in different terms? The answer provided by PPBS is that such a comparison—and the resulting allocation of funds among programs—is a political decision, not subject to the rational approach of PPBS.

The overlapping of programs and agencies in PPBS provides difficulties for governmental accounting. Traditionally, each agency recommends a budget with **line items** for each staff member's salary, for each item of equipment, and for each type of supply, for each classification of travel, and for each capital expenditure. In PPBS, staff members from several agencies may spend part of their time on a given program, so program budgeting must allocate agency expenditures among programs. (Although some proponents of PPBS have argued that government should be reorganized so that agencies coincide with programs, this has proved unfeasible, because programs

---

[2] C. West Churchman, *The Systems Approach* (New York: Dell Publishing Company, 1968).

change much more rapidly than agencies could be reorganized.) Thus two budgets must be created when PPBS is used: a line item budget and a program budget, with **crosswalks** to explain which parts of which line-items appear in each program, and vice versa. Figure 15–1 illustrates the crosswalking problem for a case where five departments from two agencies each contribute time and other resources to a single subactivity.

When President Johnson ordered federal agencies to adopt PPBS, it was also embraced by several state governments and even some cities. But because of the extra paperwork required of the executive branch by PPBS, the need for elaborate information systems to provide feedback on goal attainment, and the difficulty that some legislators experienced in following the crosswalks, PPBS has decreased in popularity in recent years.

Benefit/cost analysis is an economic technique used to evaluate individual projects as well as to decide among alternatives. It is used mainly in the Department of Defense and water resources projects, but has been experimentally applied to programs in education, transportation, and environmental protection. Each of the products and services, or "benefits," of a public program or project is measured in terms of its dollar value to society for each year of the project's proposed or expected life. Benefits are summed for each year, then discounted to present value and divided by total project cost. If the resulting benefit/cost ratio exceeds unity, the project is considered worthwhile. If sufficient resources are not available to fund all worthwhile projects, those with the highest benefit/cost ratios are funded.

As an example, suppose the U.S. Army Corps of Engineers proposes a dam which will provide flood control and recreation benefits. Flood control benefits are measured by comparing the monetary value of actual flood damages done in the past with the reduced value of damages expected if the dam is built. Recreation benefits are measured by multiplying the number of expected visitors to the lake created by the dam times some value for each visit (and netting out the value of former recreation visits to the river). These benefits, expressed in dollars, are projected for each year of the dam's expected life and discounted to present value by formula:

$$PV = \sum_{i=1}^{N} \frac{Bi}{(1 + r)^i}$$

where Bi is the annual benefits in year i, and r is the interest rate. The present value is then divided by total project costs to obtain the

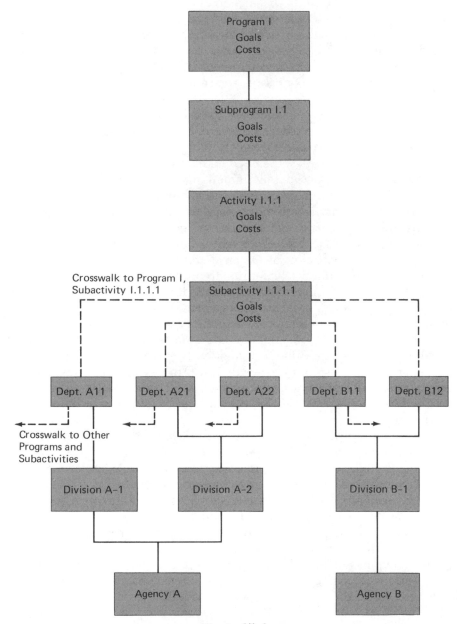

Figure 15–1
Crosswalking in PPBS

benefit/cost ratio. If the ratio exceeds unity, the present value of benefits exceeds the present value of costs, and the project is considered worthwhile.

The interest rate is a subject of much controversy in benefit/cost analysis. A lower rate results in a higher present value of benefits, and a higher benefit/cost ratio. Some people argue that a high rate, such as the rate of profit earned by corporations, should be used, so that investment in a public project will not be justified unless it provides the same "return," in terms of benefits, as private investments do in terms of profits. Others argue that public investments should not be evaluated on the same basis as private investments, and that a lower rate, such as the rate of interest paid on government bonds, should be used. The latter view has prevailed to date.

Zero-base budgeting (ZBB), developed as a governmental accounting and planning tool, was adopted by both governments and businesses under the impetus of the Carter Administration.[3] Each "decision unit" (generally an administrative unit large enough to have its own budget) develops a "decision package": a set of alternative combinations of activities designed to meet the unit's objectives. Each combination represents a different level of effort and funding, beginning with a minimum level—which is funded at an amount *below* the current budget. Each other element in the decision package includes one or more increments to the minimum level, and is ranked according to its perceived importance.

Information on objectives, activities, costs and benefits, and workload and performance measures is provided by the decision unit for each element in the decision package. Higher-level administrators can then decide (1) whether the benefits of the minimum level justify any funding whatever for the decision unit, and (2) which increments, if any, are justified. The ranking of increments provides a straightforward way of adding or deleting activities if the available budget funds increase or decrease.

Suppose, for example, that you have just made your final monthly car payment of $139.50. Your car is now four years old and in bad shape. You, as the decision unit, establish the following decision package:

1. Buy a stripped-down version of an inexpensive car. After trade-in allowance, your monthly payment will be $109.75 (below your current level of expenditures).
2. Buy the inexpensive car, but add some luxury options such as air-conditioning and a stereo radio. This would require a monthly payment of $139.50 (your current level of expenditure).
3. Buy a more expensive car, but without luxury options, at a monthly cost of 159.50.

[3] The discussion which follows is adapted from Peter A. Pyhrr, "The Zero-Base Approach to Government Budgeting," *Public Administration Review*, vol. 37, no. 1 (January/February 1977), pp. 1–8.

4. Buy a more expensive car, with options, at a monthly cost of $179.50.

The first decision to be made—the zero-base decision—is whether to buy a car at all. Do you need a car for basic transportation (the minimum benefit level)? Then you must decide what increments to the basic package are justified by their additional benefits in such terms as comfort, entertainment, and prestige. Your decision might be partially based on whether or not you get a raise (i.e., whether available budget funds increase).

Zero-base budgeting requires that each decision unit justify its very existence in each **budget cycle** (usually a fiscal year; in some state governments, there is a two-year budget cycle). Traditionally, administrators only had to justify additions to their previous budget. ZBB requires a great deal of analysis, communication, and paperwork, however; and many bureaucrats feel threatened by its implications. (The added paperwork is a major cost that can be analyzed using benefit-cost analysis for deciding whether ZBB is worthwhile).

Table 15–1 summarizes the main characteristics and disciplinary foundations of the policy and planning tools we have discussed.

CONTROLLING AND ORGANIZING

Each of the planning and decision-making tools outlined above has implications for control, because each requires the setting of goals or objectives which can later be compared with what actually happens. Because of the measurement problem faced by government, however, it is sometimes difficult to determine the extent to which goals were achieved in a given period. Thus a public administrator can elude effective control more easily than can a business manager.

Although *effective* control—seeing that an agency's objectives are achieved—can be eluded by a public administrator, public organizations are generally laden with *procedural* controls. The history of public administration is filled with examples of the misuse of public funds; hence along with the professionalization of administration which began in the late nineteenth century has come an ever-tighter system of controlling public expenditures. Moreover, procedural controls have often been extended to all activities of public agencies—not merely those directly involved with spending money. Thus elaborate systems of internal review have developed in many public agencies, which often unnecessarily delay needed action.

These procedural controls are facilitated by an intensely steep hierarchical organizational structure in public agencies. That is, there

Table 15-1
Policy and Planning Techniques Used in Management
of Public Organizations

Technique	Management Function(s)	Disciplinary Foundation(s)	Key Elements
Econometric Modeling	Policy making	Macroeconomics	Many equations; endogenous and exogenous variables; effects of policy alternatives.
Delphi	Policy making	Behavioral science	Panel of experts; independent judgments (scenarios); revision of judgments; consensus or set of policy options
Cost Effectiveness	Planning and decision making	Microeconomics, quantitative methods	Alternative approaches to reaching a common goal; impact per dollar spent
Management by Objectives	Planning and controlling	Behavioral science, information systems	Quantification of goals; self-determination of goals; accountability
Planning-Programming-Budgeting-Systems (PPBS)	Planning, decision making, and controlling	Managerial accounting, economics, and information systems	Programs and activities; measures of effectiveness (impact, output, input); crosswalks
Benefit/Cost Analysis	Planning and decision making	Microeconomics	Project, dollar measures of project benefits; discounting and discount rate; costs; benefit/cost ratio
Zero-Base Budgeting (ZBB)	Planning and decision making	Managerial accounting, economics	Decision unit; decision package; minimum level; increments; budget cycle

are many levels in the hierarchy, and thus many "officials." Actions proposed by occupants of lower "slots" in the organization must often be approved and/or modified and forwarded by officials at each higher level—until either the orginal idea is lost, or final approval comes too late.

Another problem created by the highly bureaucratic form of government organization is the tendency to treat clients as objects rather than people. Hummell[4] presents an illustration of a new-car

[4] Ralph P. Hummell, *The Bureaucratic Experience* (New York: St. Martins Press, 1977).

buyer attempting to register his vehicle and discovering he lacks a necessary form. As he is shunted about from office to office, his feelings of pride and status turn into anger and frustration.

Nevertheless, bureaucracy is a rational system for accomplishing group objectives and is necessary in both public and private organizations. It attempts to substitute efficiency, scientific reasoning, and value-neutrality for individual whim. Max Weber himself was aware of the dangers of bureaucracy—the tendency for controls rather than objectives to become the administrator's ends, and the dehumanizing both of members of the bureaucracy and of clients.[5]

These problems of bureaucracy are present in any large organization, whether in government or in business, but are probably more severe in government agencies. Why does government seem to succumb to the ills of bureaucracy more than the private sector? Again we return to the measurement of objectives. It is far easier in government to measure compliance with procedures than achievement of societal objectives.

Because of the cumbersomeness of established bureaucracies, newly elected officials often use *reorganization* as a way to reassert executive control over government. Another approach is to simply create a new agency to achieve an executive's objectives, bypassing an existing bureaucracy. For example, Richard Nixon was criticized for encouraging Henry Kissinger and his staff to bypass the State Department in conducting U.S. foreign policy (before Kissinger was made Secretary of State).

STAFFING AND DIRECTING

Government personnel include elected officials, appointees, and professionals or "civil servants." Professionals are usually covered by some kind of **merit system**, which is set of procedures for hiring, promoting, and discharging employees based upon professional rather than political criteria. Appointees generally serve at the pleasure of an elected official, or are appointed for a fixed term. Elected officials may or may not be legally limited to one or two terms.

Relationships among these three groups are sometimes difficult. Elected officials and their appointees have objectives which may be thwarted by a civil service resentful of change. On the other hand, civil servants object to "political" appointees with little technical knowledge of an agency's activities.

Staffing governmental agencies has three major difficulties. First,

[5] Max Weber, *The Theory of Social and Economic Organizations* (New York: The Free Press of Glencoe, 1964; first copyright, 1947).

existing merit system staff, because of merit system rules, cannot simply be replaced, so officials can only install "their" people in non-merit "slots," generally at the highest levels of an agency. Second, recruitment of new staff must follow detailed procedures, established to prevent favoritism. Often, competitive examinations are required, and/or applicants may be screened by a separate personnel agency. Third, salary levels in government are usually below comparable salaries in the private sector, so top-quality people are hard to recruit. (This is less true in the federal government than in state and local governments—but at the highest levels of management, even in the federal government, pay is lower than in the private sector.)

The contingency theory of leadership—the idea that the correct leadership style depends upon the characteristics of the leader, the subordinate, and the situation—applies to public as well as private organizations. The situation in government, however, is often (although not always) characterized by routine performance of highly structural tasks in an evironment of strict rules and regulations. Partly because of this situation, the people attracted to government service tend to be motivated more by security than by the need to innovate. Thus the prevalent leadership style in public organizations is directive rather than permissive.

Government employees must be motivated almost entirely without financial incentives, because salaries and promotions are subject to strict procedural controls. Bonus systems are almost never possible, for example. Thus employers must be either self-motivated (through achievement, affiliation, or power rewards inherent in the job) or motivated with nonfinancial rewards such as praise or increased responsibility. Herzberg's job enrichment concept may prove to be very useful in government—although the steep hierarchy and detailed procedural controls often found in government bureaucracies make job enrichment problematic.

The growing movement toward unionizing merit system employees in government adds a countervailing bureaucracy to existing bureaucratic problems. Although unionization could lead to higher salaries for government workers, thus making recruiting easier, it will not ease the structural rigidities of government bureaucracy—on the contrary, it will probably intensify them.

One promising development, however, is **productivity bargaining**, in which public employees agree to new, more efficient production technologies or increased output in exchange for higher wages or better fringe benefits. Productivity bargaining is most applicable in the delivery of services such as garbage collection, road maintenance, rapid transit, and police and fire protection, where measurement of

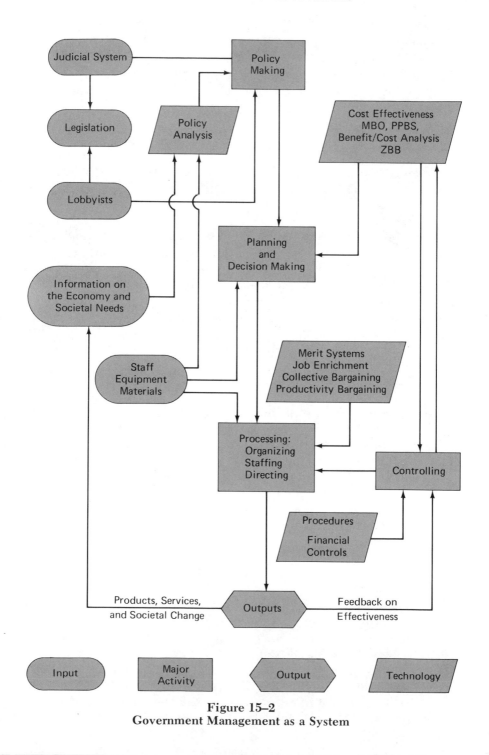

Figure 15–2
Government Management as a System

output per unit of input is clear-cut. It has been most widely used by municipal governments.

GOVERNMENT MANAGEMENT AS A SYSTEM

Figure 15–2 draws together much of the preceeding discussion and illustrates how government can be viewed as a system which takes internal and external inputs and uses various technologies to process them into outputs for society. (A technology is a way of doing something. It may be facilitating or constraining. Figure 15–2 focuses on management technologies rather than production technologies.)

The major activities of government are viewed as (1) policymaking, which combines external inputs of information about society, lobbying, legislation, and court decisions with internal staff inputs, and operates through the technology of policy analysis; (2) planning and decision making, which uses many of the technologies described in this chapter to define objectives and alternative ways to accomplish the objectives; (3) processing, which includes organizing, staffing, and directing and which is aided by the technologies of productivity bargaining and job enrichment and constrained by bureaucratic structure, merit systems, and collective bargaining; and (4) controlling, which also makes use of the technologies of planning as well as procedural and financial controls.

The essentials of management apply to public as well as private organizations. Because of the different kinds of goals emphasized by government organizations, however, and because of certain unique constraints on measuring objectives, organizing, and motivating employees, government managers have developed specialized technologies and adapted other technologies used in the private sector. Still, like any organization, a government agency must ultimately produce a product or service that is valued by society.

The penalty for not producing an output valued by society is extinction. In the private sector, declining profits are a signal of unsatisfactory performance. If performance does not improve, the firm will exhaust its financial resources and go bankrupt. In the public sector, the signals of poor performance are less clear and slower to be perceived. Eventually, however, a public agency which does not perform will be denied funding—the equivalent of bankruptcy.

REFERENCES

THE AMERICAN ACADEMY OF POLITICAL AND SOCIAL SCIENCE, *Theory and Practices of Public Administration: Scope, Objectives and Methods.* Monograph 8. Philadelphia: The Academy, 1968.

Anthony, R.N. and David Young, *Management Control in Nonprofit Organizations*, Homewood, Ill. R. D. Irwin, Inc., 1984.

Buchele, Robert B., *The Management of Business and Public Organizations*. New York: McGraw-Hill Book Company, Inc., 1977.

Buchholz, Rogene A, Essentials of *Public Policy for Management*. Englewood Cliffs, N.J., Prentice-Hall, Inc., 1985.

Gulick L., and L. Urwick, eds., *Papers on the Science of Administration*. New York: Augustus M. Keeley, 1937.

McCurdy, Howard E, *Public Administration: A Synthesis*. Menlo Park, Calif.: Cummings Publishing Company, 1977.

Sharkanski, Ira, *Public Administration*. Chicago: Markham Publishing Company, 1972.

Starling, Grover, *Managing the Public Sector*. Homewood, Ill.: The Dorsey Press, 1977.

Waldo, Dwight, ed., *Public Administration in a Time of Turbulance*. Scranton, Pa.: Chandler Publishing Company, 1971.

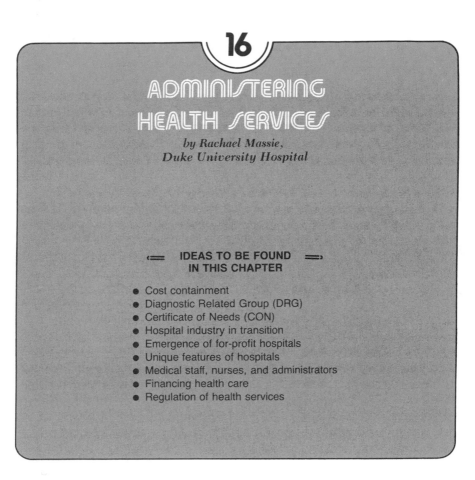

16

ADMINISTERING HEALTH SERVICES

*by Rachael Massie,
Duke University Hospital*

⇐ **IDEAS TO BE FOUND** ⇒
IN THIS CHAPTER

- Cost containment
- Diagnostic Related Group (DRG)
- Certificate of Needs (CON)
- Hospital industry in transition
- Emergence of for-profit hospitals
- Unique features of hospitals
- Medical staff, nurses, and administrators
- Financing health care
- Regulation of health services

Health care delivery in the United States is a large, unique industry, and one that is in transition. Health care is provided in a number of settings—physicians' offices, dentists' offices, local health departments, urgi-care centers, health maintenance organizations, and home health agencies. The hospital, however, is the most intricate setting and is "the institutional center of the health care delivery system."[1] This chapter will focus on the factors that make the administration of hospitals a complex and challenging field for management.

<table>
<tr><td>**MAGNITUDE
OF THE INDUSTRY**</td><td>The health services industry has grown significantly over the past several decades. In 1983, health</td></tr>
</table>

care expenditures totalled $355.4 billion, accounting for 10.8 percent of the Gross National Product (GNP). This translates into an annual expenditure of $1,459 for every man, woman, and child in the United

[1] Steven Jonas, *Health Care Delivery in the United States*, 2nd ed. (New York: Springer Publishing Co., 1981), p. 169.

States. Forty-one percent of these expenditures were for hospital care. The number of people employed in the health care industry in 1983 was 7.9 million; of these, 4.3 million were employed by hospitals.[2]

Types of Hospitals   There are over 6,700 hospitals in the United States; of these 6,100 are short-stay, general hospitals, the type of community facility that is typically thought of as a "hospital." But hospitals vary a great deal in size, average length of stay, type of specialty care proveded, ownership, and teaching affiliation. Although all hospitals have much in common, specific management problems vary according to the type of hospital.

Size of Hospital   Hospital size refers to the number of beds available for patients. A hospital in a small, rural community may have as few as 50 beds; a hospital in a metropolitan area or an academic medical center may have in excess of 1,000 beds. The typical community hospital has 200 to 300 beds.

Length of Stay   Length of stay may be short-stay, where the average number of days the patient spends in the hospital is less than 30 days, or long-term, where the average length of stay is longer than 30 days. Most long-term hospitals are psychiatric or rehabilitation centers; a few are for treatment of tuberculosis or other respiratory ailments.

Type of Specialty Care Provided   The majority of hospitals are general hospitals where a full range of inpatient medical and surgical treatment is provided. Outpatient care may also be available in emergency departments and clinics. Some hospitals offer only specialized care, such as orthopedic, pediatric, obstetrical, or psychiatric.

Ownership   Ownership may be public (federal, state, or local government) or private (not-for-profit or proprietary.) Because of their service tradition, most hospitals originated as and remain not-for-profit, community-owned institutions, many are church affiliated. However, in the past few decades, for-profit hospitals have emerged, and some not-for-profit hospitals have developed for-profit subsidiaries. Some community-owned hospitals are being purchased by for-profit hospital chains.

Teaching Affiliation   A number of community hospitals are affiliated with training programs for physicians, nurses, or other health care givers. Some hospitals are academic medical centers,

[2] *Health United States* (Department of Health and Human Services, 1984).

owned by state or private universities where education and research as well as health care are primary goals.

SOCIAL HISTORY AND TRADITIONS

More and more hospitals are coming to be thought of and to be managed as businesses. In the past, however, hospitals were largely social institutions, and their social history and service orientation continue to influence them today. During the Roman Empire, the Christian belief in obligation to care for the sick and needy extended to the whole community, and early hospitals flourished as social service centers for the sick, the poor, and the religious pilgrim. Only the rudiments of nursing care were provided. Even after many hospitals changed to secular hands and public philanthropy during the Renaissance the hospital's philosophy remained one of social service. Hospitals were where the aged, mentally incompetent, crippled, or orphaned were kept. The sick who were not poor were cared for at home.

In the seventeenth century physicians took over the care of patients in hospitals and transformed the mission of hospitals from social services to medical services provision and eventually medical research and medical education. In the twentieth century, the hospital "emerged as *the* place where people from any social class went to receive the highest quality medical care."[3]

Today's hospitals, though maintaining a service orientation, operate in a highly technical medical mode. With sophisticated technology and highly trained professionals performing diagnostic tests and procedures, it is no wonder that hospitals have come to be called "the physicians' workshop." Nonetheless, three principles that guided early hospitals are common to the modern hospital: "a service orientation, a universalistic (serve anyone and everyone) approach, and a custodial orientation."[4]

AN INDUSTRY IN TRANSITION

As outlined above, hospitals have changed from a place for high-touched "TLC" to high-tech. Furthermore, as national emphasis has shifted from access to care toward cost containment, hospitals are no longer thought of as strictly service institutions, but are being recognized as business organizations.

The change in emphasis from access to cost containment is

[3] Frederic D. Wolinsky, *The Sociology of Health* (Boston: Little, Brown and Company, 1980), pp. 345–347.
[4] Frederic D. Wolinsky, *The Sociology of Health*, p. 346.

reflected in the health care legislation enacted during the past 40 years by the federal government. From the 1940s to the 1960s, the concern was for access to care—providing as much service as possible to as many people as possible, particularly to the poor, elderly, and rural or ghetto dwellers. Toward this end, in 1948 the federal government enacted the Hill-Burton Act which provided federal funds to construct hospitals. In return, the hospitals incurred an obligation to provide a certain amount of free care to the poor each year until the hospital's Hill-Burton obligation expired.

In the 1960s, human rights were of keen interest. The prevailing attitude at that time was that health care was a right and no one should be denied access to it. So in 1965, the federal government enacted legislation to provide health care for the elderly (Medicare) and for the indigent (Medicaid.) The Medicare/Medicaid legislation dramatically increased government involvement in the health care industry as the government became a large purchaser of health services. However, this legislation provided for payment based on the hospital's cost of providing the service rather than the generally higher stated price. Payments to hospitals were termed **reimbursement**. Under this reimbursement system there were no real incentives to keep costs down, and the provider's interest was in providing as much high quality care as possible. In retrospect, it is no surprise that health care costs skyrocketed.

Operating costs not directly related to providing care to Medicare patients (for example, depreciation of buildings and equipment, debt principal, interest expense, bad debts, overhead associated with the hospital's gift shop) were disallowed from inclusion in the Medicare cost determination. These costs are, of course, a real part of the cost of doing business and must be covered from other sources of revenue.

With the huge amount of money being spent on health care, the government and executive officers of industries who pay employee health insurance premiums (and hence health care managers) have become very concerned with cost containment, efficient delivery of care, and the types of health services which should be offered. The latest federal health care payment system, enacted in 1984, reflects this concern. Unlike the original Medicare legislation which paid hospitals based on the allowable cost incurred, this current Medicare program makes payments to hospitals based on prospectively priced **Diagnosis Related Group (DRGs)**.

Under this DRG method hospitals are paid a fixed amount according to the patient's diagnosis. Certain adjustments are made in the payments to allow for medical complications, a required, extremely long-length stay, or extraordinary resource use. But for the most part, payment is fixed. This means that the customer, not the provider, determines the price. If the hospital can deliver care to a patient for less than the stated amount, the hospital can keep the "profit." If the hospital uses more resources to provide the care than the DRG amount, then the hospital loses money on that patient. This payment system obviously is designed to provide incentives to hospitals to provide care as efficiently as possible and to consider carefully what services each patient needs.

In many states, Medicaid, which is funded partially by states and partially by the federal government, is also using DRG based programs. Some other states, the Blue Cross and Blue Shield organizations, and other commercial insurance companies are considering adoption of this type of payment system. If all third-party payers adopt this kind of system, there will be no one to whom those unpaid operating costs can be shifted—except to those patients who pay directly from their own pockets.

The determination of the best method for achieving cost containment has been controversial. Some think that regulation is the best way, while others think that removal of regulation in favor of market place competition is the solution.[5]

An example of the latter philosophy is the removal of the 1974 federal requirement for state review of those plant and program changes where capital expenditures are required. The National Health Planning and Resources Development Act had required states to institute **Certificate of Need** (**CON**) programs or lose federal financial support. When a hospital wanted to add more beds or an expensive piece of equipment, such as a magnetic resonance imager, or to begin a helicopter emergency transport service, the hospital had to apply for a Certificate of Need and justify its need. If one area hospital was judged to be meeting the community or state need for the service, another hospital wishing to provide that service was denied permission to provide the service. If the need was not justified, the hospital could not carry out the expansion or add the new equipment or program without sanctions. The rationale was that the unnecessary duplication of services added to the total cost of health care so only those for which there is a demonstrable need should be added. Many states have elected to keep their health planning agencies and continue CON programs under support solely from state funds.

The byproduct of this type of control is sometimes the prevention of competition. Proponents of competition would say that who-

---

[5] C. C. Havighurst, "Controlling Health Care Costs: Strengthening the Private Sector's Hand," *Journal of Health Policy, Politics and Law*, vol. 1, no. 4 (Winter 1977), pp. 471–498.

ever wants to provide the service should do so, and the one that provides it best and/or for the lowest price will succeed.

Since hospital care is expensive compared to health care provided in other settings (e.g., home health care and outpatient surgical centers), the thrust of many of the other cost containment efforts have been directed toward incentives to decrease the number of hospitalizations and the length of stay. The Medicare Diagnosis Related Group (DRG) program, the Peer Review Organization (PRO), and changes in health insurance policies to exclude inpatient coverage for procedures which could be performed on an outpatient basis are all designed to decrease hospital utilization. Since most hospital costs are fixed, decreases in utilization (volume) have significant financial impact on hospitals.

The change in focus from access to cost containment and the types of pressures cost containment have brought to this industry have caused hospitals to be perceived more than ever like businesses. It has always been true that hospitals needed to operate in a sound business manner just to be able to continue to provide their service, but with new cost containment efforts, this has never been more true. As a result of increased financial pressures many hospitals are faltering and others have already closed. This new cost conscious environment has been particularly hard on small rural hospitals where occupancy has dwindled. The struggle of these small communities to maintain a hospital within their locale is a reminder that access to care is not unimportant. However, the pendulum has decidedly swung toward concern for cost containment and sound business practices. Proper balance between access to service and cost containment will remain a critical issue.

EMERGENCE OF FOR-PROFIT HOSPITALS

Since the health care industry commands such a large portion of the GNP, the development of health care organizations as for-profit enterprises is not surprising. Futhermore, as for-profit hospitals point out, corporate ownership provides these hospitals with a new source of funding not available to not-for-profit hospitals through the selling of corporate stock. Because of the tradition of service in the hospital industry, some in the health care field feel that for-profit hospitals are controversial. There is debate regarding whether for-profit hospitals can provide quality care for the same cost as not-for-profit hospitals. For-profits, on the other hand, claim sound management enables them to provide excellent quality care in a more efficient manner.

One criticism leveled toward for-profit hospitals is that they must "skim the cream" of the market in order to pay dividends. "Cream skimming" is providing only those services that are profitable and not offering those that are not highly profitable. Most not-for-profit community hospitals feel a social obligation to offer a full range of services so that whatever is needed will be available. Location of the hospital is important to the type of patient admitted. For-profit hospitals often choose to place their facilities in well-to-do suburban areas and not in the heart of the inner city ghetto where the proportion of free care to the indigent may be high.

A report by the Center of Health Studies,[6] a division of the Hospital Corporation of America, discusses some of the differences and similarities between these two types of hospitals and addresses some frequently raised points of controversy.

> Investor owned hospitals differ from not-for-profit hospitals in a number of ways, though they are similar in more ways than one might think. The primary difference is tax status. Investor owned hospitals must pay federal, state and local taxes whereas not-for-profit hospitals do not. Additionally, investor owned hospitals cannot receive tax deductible donations or be eligible for government grants as can not-for-profit health care organizations. In order for not-for-profit firms to retain this favorable tax status, they cannot allow any part of net earnings to inure to the benefit of a shareholder or any other individual.
>
> Another difference between tax exempt and investor owned hospitals is their source of capital. Investor owned firms have access to equity capital markets whereas not-for-profit corporations rely upon philanthropic donations and tax-exempt bonds for capital needs. Recently, however, a number of not-for-profit firms have set up wholly owned, profit making subsidiaries in order to access lower cost capital available through equity markets.

The report points out that the distinction between the two types of hospitals is fuzzy when considering the need to be financially sound. Both investor-owned and not-for-profit hospitals must generate more revenue than the amount needed for their operating expense. "Profits" are essential for:

> 1. Cash flow, needed to avoid such things as borrowing at inopportune times, forfeiting purchase discounts, or even becoming insolvent. -2. Replacement of existing equipment or the purchase of new equipment for continued or improved operations. -3. A return on the hospital's permanent capital base to insure

---

[6] The Center for Health Studies, *Update on Health Care Cost—An Executive Briefing Paper.* (Nashville, Tenn.: The Center for Health Studies January 1984).

continued access to debt capital. -4. Funds for innovations, expansions or replacement of the facilities and services important for providing higher quality health care at less cost.

In addition to these common needs for profit, investor-owned hospitals must also provide dividends to shareholders. A common criticism of invester-owned hospitals is that they make excessive profits in order to provide unconscionable cash dividends to investors, luring still more investors into the industry. Evidence to support this idea, however, is lacking. . . . Overall, except for this payment of shareholder dividends, both investor-owned and not-for-profit hospitals must make profits for the same reasons.

The report further states that investor-owned hospitals typically do not make greater profits than voluntary not-for-profit hospitals, and that there is little difference in the profit margins of investor-owned and not-for-profit hospitals. Not-for-profits have a 4.8% average profit margin while investor-owned hospitals have an average margin of 5%.

As a response to the issue of for-profit hospitals' avoiding certain unprofitable services, (leaving the not-for-profits to provide those services), the report states that, "the not-for-profits were more likely to offer profitable services such as open heart surgery, cardiac catherization, and CT scanning, but were more likely to offer unprofitable ones like premature nursery. . . . In short, except for cardiac care, . . . The investor-owned system hospitals and not-for-profit hospitals were similar, both in terms of service sophistication and willingness to offer unprofitable services."

Most for-profit hospitals belong to a system of hospitals, but there are also several not-for-profit hospital systems. Hospitals have joined together to increase their buying power and produce efficiencies in operation. These multi-institutional arrangements appear to be the trend for the future.

UNIQUE FEATURES OF HOSPITALS   As hospitals are businesses, all the functions of management come into play in the health care setting. However, there are unique features of hospitals that affect their management.

1. One of the most significant characteristics as identified by Kaluzny and associates is that *"the raw materials of health service organizations are human beings."*

In the human services of medicine, education, welfare, and law, the aim is not merely to turn out some measured product of a given quality at a given cost but to serve human beings in need of help. In manufacturing, we do not concern ourselves with the tortures through which fibers, plastics, materials, or the like are put in the course of the production process. In the human services, we are concerned that the course of providing health includes some sensitive recognition of and responsiveness to the human quality of the structure of flesh and bone being processed. Responsiveness and recognition themselves may constitute the service and its benefit. Without it, the encounter is dead and the service provided to a mere object albeit not one of fiber or plastic or metal.[7]

This difference has important implications for management— the ethical and social values applications of its technology. Questions about the limits of scientific endeavor arise in several areas, such as genetic technology, the right-to-death, and the right-to-life for severely handicapped or retarded infants. In addition, the people processed by the organization interact with the health care plan and influence the process.

2. *The "customer" is not necessarily the one who receives the service.* This is a distinctive feature of hospitals because it *is* difficult to clearly identify the customer. Obviously, it is *the patient* who receives the treatment, but it is seldom the patient who chooses the hospital or who pays the bill.

It is the physician who determines when hospitalization is necessary and chooses the hospital to which the patient will be admitted (i.e., one in which the physician has been granted admitting privileges). Then the physician determines what tests and procedures will be performed (i.e., what hospital resources are utilized) and how long the patient will stay in the hospital. The physician directs what care will be given the patient and gives orders for patient care to the nurses—who actually work for the hospital and not for the physician.

The government or the insurance companies are the customers if the customer is defined as the one paying the bill. Third-party payments account for about 90% of revenues in health care.

3. *Important Role of Professionals* Professionals and paraprofessionals—physicians, nurses, pharmacists, physical therapists, and so forth—comprise a large percentage of the people who work in hospitals. The proportion of professionals to other types of employees is higher in hospitals than in many other organizations.

Professionals tend to be highly autonomous in their outlook

[7] Eliot Friedson, in Arnold Kaluzny, D. Michael Warner, David Warren, and William Zelman, eds., *Management of Health Services* (Englewood Cliffs, N.J.: Prentice-Hall, Inc., 1982), p. 56.

and bring their own set of personal goals to the institution. Their goals may not always be in congruence with the goals of management. Since management is getting work done through other people this presents a particular challenge to management.

> Professionals often have motivations that are inconsistent with good resource utilization, and their success as perceived by their professional colleagues reflects these motivations. The professional standards simply relate to the standards of their professional colleagues and may be inconsistent with organizational goals. They perceive the rewards of achieving organizational goals as less potent than those for achieving professional objectives. Professionals by nature prefer to work independently . . . the essence of management is getting things done through other people . . . In professional organizations the professional quality of the people is the primary importance and other considerations are secondary. Therefore, managers of professionals spend much of their time recruiting good people and in seeing that they are kept happy . . . Professional education does not usually include education in management and quite naturally stresses the importance of the profession rather than of management. For this and other reasons professionals tend to underestimate the importance of the management function. Bluntly, they tend to look down on managers . . . Financial incentives tend to be less effective with professional people either because they consider their current compensation to be adequate or because their primary satisfaction comes from their work . . . Professionals tend to give inadequate weight to the financial implication of their decisions. The physician feels that no limit should be placed on the amount spent to save a human life, although in a world of limited resources such an attitude is unrealistic.[8]

Because physicians serve as gatekeepers of hospital utilization and the resources used for patient care, the most important professionals in the hospital are physicians. William Anlyan has described the relationship between physicians and hospitals as "symbiotic." Physicians depend upon hospitals for sophisticated services and facilities not available in their offices. Hospitals rely on physicians to bring them their patients, (the hospital's livelihood) and on the physicians' expertise in managing complex technologies within the hospital.[9]

[8] Robert N. Anthony and Regina E. Herzlinger, *Management Control in Non-profit Organizations* (Homewood, Ill.: Richard D. Irwin, Inc., 1980), pp. 45–46.

[9] William Anlyan, in Duncan Yaggy, ed., *Physicians and Hospitals: The Partnership at The Crossroads* (Durham, N.C.: Duke University Press, 1985), p. viii.

The Medicare DRG payment system and the Peer Review Organization's requirements increase the hospital's dependence on physician behavior. Not only does the hospital depend on the physician to admit patients to the hospital in the first place, but also payment amount or approval of coverage of a particular patient's hospitalization may depend upon how completely and accurately the physician documents information in the patient's hospital record. So, the hospital manager is in the predicament of needing to please the medical staff and at the same time, to exert more control over their behavior. Physicians, by the nature of their professional autonomy, will resist control. The hospital administrator frequently does not have as much influence within the hospital as the manager of a business within his or her organization.

ORGANIZATIONAL STRUCTURE

The organizational structure of hospitals has been referred to as a wobbly three-legged stool. The legs are the board of trustees, the medical staff, and the administration.

The *board of trustees* bears ultimate responsibility for the actions of the hospital's management and medical staff. The board makes the overall governing policies and sets the hospital's bylaws. The differences between the boards of trustees of corporate business enterprises and most hospitals are based on the fact that, industry is an economic enterprise with social overtones. The hospital, on the other hand, is a social enterprise with deepening economic overtones. A hospital's board is frequently composed of community and business leaders. They do not own or have financial interest in the hospital and are accountable for the conduct of the institution to the public rather than to shareholders of the corporation. As long as the hospital is solvent, they are less concerned with the bottom-line than boards of business organizations. In not-for-profit hospitals, the fiscal concern may be that the surplus be kept modest in keeping with the public service nature of the hospital's goals.[10]

In the community hospital, the *medical staff* is the group of physicians to whom the board of trustees has granted privileges to admit patients. The medical staff is not paid by the hospital. (In some hospitals, such as Veterans Administration hospitals, the physicians are employed and paid by the hospital.) The medical staff is not responsible for seeing that the hospital is available and there is no direct reporting relationship to administration. However, the medical

[10] Everett A. Johnson and Richard L. Johnson, *Hospitals in Transition* (Rockville, Md.: Aspen Systems Corp., 1982), pp. 72–73.

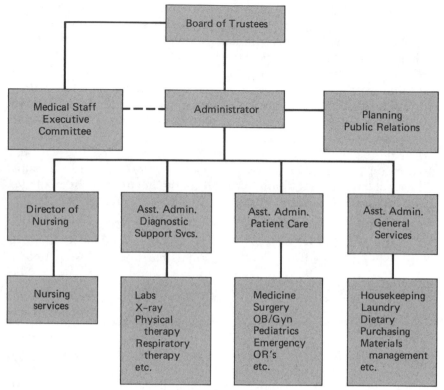

Figure 16–1
Organizational Structure for a Community Hospital

staff is responsible for the quality of medical care given patients and for the conduct of its members in accordance with the medical staff by-laws established by the board. The medical staff is accountable to the board of trustees and has responsibility to participate in the functioning of the hospital by serving on hospital committees and directing technical and clinical services.

Administration is responsible directly to the board for management of the hospital and implementation of policies approved by the board. Administration is responsible for the financial, hotel service, physical plant, and personnel functions of the hospital. All the people who work in the hospital, aside from most of the physicians, formally report through administration channels.

The organization chart illustrated in Figure 16–1 depicts the formal hierarchical lines of authority and departmentalization within the hospital. The operating divisions may be grouped in a number of

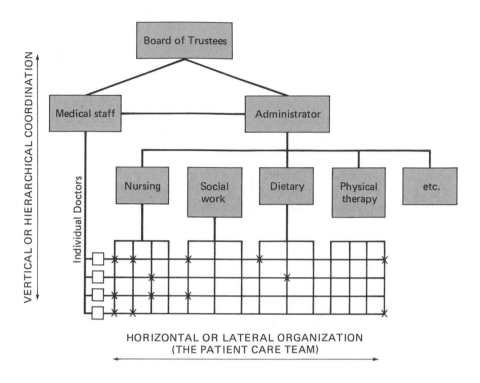

(X) Indicates a member of both a department and a patient care team.
Figure 16–2
D. Neuhauser, "The Hospital as a Matrix Organization," *Hospital Administration (Fall 1972), p. 20.*

ways, but frequently are divided into nursing, general (hotel) services, patient care, ancillary diagnostic/therapeutic support, and finance. The hospital medical departments are usually organized according to medical specialty—surgery, cardiology, pediatrics, obstetrics, and so forth. Patient care areas are grouped in this manner.

Patient care, however, is actually accomplished through a matrix organizational structure, with the medical staff directing the specialized members of the medical care team in each of the various departments. Since the medical staff do not work for the hospital *per se*, the relationships to hospital personnel are "dotted-line" relationships in terms of hospital policy, but are very real reporting relationships when it comes to patient care. The matrix organizational structure within the hospital, as diagramed by Duncan Neuhauser, is shown in Figure 16–2.

FINANCING HEALTH CARE

The primary source of payments to hospitals is through third-party payment. Berman and Weeks indicate that hospital revenues are from the following sources:[11]

Blue Cross payments	30%
Government agencies (Medicare, Medicaid, etc.)	30%
Commercial and independent insurance	30%
Self-Pay	10%

Most people are covered by some form of health insurance. The Health Insurance Institute reports that in 1978 an estimated 90% of the population had some form of health insurance and that this insurance covered approximately 86% of all services provided by hospitals.[12] The result is that very few people pay directly for hospital care. Many times health insurance policies do not include visits to physicians' offices or dental care, but most do cover at least a large percentage of the hospital stay and the physician's fee for in-hospital care. In addition, insurance premiums are frequently paid in whole or in part by employers. These arrangements insulate the patient from awareness of how expensive health care really is and provide little economic incentive to restrict the purchase of health care in quantity or quality. To counter this problem, under some insurance policies, the patient must first meet a deductible, and is then responsible for a percentage of his hospital charges.

Third-party payers, i.e., the government and insurance companies, typically make payments based on agreements with the hospital. Third-party payers view themselves as wholesale purchasers of care. Medicare payment is based on a fixed amount per case (as described earlier in this chapter). Medicaid payment amount and method vary from state to state to state but typically payments are based on a scheduled amount determined by Medicaid. There usually is a per diem limit for hospitalization payments under Medicaid. This amount is almost always less than the cost of providing the service. Blue Cross and other commercial insurance companies may pay full charges, or they may negotiate with hospitals to pay cost-plus or a percentage of charges. Health maintenance organizations and other prepaid care plans seek discounts from hospitals in exchange for an agreement to

[11] Howard J. Berman and Lewis E. Weeks, *The Financial Management of Hospitals* (Ann Arbor, Mich.: Health Administration Press, 1982), p. 86.
[12] Health Insurance Institute, in Kaluzny et al., *Management of Health Services* (Englewood Cliffs, N.J.: Prentice-Hall Inc., 1982), p. 369.

have their subscribers admitted to the contracted hospital when hospitalization is required. Since many insurance companies pay less than full charges and government payers often pay less than cost, the hospital must charge someone to meet the remainder of its full financial requirements. This lot falls to uninsured individuals or self-payers.

Hospitals do receive some funds through gifts and donations, but philanthropy accounts for only about 1% of the payments for health care in the United States.[13] In the past, this amount was more than twice what it is today.

Hospitals owned by federal, state, or local governments may receive an appropriation to cover their shortfall.

STAFFING   Hospitals are labor intensive. In 1982 labor costs averaged 56.7% of operating expenses. Hospitals employ people with a wide variety of skills. The range goes from an unskilled janitor or food service worker to the most highly educated and specialized paraprofessional and professional. A patient in the hospital may have as many as 25 or 30 different employees visit his room on any given day. These may include the cleaning person, different nurses on each of three shifts, nurse's aides, physicians, respiratory therapists, radiology technicians, blood drawers, social workers, nurse clinicians, and business office representatives.

Working in a hospital places considerable demands on its employees. Hospitals must be open 24 hours a day, 365 days a year. This means that employees must work shifts; they must work weekends and holidays. In recognizing the personal needs of its employees, and to decrease turnover, a hospital may elect that every employee shall have every other weekend off, or at least every third weekend off.

Because the nature of illness and injury is most often unpredictable, it is difficult to predict the demand for services at any particular moment; however, the expectation is that the hospital must be prepared to handle any number of circumstances and be staffed accordingly.

Health care personnel are highly specialized. The hospital must have available not just the proper number of personnel but personnel with the right combination of skills. Even nurses are often specialized today, particularly in intensive care settings. For example, a nurse familiar with caring for patients with acute spinal cord injuries may

[13] Health Insurance Institute, in Kuluzny et al., *Management of Health Services*, p. 369.

not be skilled in caring for pediatric patients who have had open heart surgery.

To accomplish these objectives, the hospital must employ more than the critical number of employees necessary to provide the service, and scheduling becomes a very complex task.

MANAGEMENT CONTROL Control issues for hospitals are similar in some ways to the control issues in public administration as described by Lawrence Lynch in Chapter 15. The difficulty in defining goals for which conclusive measurements can be obtained makes management control difficult for hospitals.

The definition Anthony and Herzlinger use for not-for-profit organizations applies well to hospitals: "an organization whose goal is something other than earning a profit for its owners. Usually its goal is to provide services."[14] They point out that the distinction between these two types of organizations can cause many management control problems that are peculiar to not-for-profit organizations.

> In a profit-oriented company, . . . success is measured, to a significant degree, by the amount of profit that these organizations earn. This is not to say that profit is their only objective or the only measure of their success. . By contrast, in not-for-profit organizations, decisions made by management are intended to result in providing the best possible service with the available resources; and success is measured primarily by how much service the organizations provide and by how well these services are rendered. . . "Service" is a vague, less measurable concept than profit. It follows that it is more difficult to measure performance in a non-profit organization. It also is more difficult to make clear-cut choices among alternative courses of action in such an organization because in a non-profit organization, the relationship between cost and benefits and even the amount of benefits are difficult to measure. Despite these difficulties, an organization must be controlled. Its management must do what it can to assure that their resources are used efficiently and effectively. . . . In many not-for-profit organizations, however, outputs cannot be measured in quantitative terms; furthermore, many not-for-profit organizations have multiple objectives and there is no feasible way of combining these measures of several outputs [to achieve a single measure of goals].

[14] Anthony and Herzlinger, *Management Control in Non-Profit Organizations*, p. 31–32, 35.

The absence of a single satisfactory overall measure of perform-ance that is comparable to the profit measure is the most serious management control problem seen by Anthony and Herzlinger in a not-for-profit organization. Even when organizational outputs can be measured in financial terms, the income statement for a not-for-profit organization must be viewed in a fundamentally different way than a for-profit company's income statement.

> If one accepts the premise that the patient charges are a good measure of output and if a hospital's revenues exceed expenses, this is a signal that its prices are too high or that it is not rendering enough service for what it charges. If revenues are less than expenses, the hospital's services are being produced at an expense which is more than the value which people assign to these services.

However, excess of revenuesover expenses must be used to support the total financial requirements of the institution, i.e., work-ing capital, replacement of physical plant, and introduction of new technology or new services.[15]

The service nature of a hospital presents special concerns. "Unlike many manufactured goods, services cannot be stored. If the facilities and personnel that are available to provide a service today are not used today, the revenue from that capability is lost forever."[16] It is more difficult to keep track of the quantity of services rendered than the quantity of goods produced or sold. Hospitals can certainly measure the number of bed-days used (the sum of the number of occupied beds in the hospital per day), the number of clinic visits, or the occupancy rate, but this does not necessarily measure the amount of service actually given or the resources used. But like any business organization, the key to control is to identify objectives to the performance and compare performance to criteria.

But control issues of hospitals do resemble those of profit organizations. Anthony and Herzlinger describe both the differences and similarities between the two types of organizations:

> Indeed, were it not for the difference in objectives—service rather than profit—their management control problems would be similar to those of their profit oriented counterparts. . . . These organiza-

[15] James D. Suver and Bruce R. Newmann, *Management Accounting for Health Care Organizations* (Oak Brook, Ill.: Hospital Financial Management Organization, 1981).

[16] Anthony and Herzlinger, *Management Control in Non-Profit Organizations*, p. 41.

tions do have fewer competitive pressures than the typical business, most of their revenue is received from third parties rather than directly from clients, they are dominated by professionals, and they have no clear cut line of responsibility to a defined group of owners. Spurred on by public concern about the rising cost of health care and by the necessity for justifying their fees on the basis of a plausible measurement of cost, . . . hospitals have made dramatic improvements in their management control systems in recent years.[17]

One of the essentials to a hospital's solvency is that it maintain a viable occupancy rate. Occupancy rate is the number of beds used divided by the number of beds available. "Available" means a bed that is physically there and staffed with a nurse and other personnel to care for a patient. The average occupancy rate for a short-stay general hospital in 1982 was 75.3%. Generally, a hospital needs to be at this occupancy level to remain solvent. Each day the first thing that every hospital administrator does is check the census, the number of patients that are in the hospital. Even small fluctuations in average occupancy rate have significant impact.

The DRG payment system, which pays hospitals by diagnosis, makes it important for hospital management to know the cost of providing care for each diagnosis. This is similar to industries' tracking costs by product-line. Many different resources are used to care for patients so hospitals need a sophisticated information system to obtain this type of information.

QUALITY ASSURANCE   Equally important to management control is quality control. In health care, quality control is referred to as *quality assurance*. Ethics, as well as a financially prudent management perspective to avoid malpractice settlements, require that managers of hospitals be certain that the care provided is at an acceptable level of quality.

In manufacturing industries, the competition of the market place is considered to be the ultimate quality assurance mechanism. If the product is not of sufficient quality or of sufficient value for the price, then the consumer tends not to buy that product. In health care and related industries the consumer is not in a position to evaluate the quality of the service from a clinical point of view. In addition, the consequences of the lack of quality can have far reaching effects since the product is the patient's well being and perhaps his life. Therefore, it is up to the guardian of the common good (e.g., the government) and the providers of care to assure that quality is of an adequate level.

[17] Anthony and Herzlinger, *Management Control in Non-Profit Organizations*, p. 31.

Quality of care is difficult to measure. "It generally refers to the organization's ability to provide service according to accepted professional standards and in a manner that is acceptable to the patient."[18] William Jesse has defined good quality as "(1) obtaining the optimal achievable benefit of hospitalization for each patient, within the limitations of the patient's illness, age, underlying chronic disease or diseases, and other patient related factors influencing the outcome of care, (2) achieving these benefits with minimal expenditure of resources, (3) avoiding injury or additional disability (i.e., iatrogenic illness, hospital acquired infection, hospital incurred trauma, etc.)."[19]

Avedis Donabedian outlines three aspects of quality: structure, process and outcome.[20] The first is the structure put into place to assure that the setting is conducive to giving quality care; this includes an adequate physical plant, hygienic environment, criteria for physicians' being granted medical staff privileges, policies, and so forth. Other structured components include licensing laws and standards set by various accreditation agencies. One of the criteria for accreditation by the Joint Commission on the Accreditation of Hospitals is that a quality assurance program be in place within the hospital. Because so many other factors are not within the control of hospital administration, the most prevalent forms of quality assurance in place are structural in nature.

Process and outcome measures are more difficult. Process measures focus on how things are done. Examples of process assessment activities might include observation or an audit of patients' charts by a nurse or physician. The activities noted in the charts will be compared against certain criteria in the evaluation of quality.

Because of the difficulty in defining health and because of the uncontrollable factors affecting outcome, outcome measures are the least likely to be used. They are, however, the most significant in terms of evaluating the service rendered. One way to measure outcome is to profile various important quality indicators: death rate, post-operative complication rate, drug reactions, incidents (falls, medication errors, etc.), second surgical procedures under one admission, equipment failures or malfunctions, and level of functioning on discharge.[21]

[18] Kaluzny et al., *Management of Health Services*, p. 29.

[19] William F. Jesse, *Identifying Health Care Quality Problems* (Chapel Hill: N.C.: Department of Health Administration, School of Public Health, 1982), p. 5.

[20] Avedis Donabedian, *The Definition of Quality and Approaches to Its Assessment* (Ann Arbor, Mich.: Health Administration Press, 1980).

[21] William F. Jesse, *Identifying Health Care Quality Problems*, p. 21.

Table 16-1
Regulations Affecting Health Facilities[a]

Agency or Authority	Capital Construction	Cost and Charges for Service	Personnel Standards	Professional Performance (Peer Review)	Working Conditions	Training and Education	Patients' Rights	Accounting
Medicare	F	F	F	F	F	F	F	F
Medicaid	FS	FS	FS	FS	FS	FS	FS	FS
Public Health	SL		FSL		FSL			
Joint Commission for the Accreditation of Hospitals	P		P	P			P	P
Blue Cross, intermediary, and private insurance	FSP	FSP	FSP	FSP				
State Insurance Commissioner	S	S			S			
State Licensing Agency	S		S		S			
Fire marshal	S							
Equal Opportunity Office			FS			FS		
National Labor Relations Board and State Department of Labor			FS		S			
State rate review	S	S						S
Internal Revenue Services		F						
Planning Agency	FSL							
Peer Review Organization				FSP				
American Medical Association			P			P		
American College of Pathology			P					
American Institute of Certified Public Accountants								P
Office of Civil Rights							FS	

[a]F, federal; S, state; L, local; P, private or voluntary.
Source: Adapted from Kaluzny, Warren, Warren and Zelman, *Management of Health Services* (Englewood Cliffs, N.J.: Prentice-Hall, Inc., 1982) p. 395.

LEGISLATION AND REGULATION

The external environment is important to any organization. One of the principal components of the external environment of the hospital industry is regulation. Regulations affecting the health care industry are not only governmental;

hospitals are also subject to regulation by private agencies that set standards for accreditation or membership. The scope of various regulatory agencies affecting the day-to-day operations of a hospital is shown in Table 16–1.

The level and scope of regulations impacting on health facilities result in a multiplicity of authority and accountability. The American Hospital Association has noted that "key decisions relating to patient care, terms of hospital payment, capital investment, and planning cannot be made without participation by a regulatory agency. . . . Reduction of managers' authority correspondingly limits their ability to determine the mix of factors to produce health care services. . . . Within the hospital, increasing regulation has the effect of reducing the decision latitude of the administrator and the board of trustees and the medical staff." Other problems cited as results of legislation and regulation include lack of incentives for certain types of undertakings, for example, shared services because of tax policies, or cost shifting to finance non-reimbursable activities such as community services.[22]

Many of the regulations and standards in existence are to ensure quality and safety. But legislation involving Medicare, Medicaid, and other government-sponsored payment programs and controlling resource use has a direct financial impact on providers of health services.

The hospital administator must be aware of federal, state, and local regulations which influence financial management of a hospital, the amount of service offered, or the amount and use of resources available to provide these services. The hospital administrator must have a thorough knowledge of existing regulations, changes in those regulations as they occur, and the political context in which these changes take place. Because of the tremendous impact regulation has on the hospital, the hospital administrator must get to know legislators and city and national leaders who may be helpful to health care.[23]

PROs (Peer Review Organizations) were legislated in 1984 to replace Professional Standard Review Organizations as part of the new DRG Medicare package. The PRO is an organization under contract, awarded by bid to the Federal Government, to review Medicare admissions and to determine whether the services provided were necessary, at an acceptable level of quality based on a criteria developed by the PRO, and provided in the appropriate setting. If the PRO determines that a hospital admission was unnecessary, they can deny Medicare payment for the entire patient stay.

[22] Arnold Kaluzny et al., *Management of Health Services*, p. 394–96.
[23] Arnold Kaluzny et al., *Management of Health Services*, p. 396.

In addition, there are a myriad of laws dealing with malpractice, licensing, the institutionalization of the mentally ill, abortion, rendering care to minors, and informed consent with which the hospital administrator must be familiar in order to make decisions in the hospital on a day-to-day basis.

CONCLUSION   This discussion of hospital administration has been limited to the unique aspects of this field of management. Two elements of management having particular expression in the hospital setting—information systems and marketing—were not discussed here because they are covered in Chapters 9 and 11 respectively.

Administration of hospitals requires all the essentials of management that have been discussed in this book. In order for hospitals to be in a position to continue to provide health care, they must be well managed. Hospitals, however, are more than just businesses. They have a social responsibility to provide a service to the community, and the values attendant to the mission of providing *care* to the ill must be integrated into management decisions.

REFERENCES

ANTHONY, ROBERT N. AND REGINA E. HERZLINGER, *Management Control in Nonprofit Organizations*. Homewood, Ill.: Richard D. Irwin, Inc., 1980.

BERMAN, HOWARD J. AND LEWIS E. WEEKS, *The Financial Management of Hospitals*. Ann Arbor, Mich.: Health Administration Press, 1982.

JESSE, WILLIAM F., *Identifying Health Care Quality Problems*. Chapel Hill, N.C.: Department of Health Administration, School of Public Health, 1982.

JOHNSON, EVERETT A. AND RICHARD L. JOHNSON, *Hospitals In Transition*. Rockville, Md.: Aspen Systems, 1982.

JONAS, STEVEN, *Health Care Delivery In The United States*, 2nd ed. New York: Springer Publishing Co., 1981.

KALUZNY, ARNOLD D., MICHAEL WARNER, DAVID G. WARREN, AND WILLIAM ZELMAN, *Management of Health Services*. Englewood Cliffs, N.J.: Prentice-Hall, Inc., 1982.

RAKICH, JONATHAN S., BEAUFORT B. LONGEST, JR., AND THOMAS R. O'DONOVAN, *Managing Health Care Organizations*. Philadelphia: W. B. Saunders Co., 1977.

SUVER, JAMES D. AND B. R. NEUMANN, *Management Accounting for Health Care Organizations.* Oak Brook, Ill.: Hospital Financial Management Association, 1981.

Update On Health Care Costs. Nashville, Tenn., The Center for Health Studies, January 1984.

VENINGA, ROBERT L., *The Human Side of Health Administration.* Englewood Cliffs, N.J.: Prentice-Hall, Inc., 1982.

WOLINSKY, FREDRIC D., *The Sociology of Health.* Boston: Little, Brown and Co., 1980.

YAGGY, DUNCAN, ed., *Physicians and Hospitals: The Great Partnership at the Crossroads.* Durham, N.C.: Duke University Press, 1985.

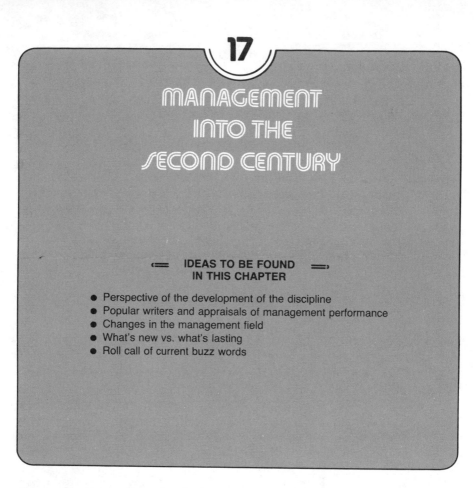

MANAGEMENT INTO THE SECOND CENTURY

⟸ IDEAS TO BE FOUND ⟹ IN THIS CHAPTER

- Perspective of the development of the discipline
- Popular writers and appraisals of management performance
- Changes in the management field
- What's new vs. what's lasting
- Roll call of current buzz words

Last chapters of textbooks are usually anticlimactic: they either merely summarize or they attempt to look into the crystal ball of the future. Readers often don't make it to the last chapter or unlike the readers of detective stories, they are groggy and don't care "whodunnit." This last chapter of the fourth edition almost turned out to be similar to the last chapter of each of the first three. The author's reflections, however, pointed to a different role this time: to provide prospective to the 100-year development of the management field, to evaluate its progress, and to sift out the lasting "essentials" from the flood of buzz words that emerge in cycles.[1]

[1] Author's note: The subjective nature of this last chapter should raise this question in the reader's mind. What are the author's qualifications for such judgments?
1. He has been involved in the management field for 40 percent of its existence.
2. Beginning as a young academic, he observed from the side of the road; later, he participated in driving down the road by writing articles and books; finally, he is viewing the flow of ideas from the side of the road again.
3. As a member of the Academy of Management, he has seen it grow from a few members to over several thousand; the AACSB (the American Association of Collegiate Schools of Business) attained power and prestige during this period.

DEVELOPMENT OF DISCIPLINE IN PERSPECTIVE The title of this chapter is in keeping with the trend of centennials and bicentennials experienced in the United States during the last two decades. These celebrations might serve to remind us how old an institution is or they might serve to indicate how young it is. It depends on one's perspective and basis of comparison. To someone new in the management field, 100 years seems like a long time until one recognizes that relative to other disciplines, management is a "new kid on the block."

An Analogy The father, professional engineering, was already established on May 26, 1886, when Henry R. Towne presented his paper signaling the birth of the new child, management. The mother, political economy or economics, nurtured this child in universities by taking custody in the emerging schools of business (Wharton, the oldest, was formed in 1881). Not until after World War II (more precisely after 1960 and the Carnegie and Ford Foundation reports) did management mature to adulthood (with its own Academy Journal). Then came the marriage of the young adult to the behavioral sciences and quantitative methods. The offspring of the *new* management fortunately inherited excellent genes from psychology, statistics, sociology, and mathematics, but it left home and often spurned its father (engineering) and mother (economics) by limiting its scope to narrow specialized topics. Its godfather (accounting), himself over 400 years old, continued to be viewed as an outside auditor and not as a blood relative.

Now let's leave the analogy and summarize the chronological facts. Table 17–1 outlines some of the key dates in the development of the management discipline.

Growth During First 100 Years The chief characteristics of management's growth can be succinctly summarized:

1. Management and business education have increasingly attracted more students, faculty, and money within the university setting; today management students comprise 10 to 25% of total registrants in individual universities.

---

4. The two great reports (the Carnegie and Ford Foundation reports) were issued about the time of the author's first text, *Management* (1961).
5. During a period of what Harold Koontz called the "management jungle," the author published a short eclectic statement—the first edition of *Essentials* in 1964.

Table 17–1
Milestones in Development of the Field of Management

Accounting—double entry bookkeeping	1494
First business school—Wharton (University of Pennsylvania)	1881
American Association of Collegiate Schools of Business (AACSB) first standards	1919
American Academy of Management	1936
first *Journal* Published	1958
first *Review* Published	1976
Report of the Ford Foundation	1959
Report of the Carnegie Foundation	1959

2. The number of trade and textbooks on management has increased while scholarly journals and individual articles have multiplied.

    a. In the 1950s only five basic texts were available in industrial management, business organization, and principles; in the 1980s the number is at least five times as many.

    b. In the 1950s few specialized scholarly journals were available to management researchers including publications of such associations as the American Management Association and leading universities, e.g., *Harvard Business Review* and the *Journal of Business* (University of Chicago).

    c. By the 1980s the best-seller list for nonfiction usually included three or more books on management in the top ten and for long periods. At times, the number 1 and number 2 books were on management topics (outselling sex and body building books).

3. Academic respect for management education from faculty colleagues has been gained slowly.

4. Management topics remain a "mixed breed" without an established "pedigree." (Even the AACSB's accreditation standards have a footnote advising that administration "shall be understood to include business administration and management.") Some universities have a management department among 10 or 15 departments in business while some name the entire school School of Management.

5. Internationally, management is viewed as an American phenomenon.

6. Graduate degrees in business, MBAs, have increased but with some question as to the role of undergraduate education in business; the greatest quantitative growth has been in community college offerings.

7. Professionalization of the field of management remains a debatable point but generally is less than in other fields, e.g., law, medicine, engineering.

Mixed Breed   Not only is the lineage of management not pure, but dominant concepts continually shift from one decade to the next. We have seen that for the first 50 years industrial engineers set the pattern for management thinking. From 1944–55, the major interest was in describing management and practicing "human relations." We saw in Chapter 2 that 1960 was a turning point with the introduction of the behavioral sciences and quantitative methods. Scientific verification pushed the art of management and philosophy aside. In the 1980s the popularity of management in non-fiction and on television reintroduced the simplified version of management—keep close to customers and innovate!

Within this ill-defined field, the last several decades have seen the introduction of one fad after another. A *fad* usually is very popular for a short time (a year or two), and then disappears as quickly as it has appeared. Often the new idea is stated as an acronym (a short word composed of the first letter(s) of a phrase). For example, a basic topic, closely related to the emphasis on behavioral sciences, was organization behavior (OB). Soon, a new, related topic appeared, organization climite, (OC), and then a few years later, still another, organization development (OD). One might foresee that in the next century we will see not only an OE and OF, but also an OX, OY, OZ. On second thought, the latter may not be appropriate because we already have Theories X, Y, and Z!

One reason for the introduction of new acronyms and buzz words is the publishing industry which pressures authors, publishers, and business firms to revise books every two or three years. The two main reasons for this are (1) any book with a copyright date older than a few years is considered out-of-date even if nothing truly significant has been discovered in those intervening years and (2) textbooks have become expensive and the used-book market threatens the new text market.

Management's mixed breed characteristics, or if you prefer its interdisciplinary nature, dashed the hope for development of "a general theory of management." Most of the greatly increased amount of research during the last several decades has focused on measurable, narrow topics that could be completed within a year or so. No one has been giving attention to a "philosophy of management" (with the exception of Peter Drucker and a few other philosophers who observe actual management practices) nor to longitudinal and broad theoretical matters.

Professionalization   Another topic that previously received attention was the question: Is management a profession? or Should management be a profession? Although this is not an "in"

Table 17–2
Criteria of a Profession

1. Systematic Body of Knowledge	A profession involves intellectual activity which calls for a prescribed training program.
2. Experimental Attitude	A profession searches for new ideas with research a critical element.
3. Code of Ethics	A profession is built on an ethical foundation and clear standards of behavior.
4. Service on Personal Basis	Financial return is secondary to the performance of a personal (and often confidential) service.
5. Entrance into an Association	Entry to the profession is restricted by standards set by an association in an attempt to assure quality in its members.

subject at the date of publication, it is reasonable to predict that the issue will re-emerge. For this reason, we need a clear definition and set of criteria for a profession. Table 17–2 states these criteria.

At the present time it is clear that the manager group fails to satisfy all the criteria of a profession. Although more managers are obtaining MBAs, firms do not restrict hiring to only those who have a certain degree or belong to an official association. Furthermore, many argue along with Peter Drucker that management should be open to all and should never attempt to professionalize. We have seen, moreover, that the body of knowledge required is not restricted to a common system of topics. In the last few years ethical questions have been raised by the public in reaction to failure of managers to meet ethical standards. Legal constraints have been imposed and in the future we will probably see greater attention to the ethical component of management.

POPULAR BOOKS AND APPRAISAL OF MANAGEMENT PERFORMANCE

The ultimate test of the success of management ideas is their actual, long-run performance and operations results in the competitive market. In the last decade attention has increasingly been directed to appraisal of this performance and effectiveness of leadership has been studied rigorously by researchers.

Popular interest in appraisal of management performance is evidenced by the fact that several books on the subject have become best sellers. One such best seller is *In Search of Excellence* by

Thomas J. Peters and R.H. Waterman.[2] The authors of this book, using their experience as management consultants, describe the basic characteristics of the best managed companies. They found that excellent managers have the following eight important attributes:

1. They are action-oriented.
2. They are close to their customers.
3. They seek autonomy and emphasize entrepreneurship.
4. Their focus is on production through people.
5. They emphasize underlying values and try to use values in practice.
6. They "stick to their knitting" and do not attempt to perform in areas outside their expertise.
7. They seek a simple form of organization and keep their staffs lean.
8. They keep tight controls, yet they allow loose means of maintaining control.

Peters and Waterman based their conclusions on structured interviews and reviews of literature over a 25-year period in 43 companies.

A sequel to the Peters and Waterman best-seller was entitled *A Passion for Excellence*.[3] The authors conceived their work not as a "how-to-do-it" book nor a contribution to theory, but as a description of how some companies have achieved excellence. The focus throughout is on the customer, and ways to increase revenue and innovation. It introduces new buzz words and abbreviations, such as MBWA (Managing by Wandering Around), "skunkworks," and the "home run" approach. Furthermore, it sneers at many cost concepts, such as economies of scale, cutting costs, learning curves, and other basic ideas emphasized over the years by students of the field. It is high on emotion and has a catchy style, but is weak on analytical rigor that could help managers improve operations.

Another best seller, *What They Don't Teach You at Harvard Business School*,[4] is a collection of "how to's," such as "how to read people," and "how to think on your feet." An intentionally humorous trade book that is more instructive (but less popular) is *The Official MBA Handbook or How to Succeed in Business Without a Harvard*

---

[2] Thomas J. Peters and Robert H. Waterman, Jr., *In Search of Excellence: Lessons from America's Best Run Companies* (New York: Harper & Row, Publishers, 1982).

[3] Thomas J. Peters and Nancy Austin, *A Passion for Excellence* (New York: Random House, 1985).

[4] Mark H. McCormack, *What They Don't Teach You at Harvard Business School* (New York: American Management Association, 1984).

MBA,[5] written by two recent recipients of the Harvard MBA. It makes fun of many current buzz words and could be instructive to those who have received specialized training in business.

Self appraisals or autobiographies written by famous CEOs have also been best-sellers. The most popular has been Lee Iacocca's *An Autobiography of Lee Iacocca*.[6] His success in turning around Chrysler Corporation and his charisma in television appearances have attracted many who are not even interested in management. Still another book by a famous (and in the view of some infamous) CEO is *Managing*[7] by Harold Geneen. This once powerful manager of ITT criticizes many generally accepted management ideas and focuses on control of operations with methods that differ drastically from the Peters's books. The author not only attacks many concepts presented here in *Essentials*, but he also argues that, "The secret of how to succeed in business or life is that there is no secret. No secret at all. No formula. No theory." This book, like many others written by dynamic, aggressive doers is quite weak on rational frameworks to help one attempting to learn the content of the management field. Over and over again the conclusion is that management is simple, and amenable to any hard working person—a dangerous oversimplification.

CHANGES IN THE MANAGEMENT FIELD

Increasingly, managers must understand their role under conditions of rapid change. In certain situations they will find themselves facing conditions that change as a result of forces outside their own control; they must in these situations learn to *adjust* to new developments. On the other hand, they will find that their role in society is to *promote* change and to *create* progress; they thus are involved in initiating and directing change. Modern society offers numerous opportunities that require either adjustment or creation or both.

Change is one of the most characteristic features of management. Leadership can be seen as an attempt to implement change. Much of the preceding discussion in this book testifies to continued change in management. Thus change is not new. What *is* new to managers is the recognition of the complexity and inescapability of change. What are some of the significant changes in the management field?

---

[5] Jim Fisk and Robert Barron, *The Official MBA Handbook* (New York: Simon & Schuster, 1982).

[6] Lee Iacocca, *An Autobiography* (New York: Bantum, 1984).

[7] Harold Geneen, *Managing* (New York: Doubleday, 1984).

Changes in Knowledge, Information and Techniques

Many of the past chapters in this book offer concepts and language unknown to the manager of the small factory in the last part of the nineteenth century. As we noted, the technical aspect of the management field has advanced greatly and will probably continue in its contribution to the engineering-type problems of the future.

The growth and use of economic concepts were features of the development of management in the first half of the twentieth century. Cost effectiveness studies developed not only in private firms but also in governmental and nonprofit organizations.

The field that received most attention during the last two decades has been the behavioral sciences. The marketing manager, controller, quality inspector, personnel director must interact with others; they must try to coordinate the efforts of people in performing the operations of the firm. Wherever a manager must relate with other persons, some aspect of behavioral science comes into play. The behavioral science applications to the management field have had top priority in the programs of management in the past; however, expectations should not be abnormally high. Machines are usually more predictable than people, and the advances in the technical areas of management over the past 100 years will not be so easily matched in the behavioral field. Even when scientists can identify the significant factors in individuals, groups, or societies, the relative weight of the factors constantly changes. Group identification and belongingness may be important in one period but not in another. People and their environment continually change, and the difficulties facing the behavioral scientist are great. Perhaps all that can be expected for the next few decades is a better understanding of the problem rather than a specific model which improves the predictability and control of behavior.

Changes in Scope of Management

There was a time when the field of management spoke primarily to the managers of industrial plants. Because the dominant problems of the factory system were production, the men who joined together were engineering types. The early journals, professional associations, research, publications, and participants from the universities and colleges were oriented toward technical problems and solutions. Recently managers in the public sector, managers of educational institutions, medical clinics, employment agencies, consulting firms, and staff units of religious organizations have found that they have many common problems. Thus the application of management concepts and techniques to varied types of organizations spreads and will continue to spread as the makeup of organizations changes.

The broadening of the scope of management should bring greater demand for specialization of the application of management knowledge. There will be more research studies dealing with the management of organizations concerned with poverty, voluntary groups, political units, etc. The early statements about the universality of management will find expression in specific applications and interpretations of insights in differing new contexts.

The increased scope of management has been accompanied by new social pressures to increase the utilization of groups previously under-represented on the management team. Affirmative action programs are now directed toward improving the opportunities of minority racial groups. In the 1970s, management recruiters increasingly sought qualified blacks as managers. The American Management Association has focused research on greater utilization of women as a new source of future managers.[8] Congressional relaxation of the age for compulsory retirement has enabled older managers, with their valuable experience, to continue longer to provide useful service to society. The result is that management has become more important to a much larger proportion of society.

Changes in the Issues and Problems Facing Managers

A pronounced trend in the American management scene is the *growth of educational preparation and training programs*. Each year, beginning persons at all levels of the organization (machine operators, secretaries, supervisors) enter their careers with higher levels of formal education. More companies and universities offer training programs for advanced study.

This educational trend has caused an *increase in the career mobility* of the work force. Each graduating class is expected to make an increasing number of job or career changes during the lifetime of its members. A graduating senior may expect to make at least seven changes in career or company, not including changes in geographical location *within* the company.

Another change in the workforce under the manager is a *change in composition*. Fewer jobs are available to the traditional blue collar worker. Automation and technological changes in the nature of work

[8] The concern for women as managers can best be felt by noting the great increase in number of books written on this topic in the 1970s. For example, see Rosabeth Moss Kanter, *Men and Women of the Corporation* (New York: Basic Books, 1977); Margaret Hennig and Anne Jardim, *The Managerial Woman* (New York: Anchor Press/Doubleday, 1977); Laurie Larwood and Marion M. Wood, *Women in Management* (Lexington, Mass.: Lexington Books, 1977).

have stimulated growth in white collar positions. Each year the ratio of white to blue collar changes, which means that today's manager must deal with a more educated and mobile subordinate. Furthermore, managers themselves have become more educated and mobile. Companies are finding that traditional motivational techniques no longer yield the expected results and inroads are being made into the once "loyal" members of the organization.

The white collar workers and public service employees will be a challenge to the skills of management. The question of legitimacy of organization has not been clearly defined for many of the new groups seeking or contemplating some form of collective representation. Teachers went on strike in the 1960s and will continue to use the strike as a means of power equalization. New groups have considered taking some form of collective action against what they think are autocratic institutions and practices.

The future holds much uncertainty in the relations between organizations and individuals. The security derived from educational training and the mobility of the labor market give rise to a situation where subordinates no longer automatically yield to hierarchical authority. The question of *governance* (who has rights) will continue to be crucial in interpersonal relationships.

Changes in the Environment

The world is changing. Population changes are becoming extremely significant to management personnel in organizations. These changes can be viewed as changes in (1) consumers, (2) factors of production, and (3) participants in society. The increase in the size of consumer markets and the segmentation of markets into strata (age, ethnic) are obvious changes. Consumption patterns vary and are in constant states of change, and the manager continually searches for market information to help in making sound decisions. Values, expectations, and aspirations are continually being transformed.

Population increases are favorable when viewed as expansion in consumer markets and greater availability of human resources. There are many instances, however, where the population changes are not seen as positive aspects of societal growth. When the increase in numbers increases density, unemployment, poverty, there is a question about the value of increase. The population explosion, as a problem to society, varies among countries, but in the future management must be aware of the impact of urban concentrations of people in all areas.

Some environmental changes relevant to management are pollution and social changes in the cities. Pollution (air, water, land, noise) seems to be the cost of industrialization and the exploitation of the resources of the country. What makes the topic critical in the last quarter of the twentieth century is that many **ecologists** (scientists who study humanity's relationship to its environment) foresee the possible destruction of irreplaceable resources. Managers in organizations as well as the professional and academic communities are now starting to show interest in the subject.

The crisis in the cities and urban centers increasingly affects management. The interdependence of the many factors of society make one problem the problem of many. Thus management in the 1990s may become more oriented to its sociological dimensions.

WHAT'S NEW VERSUS WHAT'S LASTING

The increasing popularity of management is encouraging, but it also raises conflicts in the minds of serious, sophisticated students. Is management a simple, common sense field? To whom should one listen—The writers of best sellers? Famous, successful, chief executive officers who rose to greatness in a different, earlier period? The writers who continually introduce new, catchy buzz words? The scholarly writings of pure researchers? The authors of the large number of textbooks which have continually been made more colorful and readable? Management consultants?

One suggested approach in balancing this mixture of pure intellectual theories and their practical application by men of action was offered by Charles Summer, Jr., several decades ago.[9] Table 17–3 is a simplified adaptation of the key ideas of his article. In fact, the title of this article is an example of an earlier buzz word, "Managerial Mind," which, after achieving great popularity, was discarded and thus isn't included in the revised list of buzz words (Table 17–4). Does the fact that an old buzz word is no longer popular mean that its idea is less important than a hot, new one that will inevitably emerge after this edition of this book goes to press? The opinion of this author is that there is much value in writings on management published over the last 100 years despite the fact that they are discarded by new writers who continually introduce new ideas.

Modern American culture, as we saw in Table 3–1, gives high status to "what's new?" whereas older cultures, such as the Japanese and Chinese, give high status to ideas and plans that have lasted hundreds of years. Yes, modern society is experiencing more changes in this decade than it experienced over previous centuries, and modern managers must keep up with these changes. *But*, a solid manager should develop the wisdom to hold on to lasting essentials

[9] Charles E. Summer, Jr., "The Manager's Mind," *The Harvard Business Review* (1959), pp. 69–78.

Table 17-3
Basic Intellectual Qualities and Modification
of the Managerial Mind

Basic Qualities		Management Modification
The Factual Attitude:		
The manager demands and seeks facts before making decisions	BUT	must use reasoning and judgment if lack of facts or time prevents the complete researching of a problem.
The Quantitative Attitude:		
The manager attempts objectivity and collects "measurable" facts	BUT	does not worship mathematical systems and thus doesn't postpone or shun judgments when action is called for.
The Theoretical Attitude:		
The manager develops an interest in searching for concepts that help catalog events into the same meaning; develops an interest in reasoning out laws to explain the relationship of one concept to the other	BUT	realizes that reasoning and quiet thought, as well as the use of theory from others, can be valuable in professional practice, provided one maintains a healthy distrust and a willingness to abandon theoretical concepts if they do not fit the specific problem.
Predisposition for Truth:		
The manager would like every word tested and traced to the abstract characteristics that connect the word to the object it represents in the real world	BUT	realizes that one cannot shrink from the problem because some statements are impossible to define precisely.
Consistency:		
The manager tries to be sure that the arguments in reasoning are valid—that premises are consistent among themselves rather than contradictory and that the statement of conclusions and decisions is also consistent with the statements of premises	BUT	cannot expect to discover scientific laws in every decision through strictly valid arguments, and sometimes finds it necessary to substitute "reasonableness" for syllogistic precision in thinking.

while adapting. If this author were to attempt to forecast a best-selling book on management in the next decade, he might predict that we would see a dynamic best seller entitled *Honesty is the Best Policy* with references to such earlier successful chief executives as Donald Danforth, Sr., ("I dare you") or J. C. Penney (ethical judgments). Change, yes, but very often what is new is old.

CHANGES IN MANAGEMENT JARGON

A revision of a book on *Essentials of Management* brings into focus a final type of change that a manager faces—the continual process of inventing and introducing new terms, acronyms, and jargon to emphasize old and basic concepts or principles. If the original edition of this book on essentials satisfactorily summarized the underlying fundamentals and principles of management, the need for continual revision of the book would seem to be unnecessary. Fundamental truth is certainly long-lasting. Yet, while the essentials do not change, this final part has shown that problems and the environment do change. Thus, updating of illustrations, refinements of analytical tools, refocusing on new problems, and reporting of new research on the essentials are needed periodically. Furthermore, a manager needs to keep up to date on the current usage of new terms, often referred to as buzz words, in order to understand modern expressions. In short, the language of management undergoes rapid changes with the introduction of new words, acronyms, and styles of expression.

While most of the essential concepts of management have roots in historical developments, the jargon of management is dynamic; "old wine is placed in new bottles." From a practical viewpoint, modern managers must continually adjust their vocabularies to new methods of expression. Often an old idea is rediscovered and given a new name. Since management is built on a number of disciplines, new terms emerge from each of these disciplines and other terms emerge that serve as gangplanks between disciplines. Therefore, it is necessary for the well-informed manager to keep current through continual reading of the professional literature. Table 17–4 will help the reader translate some of the basic, essential concepts into current language—the language of new research, new practices, and new analytical approaches.

<table>
<tr><td>**CONCLUDING**
REMARKS</td><td>Managers of organizations must always face an unfinished world. Rarely do they have all the infor-</td></tr>
</table>

mation to make a perfect decision; rarely do they have the full authority to implement the best one of their solutions; and rarely can they predict specific human responses to events.

Essentials of Management gives managers a perspective to view their present environment. They can see the past, present, and future developments of the field. They can identify the managerial processes and the techniques in the related disciplines to applications in business operational functions and activities of public agencies. But most importantly, managers may sense the need for an appropriate posture.

No matter how large or small the organization, the problems, decisions, and responses emerging from one environment have an impact upon other environments. As one of the principal characters in life's unfinished but continuing drama, the manager has the potential of determining the destiny of our society.

Table 17–4
Guide to the Managerial Jungle of Buzz Words

Current Buzz Words	Essence of Term's Meaning and Usefulness	Durable, Related Essential Concept
Contingency Approaches	Organization structure and leadership styles are contingent on the task, technology, and environment. No universals will fit all situations.	Mary Parker Follett's (1930) law of the situation. Harvard's case emphasis indicating diversity in practice.
Cost/Benefit Analysis	The quantitative examination of alternative courses of action where benefits are directly related to their costs.	Allocation of resources (costs) to the satisfaction of goals (benefits).
Delphi Technique	A group decision-making technique involving an iterative process for securing independent recommendations and support, in writing, without feedback from others.	Consultations with independent experts is valuable, especially when judgment must be used (no empirical facts available); pooled, independent judgment.
Employee Assistance Program (EAP)	A program that offers professional, confidential counseling to those troubled by problems off-the-job that interfere with work performance, e.g., marital problems, drugs and alcohol, and stress.	Problems formerly handled by family, church, or close friends. In 1942 duPont focused on alcohol problems.
Management Information System (MIS)	An all-inclusive system for providing management with information for effective decision making.	Use of all available data, e.g., accounting data library and primary collection, before making a decision.
Management by Objectives (MBO)	A systematized idea for setting clear and definite objectives for each individual at all hierarchical levels, usually through joint participation of superior and subordinate.	Control elements of targets, measuring performance, flagging variances, and taking corrective action; feedback by participation of those concerned.

Table 17–4, *cont.*

Current Buzz Words	Essence of Term's Meaning and Usefulness	Durable, Related Essential Concept
Managing by Wandering Around (MBWA)	A style of leadership that keeps in touch with people by direct contact.	Follett's coordination by direct contact with responsible people concerned (1930).
Operations Research (OR)	A scientific approach for solving problems, usually using quantitative approaches, in which an optimum is sought but where a team of diverse specialists contributes.	Utilization of quantitative models and methods whenever the subject can be stated mathematically or statistically.
Organization Behavior (OB)	The study of the behavior of individuals in organizations through emphasis on behavioral sciences, i.e., psychology, sociology, political science, anthropology.	Organizations involve people; thus managers must adjust to individuals and groups.
Organization Climate (OC)	The total of the degree and quality of environmental factors that influence participants, usually measured by their perceptions.	Humanity has evolved in civilizations through responses to challenges from outside; *esprit de corps*; morale.
Organization Development (OD)	A planned, organizationwide effort for participating in continuous rethinking (unfreezing) and changing beliefs, values, and structure to adapt to new challenges.	Groups need not get stuck in a rut; animals (human) must adapt. Creativity is basic to progress.
Organization Effectiveness (OE)	The measurement of whether the organization is attaining the goals which it has chosen.	Organizations should actually obtain results.
Profit Impact of Market Strategies (PIMS)	Analysis of strategic moves based on extensive data bases.	Look at the facts before you take action.
Planning/Program/ Budgeting (PPB)	An integrated system for rational ordering of inputs and outputs of an organization, with focus on identifiable goals. Interrelates separate budget elements and long-run goals.	Planning involves interrelating outputs (goals) with budgeted inputs (costs) or each component of a unit's activities.

Table 17–4, *cont.*

Current Buzz Words	Essence of Term's Meaning and Usefulness	Durable, Related Essential Concept
Program Evaluation and Review Technique (PERT)	A quantitative method of scheduling activities in which a network of activities must be performed in a definite sequence but uncertainty is faced. The optimum path is referred to as the critical path.	Planning and scheduling require precise description of activities and times required but actual completion is affected by uncertain factors.
Satisficing	A term coined by H. A. Simon to contrast with optimizing; an attempt to find a satisfactory solution which need not be the exact optimum.	Realistically, an approximation of reasonable solution where the theoretical optimum (e.g., an economic man) is not of practical importance.
Systems Approach	Viewing a subject as a whole composed of interdependent parts and delineated by clear boundaries.	Synthesis of elements of knowledge. Integration of component parts.
Time Management	A technique for allocation of one's time through setting goals, assigning priorities, identifying and eliminating time wasters, and use of managerial techniques to reach goals efficiently.	Work improvement, scheduling, and concepts from scientific management. Ideas from Benjamin Franklin.
Zero-Based Budgeting (ZBB)	The identification of the irreducible minimum (zero) of program costs and renewed justification for each extra program, thus providing the framework for rethinking priorities and replacement of new programs for old programs having lower value.	Incremental decision making; opportunity costs; tradeoffs; continual review of present programs; "cut out deadwood."

REFERENCES

BASS, BERNARD *Leadership and Performance Beyond Expectations* New York: The Free Press, 1985.

BENNIS, WARREN G., KENNETH D. BENNE, AND ROBERT CHIN, eds., *The Planning of Change*, 3rd ed. New York: Holt, Rinehart and Winston, 1976.

Drucker, Peter, *Temptation To Do Good*, New York: Harper and Row, 1984.

———, *Innovation and Entrepreneurship*, New York: Harper and Row, 1985.

Jacoby, Neil H., *Corporate Power and Social Responsibility: A Blueprint for the Future.* New York: The Macmillan Company, 1973.

Kahn, Herman and B. Bruce-Briggs, *Things to Come.* New York: The Macmillan Company, 1972.

Karp, H.B. *Personal Power: An Unorthodox Guide to Success*, New York: AMACOM, 1985.

Porter, Michael E. *Competitive Strategy: Techniques for Analyzing Industries and Competitors*, New York: The Free Press, 1980.

Rothschild, William E. *Putting it All Together: A Guide to Strategic Thinking*, New York: AMACOM, 1976.

Steiner, George A., ed., *Changing Business Society Interrelationships*, Los Angeles: Graduate School of Management, UCLA, 1975.

Walton, Clarence C., *The Ethics of Corporate Conduct.* Englewood Cliffs, N.J.: Prentice-Hall, Inc., 1977.

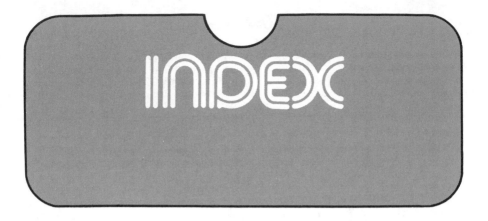

INDEX